What readers are saying about
Stripes... and Java Web Development Is Fun Again

This book is a must for anyone using Stripes, novice or pro. The author has done a great job of explaining the basics as well as the details of Stripes' amazing features while showing how to build a real-life application. A novice developer can get up to speed fast, keeping with Stripes' pragmatic approach to development: "It doesn't have to be hard." As the chapters progress, you will gain thorough knowledge of all the Stripes features. What really impressed me was the author's dedication to giving you full examples of all the possible variations; you're not left thinking, "If I just knew how to use that feature." If you want to know how to use a Stripes feature, look it up in this book—it's definitely covered. *Stripes...and Java Web Development Is Fun Again* will be on my work desk from now on.

▶ **Jeppe Cramon**
Chief Architect, TigerTeam

This book is really engaging. Since I'm familiar with Stripes, I enjoyed learning about many lesser-known nuances that Stripes provides— and those tasty little nuggets kept me reading. This book delivers a comprehensive understanding of the intellectual and technical aspects of Stripes. It has served to cement my appreciation for Stripes.

▶ **Brandon Goodin**
Coauthor, *iBATIS in Action*

At first I thought this book would be merely a welcome dead-tree reference for our team of self-proclaimed veteran Stripes developers. But somewhere along the way Frederic Daoud managed to greatly impress and humble me with his experience and in-depth knowledge of Stripes.

With its clear and well-structured chapters, the content is thorough and fast-moving. The text flows naturally from topic to topic and from chapter to chapter. The code is good, clear, and readable. The tone is personal and light, like the author is casually chatting with us, the readers. This was very appealing to me, having read truckloads of dry, almost scientific comp-sci books. And even I, as a long-time Stripes user, learned some things I didn't know.

> ▶ **Jasper Fontaine**
> Lead Developer, Codegap

As a Stripes committer, I learned a good bit from reading this book. For example, the explanation of how checkboxes are handled is very informative. In fact, I might print it out and hang it above my desk! Even seasoned Stripes developers get confused by that sometimes. Thanks, Frederic.

> ▶ **Ben Gunter**
> Committer, The Stripes Framework

I changed several of my practices after reading this book. The book contains some really great ideas, and I really was surprised I learned so much from it!

> ▶ **Aaron Porter**
> Committer, The Stripes Framework

This is a valuable resource to both newcomers and experienced Stripes developers. Although Stripes is very easy to use, this is *the* book I wish I had read when I got started! Having used Stripes for more than a year, I still found many great tips that will help me improve and simplify my code.

> ▶ **Chris Herron**
> Freelance Java Developer

Stripes

...and Java Web Development Is Fun Again

Stripes

...and Java Web Development Is Fun Again

Frederic Daoud

with Tim Fennell

The Pragmatic Bookshelf
Raleigh, North Carolina   Dallas, Texas

Many of the designations used by manufacturers and sellers to distinguish their products are claimed as trademarks. Where those designations appear in this book, and The Pragmatic Programmers, LLC was aware of a trademark claim, the designations have been printed in initial capital letters or in all capitals. The Pragmatic Starter Kit, The Pragmatic Programmer, Pragmatic Programming, Pragmatic Bookshelf and the linking *g* device are trademarks of The Pragmatic Programmers, LLC.

Every precaution was taken in the preparation of this book. However, the publisher assumes no responsibility for errors or omissions, or for damages that may result from the use of information (including program listings) contained herein.

Our Pragmatic courses, workshops, and other products can help you and your team create better software and have more fun. For more information, as well as the latest Pragmatic titles, please visit us at

> http://www.pragprog.com

ISBN-10: 1-934356-21-2

ISBN-13: 978-1-934356-21-0

Printed on acid-free paper.

P1.0 printing, October 2008

Version: 2008-10-13

To Nadia.
You are the love of my life
and the woman of my dreams.

Contents

Everything should be made as simple as possible, but not one bit simpler.
  ▶ Albert Einstein

Chapter 1

Introduction

Welcome to Stripes!

Stripes is a framework that makes developing Java web applications easier. How? It eliminates much of the configuration that traditionally has been associated with Java web development. Goodbye, XML hell!

When Tim Fennell created Stripes in 2005, he decided to leverage the features introduced in Java 5, such as annotations and generic types, to remove the need for XML configuration files. In fact, the only XML file that you'll need is the standard web.xml file that kick starts any Java web application.

But Stripes isn't just about reducing configuration. Have you ever used a framework and felt you had to do too much work *for* the framework compared to what the framework gave you in return? Have you ever received very reasonable requirements from a client but then had to fight with the framework to get the application to meet those requirements? Have you ever stopped and thought, "It's not normal for these things to be so complicated"?

Stripes is about making things simple for you, the programmer. While you develop your application, you'll notice how Stripes adapts to your code—a lot more than you have to adapt your code to Stripes. You spend your time writing *your* application, not reshaping your code in strange ways just to meet a framework's restrictions. Stripes is about making your work more enjoyable. Tim's tag line for Stripes says it all: "Java web development doesn't have to suck."

Everything in Stripes aims to be as straightforward and practical as possible. Web development inevitably involves many repetitive low-level tasks; Stripes takes care of those so that you can concentrate instead on writing clear, concise, readable, and maintainable code.

Let's briefly discuss some of the characteristics of Stripes. Stripes is a Model-View-Controller (MVC) framework and is mostly present in the controller and view parts. Stripes interacts with your model but does not intrude—your model stays independent of anything Stripes-specific. Stripes happily transfers data between your model and the controller/view without asking you to describe anything in some configuration file or do any other form of "framework hand-holding."

Stripes is not a "full-stack" framework; it works with your model but lets you decide how to map your model to a database. Plenty of high-quality frameworks exist for that, and the Stripes developers do not see value in duplicating those efforts. Moreover, not only do you probably already have a favorite solution for model-database mapping, but perhaps you even use different frameworks depending on the application. Stripes sees the value in that and does not tie you to a single solution. Stripes is very lightweight that way—it doesn't reinvent the wheel for everything, and it won't require that you learn a completely different paradigm. Stripes just focuses on the web part of web application development.

Stripes developers are very careful to avoid the "scope creep" pitfall. It's easily understandable that you'd want to add every single feature requested by users—you want to please them. In the long run, you're actually doing users a disservice because the number of features explodes, leading to a bloated, hard-to-understand, and hard-to-maintain framework. With a never-ending list of classes and methods, too many tags, and a ton of attributes, a framework becomes tedious to use. Stripes stays focused on a core set of features. At the same time, Stripes is very simple to extend so that you can easily add anything you need.

Stripes is an action-based framework. It acknowledges the stateless nature of HTTP and does its best to get the most out of it. HTTP is based on a request-response cycle: when the user clicks something in the browser, a request is made to the web application, which does its work and provides a response. The browser is refreshed with the results, and the cycle is complete. Stripes shapes itself to fit into this request-response cycle. A request is translated into an *action*, which triggers a Java method that does the work and returns a result. The framework interprets the result and provides the appropriate response. By using plain requests and responses, Stripes stays transparent and makes it easy to plug in third-party libraries and Ajax frameworks.

Another nice thing about Stripes is that you need to learn only a few basic concepts to get started. You can go a long way with a small set of features and can leave the advanced stuff for later. When your applications become more sophisticated, you can learn how to get more out of Stripes. This cuts down on complexity when you start using the framework, because you don't need to learn too many things at once before you get some gratification.

What truly makes Stripes a joy to work with is that it helps you without getting in your way. You can actually wrap your head around the framework and understand what it is doing. When you run into a situation where you need something special, you can tap in and tinker to get the required result. Stripes is not a big magic black box that works "only if used as intended" and for which the warranty is void if you tear off the sticker and open the box.

1.1 What Can Stripes Do for You?

So if Stripes is so small and simple, what does it actually do? Plenty. Here's a quick feature summary:

- *Smart binding*: Stripes goes a long way to bind URLs, parameters, and events from HTTP to Java so that your code remains simple and straightforward. The names in your view templates match the names of your Java classes, methods, and properties, so the association between the two is very clear.
- *Autoloading*: Stripes automatically discovers and loads your Stripes-related classes, so you can add, rename, and remove classes without worrying about keeping any configuration files (XML or otherwise) in sync.
- *Validation*: Stripes provides a powerful validation mechanism that is based on annotations.
- *Type conversion and formatting*: Stripes gives you strong type support by automatically converting between Strings and common Java types and making it easy to add your own data types to its conversion system.
- *Layouts*: With three tags from its tag library, Stripes gives you a simple and powerful reusable layout mechanism. You guessed it—no configuration files involved here either.
- *Localization*: Stripes tags have a default resource bundle lookup strategy so that localization is simply a matter of following the

convention and adding key-label pairs in a resource bundle.

- *Exception handling*: When an exception goes all the way up the stack without being handled, the servlet container shows a big ugly exception page. You don't want your users to see that! Stripes lets you show specific error pages for the exception types that you care about and has a general "catchall" error page for all other exceptions.

- *Interceptors*: When handling a request, Stripes goes through several life-cycle stages before providing a response. Interceptors let you write code that is called before or after any of these stages, making it easy to alter the flow, change the data, and so on. Interceptors are a great way of plugging in custom behavior.

- *Customizable URLs*: Stripes takes care of all the URL binding for you, so you can write your whole application without ever bothering with URLs. However, if you need specific URL patterns, Stripes lets you do that too.

- *Easy Ajax integration*: With the simple and transparent request-response nature of Stripes, you can Ajaxify your applications by using your favorite Ajax framework as a front end and Stripes as a back end.

- *Testing*: Stripes comes with a built-in set of mock objects that help you write automated unit tests to make sure your application works as expected.

- *Easy extension and customization*: Stripes is designed in a modular fashion with many areas to hook into. You can plug in different behavior for any part of the framework. Extensibility is an area where Stripes really shines, and if you're not used to being able to easily insert custom code into a framework, you're in for a real treat.

1.2 Getting the Most Out of This Book

Here is some information that will help you get the most out of this book.

What You Should Already Know

I assume you know the basics of Java web application development, including compiling Java code, creating a web application, packaging a WAR file, and deploying to a servlet container. You should also be familiar with JSPs and the Expression Language (EL).

If you need a refresher, you'll find a myriad of tutorials and examples on the Net. Here are a few good places to start:

The Java Tutorial http://java.sun.com/javaee5/docs/tutorial/doc/bnadr.html
The web application section of the Java Tutorial

JSP Syntax Reference. . .
. . . http://java.sun.com/products/jsp/syntax/2.0/syntaxref20.html
Handy reference on JSP syntax, EL expressions, directives, and standard JSP tags

Java with Passion! http://www.javapassion.com/j2ee
Sang Shin's online course for learning Java web application development

NetBeans Tutorial . . . . http://www.netbeans.org/kb/trails/web.html
A tutorial for creating web applications with the NetBeans IDE

Eclipse Tutorial. . .
. . . http://www.eclipse.org/webtools/community/tutorials/BuildJ2EEWebApp/
BuildJ2EEWebApp.html
A tutorial for creating web applications with the Eclipse IDE

Getting the Source Code

This book comes with a lot of source code so that you can learn Stripes by example. Of course, the text contains code snippets along with explanations. Although I've done my best to include enough context around the code shown in the book so that it makes sense, I didn't want to bombard you with pages upon pages of code listings. When you want to see the full source and navigate through the code at your mind's desire, the best thing to do is to download the source package and use your favorite text editor or IDE. While you're at it, there's a good chance you'll want to try a few things of your own. Go ahead—that's a great way to learn.

You can download the source code from this location:

http://www.pragprog.com/titles/fdstr/source_code

Conventions

I use a few simple conventions in this book, which you'll recognize if you've read other books by the Pragmatic Programmers.

Live Code
> The majority of code snippets in the book are extracted from fully functional examples. When that's the case, a bar before the code contains the path to the source file.

For example:

`getting_started/web/WEB-INF/jsp/hello.jsp`

```
<p>
  Date and time: ${actionBean.date}
</p>
```

If you've downloaded the source code package, you'll find the file using that path. If you're reading the PDF version of this book with a PDF viewer that supports hyperlinks, it's even easier: just click the bar, and the code will appear in a browser window. If your browser mistakenly tries to interpret the file as HTML, just view the page source, and you'll see the real code.

Joe Asks...

Joe, the mythical developer, sometimes pops up to ask questions about what I'm discussing in the text. I answer these questions as I go along.

Tim Says...

Tim Fennell, who created Stripes, has some wisdom to share every now and then. Look for these *Tim Says...* sidebars to read his rationale, recommendations, and colour (he's English, so he spells it with a *u*) commentary.

Road Map

This book is organized in three parts. Part I is about learning the different parts of Stripes and how they work. After setting up a development environment and getting a "Hello, World!" example running to make sure everything works, you start building the sample application that you'll keep improving throughout the book. In Part II, you are ready to use Stripes to add more sophisticated functionality to the application. By Part III, you'll move on to some of the more advanced features of Stripes and will also learn how to integrate third-party libraries such as Hibernate, Spring, Guice, JUnit, and jQuery.

Stripes Version

This book covers Stripes 1.5. If you are using a previous version of Stripes, consider upgrading to 1.5 for your next project because this version has many interesting new features that make developing with Stripes even more enjoyable.

1.3 Acknowledgments

Writing this book has been a very fulfilling, challenging, enlightening, and rewarding experience. I have several people to thank. Without them, my lifelong dream of writing a computer book (admittedly, a geek's dream) would not have come true.

Dear Nadia, being married to you has made me happier than I could ever imagine. You never stop believing in me, and for that I'll always be grateful. You are a wonderful wife, a fantastic mother, and the most beautiful person I have ever known. I love you.

Lily Nadine, thank you for being such a bright, active, bouncing, laughing, happy baby. Every day, you bring us a tremendous amount of joy.

Merci Papa et Maman, Wasfi et Viva, d'être des parents si merveilleux. Vous faites toujours tout pour moi et j'en suis très reconnaissant. Merci à vous deux d'avoir chacun eu le courage de surmonter de graves problèmes de santé. Je vous admire. Que Dieu vous bénisse.

Thank you, Tim Fennell, for creating such an excellent framework. I was actually able to read and understand all the source code! You truly did a fantastic job. Thank you for collaborating with me on this book, contributing the *Tim Says...* boxes, reviewing my work, making suggestions for improvement, and answering my questions. Thank you also for welcoming me as a Stripes committer. Finally, thank you for being such a great person. Being brilliant and humble at the same time is a rare and terrific combination.

Thank you, Andy Hunt and Dave Thomas, the Pragmatic Programmers, for giving this book a chance in the first place. Special thanks to Dave for being patient with all the back-and-forth for the book cover and to Andy for offering advice and always answering my questions so promptly and helpfully.

Thank you, Jackie Carter, for tirelessly reviewing my work, offering advice, always being positive, and helping me make this book better.

Thank you, Tony George and Steve Francisco, for reviewing my early drafts back when I had not yet found a publisher. You dedicated your free time to help me, and I truly appreciate it.

Thank you, Ben Gunter, for answering all my questions and for contributing such great features to Stripes.

Thank you, Aaron Porter, Chris Herron, Ben Gunter, Brandon Goodin, Jasper Fontaine, Tim Fennell, and Jeppe Cramon, for participating in the book's technical review.

Thank you, Remi Vankeisbelck, Will Hartung, Jasper Fontaine, and Jeppe Cramon, for reviewing my outline and offering your suggestions.

Thank you, Aaron Porter, for contributing Stripersist and the client-side validation code and agreeing to having them featured in this book. Special thanks for your patience in answering all my questions!

Thank you, Oscar Westra van Holthe-Kind, for contributing the Stripes security package.

Thank you, Martijn Dashorst and Eelco Hillenius, for answering my questions and offering advice on undertaking the tremendous challenge of writing a computer book.

Finally, thank you, Stripers, for forming such a bright, helpful, dynamic, lively, and friendly community. That's what Stripes is all about.

Part I

Learning the Controls

Chapter 2

Stripes 101: Getting Started

The best way to get started with a framework is to dive in and get a simple example up and running. So, let's do that.

2.1 Setting Up a Stripes Application

First, you will need to set up a Stripes web application development environment:

1. Install the development tools.
2. Install the Stripes framework and dependencies.
3. Configure the web application to use Stripes.

This is a one-time job. You'll be able to reuse this environment for all of the book's examples as well as your own masterpieces.

The Development Tools

Install the following development tools. Note that every version number is a minimum version—higher versions should work as well. You are probably already familiar with these tools. If not, refer to the installation instructions on the indicated website.

- Java Development Kit (JDK), version 1.5: http://java.sun.com.
- A servlet container that supports Servlet 2.4 and JSP 2.0. There are several; here are just a few examples:
  - Jetty version 5.0: http://jetty.mortbay.com
  - Resin version 3.0: http://www.caucho.com
  - Tomcat version 5.5: http://tomcat.apache.org

> **Using Third-Party Libraries with Stripes**
>
> Stripes has very few dependencies. However, as you build more sophisticated applications, you'll probably want to add other libraries—to manage database transactions, for example. Instead of being a full-stack framework, Stripes is designed to integrate well with third-party libraries so that you are free to choose the best tools for your applications.

- (Optional) Apache Ant, version 1.7.0: http://ant.apache.org, if you want to use the build scripts that come with the book's sample code.
- A text editor or an IDE to work with the source code. I'm sure you already have some favorites. Mine are VIM[1], Eclipse[2], and NetBeans[3].

Once all the tools are installed, create a web application. This can involve a wizard in your IDE or just creating a project directory with subdirectories for the source code and web application files. If you want the easy way out, just use the book's source code.

Stripes Framework and Dependencies

Next, get the Stripes distribution, version 1.5 or higher, from http://www.stripesframework.org. You'll need to copy the required JAR files into the WEB-INF/lib directory of your web application:

- stripes.jar: The Stripes framework, of course
- commons-logging.jar: Required by Stripes

You'll also need to copy StripesResources.properties to a location that's on the web application's class path, such as the WEB-INF/classes directory.

The Java Standard Tag Library (JSTL) is not a Stripes requirement, but it's very useful when developing Stripes applications with JSPs, as you'll see throughout the book's examples. To install the JSTL, copy the following two JARs from http://jakarta.apache.org/taglibs (or the book's sample code) to your WEB-INF/lib directory:

- jstl.jar
- standard.jar

---

1. http://www.vim.org
2. http://www.eclipse.org
3. http://www.netbeans.org

The web.xml Configuration

Finally, as with any standard Java web application, you'll need the WEB-INF/web.xml file. This is where you configure the web application to use Stripes. The two elements that handle incoming requests are the *Stripes filter* and the *dispatcher servlet*. Here is how you set them up in web.xml:

getting_started/web/WEB-INF/web.xml

```xml
<?xml version="1.0" encoding="ISO-8859-1"?>
<web-app version="2.4" xmlns="http://java.sun.com/xml/ns/j2ee"
  xmlns:xsi="http://www.w3.org/2001/XMLSchema-instance"
  xsi:schemaLocation="http://java.sun.com/xml/ns/j2ee
  http://java.sun.com/xml/ns/j2ee/web-app_2_4.xsd"
>
❶    <filter>
       <filter-name>StripesFilter</filter-name>
       <filter-class>
         net.sourceforge.stripes.controller.StripesFilter
       </filter-class>
       <init-param>
❷        <param-name>ActionResolver.Packages</param-name>
         <param-value>stripesbook.action</param-value>
       </init-param>
     </filter>

❸    <servlet>
       <servlet-name>DispatcherServlet</servlet-name>
       <servlet-class>
         net.sourceforge.stripes.controller.DispatcherServlet
       </servlet-class>
       <load-on-startup>1</load-on-startup>
     </servlet>

❹    <filter-mapping>
       <filter-name>StripesFilter</filter-name>
       <servlet-name>DispatcherServlet</servlet-name>
       <dispatcher>REQUEST</dispatcher>
       <dispatcher>FORWARD</dispatcher>
     </filter-mapping>

❺    <servlet-mapping>
       <servlet-name>DispatcherServlet</servlet-name>
       <url-pattern>*.action</url-pattern>
     </servlet-mapping>

❻    <welcome-file-list>
       <welcome-file>index.jsp</welcome-file>
     </welcome-file-list>

     </web-app>
```

That's a lot of XML, but don't worry—you have to do this only once, and then you can use this configuration as a base for every Stripes application you write. You'll need only to edit web.xml to enable some of Stripes' more advanced features, and even then it's the "once and for all" type of configuration. You won't have to work with XML files—or any other configuration files—for everyday work.

Here's what is now set up in this web.xml file:

❶ The Stripes filter declaration.

❷ A parameter to the Stripes filter. More details on this in a minute.

❸ The dispatcher servlet declaration.

❹ A mapping to make the Stripes filter intercept all requests that go through the dispatcher servlet.

❺ A mapping that makes the dispatcher servlet handle all .action requests.

❻ This says to use index.jsp as a default file when the user accesses the application with the base URL, such as http://localhost:8080/getting_started. We'll see how that works a little later.

Have a look at an illustration of this configuration in Figure 2.1, on the facing page. All .action requests are intercepted by the Stripes filter and then handled by the dispatcher servlet that looks for the action bean that is bound to the URL. Stripes instantiates the action bean and uses it to handle the request. The action bean can produce a response directly or forward to a JSP, which in turn produces the response.

A value for the ActionResolver.Packages initialization parameter is given to the Stripes filter in ❷. As promised, let's take a closer look at what this parameter does.

The Search for Action Beans

Action beans are the basic building blocks of a Stripes application. Because they are so essential, Stripes automatically loads them at startup by scanning the class path. But it does need a starting point: at least one package *root* from which to begin the search. So, you must choose the package(s) in which you'll be placing your action beans and indicate the package roots, separated by commas, using the Stripes filter's ActionResolver.Packages initialization parameter. For each package root, Stripes will examine the classes in that package *and all subpackages*. Every action bean that it finds will be registered.

Specifying the Action-Resolver.Packages parameter is mandatory.

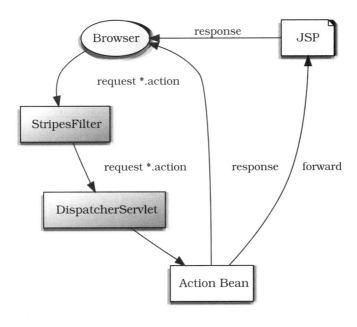

Figure 2.1: A MINIMAL STRIPES CONFIGURATION

All action beans in the examples will be in the stripesbook.action package. So, this package is indicated at ❷ in the web.xml file. Using stripesbook would also work, but being as specific as possible down the package hierarchy reduces the number of classes to be examined and speeds up the startup process.

I really like this feature of Stripes. You configure the packages for your action beans once and for all, and then you're free to add, rename, and remove as many action beans as you want. As long as you use one of those packages, you don't have to worry about editing a configuration file. Add an action bean, and Stripes will automatically load it. Remove an action bean, and you don't have to remember to remove something in a configuration file to keep things "in sync." Working with action beans is the most frequent thing you're doing in a Stripes application, so freeing you of configuration annoyances saves you a lot of time and effort.

That is all the setup and configuration you need. You're now ready to write some application code.

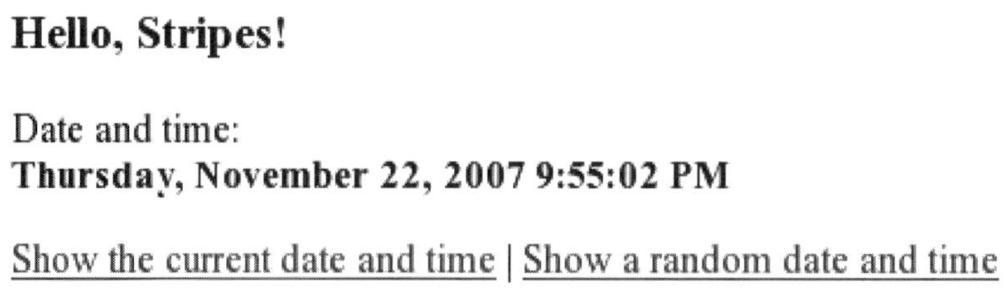

Hello, Stripes!

Date and time:
Thursday, November 22, 2007 9:55:02 PM

Show the current date and time | Show a random date and time

Figure 2.2: A GREETING FROM STRIPES

2.2 Hello, Stripes!

As a "Hello, World!" example, we'll use the page shown in Figure 2.2. When you start the application, the page displays the current date and time. The two links at the bottom update the display: the first link refreshes the current date and time, and the second link displays a random date and time instead.

Although this example does not do much, it will help you get started with Stripes. By displaying the current date and time, you'll learn how to obtain data from an action bean and display it in a JSP. Having two links shows you how to trigger different event handlers on the action bean. You'll gain a clear understanding of how the view (JSP) and the controller (action bean) work together. Of course, let's not forget the benefit of getting a Stripes application up and running in the first place!

You've already set up a web application skeleton. All you need to get this example working is one action bean (HelloActionBean) and one JSP (hello.jsp). The file structure of the complete example will look like this:

```
WEB-INF/lib/stripes.jar
WEB-INF/lib/commons-logging.jar
WEB-INF/lib/jstl.jar
WEB-INF/lib/standard.jar

WEB-INF/web.xml

WEB-INF/classes/StripesResources.properties
WEB-INF/classes/stripesbook/action/HelloActionBean.class

WEB-INF/jsp/hello.jsp

index.jsp
```

Let's write the HelloActionBean class.

Writing the Action Bean

The action bean provides the date to be displayed and changes it when the user clicks one of the links. Action beans, action beans, all this talk about action beans, but what exactly is an action bean, in terms of *code*? It's a Java class that implements the ActionBean interface:

```java
public interface ActionBean {
    public void setContext(ActionBeanContext context);
    public ActionBeanContext getContext();
}
```

This is just a getter and a setter method for the ActionBeanContext, which contains the current request and response objects along with other useful information about the current request. Stripes takes care of providing the ActionBeanContext to action beans, so you can always count on having easy access to this information in your action beans by calling getContext().

Often, within an application, you'll write an abstract base class that implements the ActionBean interface and have your concrete action beans extend this base class. This also gives you a single place for adding any code that you want to make available to all your action beans.

There is only one action bean in this simple example, so we won't bother creating a separate abstract base class. Let's look at the code for HelloActionBean:

getting_started/src/stripesbook/action/HelloActionBean.java

```java
package stripesbook.action;

import java.util.Date;
import java.util.Random;
import net.sourceforge.stripes.action.ActionBean;
import net.sourceforge.stripes.action.ActionBeanContext;
import net.sourceforge.stripes.action.DefaultHandler;
import net.sourceforge.stripes.action.ForwardResolution;
import net.sourceforge.stripes.action.Resolution;

❶ public class HelloActionBean implements ActionBean {
    private ActionBeanContext ctx;
    public ActionBeanContext getContext() { return ctx; }
    public void setContext(ActionBeanContext ctx) { this.ctx = ctx; }

❷  private Date date;
    public Date getDate() {
        return date;
    }
```

```
        @DefaultHandler
❸       public Resolution currentDate() {
            date = new Date();
            return new ForwardResolution(VIEW);
        }
        public Resolution randomDate() {
            long max = System.currentTimeMillis();
            long random = new Random().nextLong() % max;
            date = new Date(random);
            return new ForwardResolution(VIEW);
        }
        private static final String VIEW = "/WEB-INF/jsp/hello.jsp";
}
```

The class implements the ActionBean interface (❶) with a standard get-ter and setter. Next, the date property is defined at ❷. The JSP will access this property using the Expression Language (EL) to display the date. Finally, the currentDate() event handler (❸) refreshes the current date, while randomDate() produces a random date. Both event handlers set the date property and then forward to /WEB-INF/jsp/hello.jsp using a ForwardResolution. The next step is to create the hello.jsp file.

Writing the JSP

The hello.jsp file is responsible for displaying the page that we see in Fig-ure 2.2, on page 16. Most of it is plain HTML, but there two interesting parts: displaying the date and time and creating links that trigger event handlers on the action bean.

Let's look at the source for hello.jsp:

getting_started/web/WEB-INF/jsp/hello.jsp

```
<%@page contentType="text/html;charset=ISO-8859-1" language="java"%>

<%@taglib prefix="s" uri="http://stripes.sourceforge.net/stripes.tld"%>
<%@taglib prefix="fmt" uri="http://java.sun.com/jsp/jstl/fmt"%>

<!DOCTYPE HTML PUBLIC "-//W3C//DTD HTML 4.01//EN"
  "http://www.w3.org/TR/html4/strict.dtd">
<html>
  <head>
    <title>Hello, Stripes!</title>
  </head>
  <body>
    <h3>Hello, Stripes!</h3>
    <p>
      Date and time:
      <br>
```

```
    <b>
❶    <fmt:formatDate type="both" dateStyle="full"
       value="${actionBean.date}"/>
    </b>
  </p>
  <p>
❷    <s:link beanclass="stripesbook.action.HelloActionBean"
       event="currentDate">
       Show the current date and time
    </s:link> |
    <s:link beanclass="stripesbook.action.HelloActionBean"
       event="randomDate">
       Show a random date and time
    </s:link>
  </p>
  </body>
</html>
```

After the standard **page** directive that declares the page as a Java JSP, the **taglib** directives import the Stripes tag library and the JSTL's formatting tags. I'll use the prefix s to represent the Stripes tag library; most people use either s or stripes. The fmt prefix is standard for the JSTL's formatting tags.

The code at ❶ displays the value of the date property from HelloAction-Bean. The ${actionBean.date} expression calls the getDate() method on the current action bean, and the *<fmt:formatDate>* tag formats the result by displaying both the date and the time in full.

At ❷, the *<s:link>* tag creates a link to the currentDate() event handler of HelloActionBean. Notice how clear this is in the tag: the beanclass= attribute contains the fully qualified class name of the action bean, and event= tells us the name of the method. The link to randomDate() is created in the same way. When we read this code, we know exactly which class and method is called by each link.

Just like that, we've made two types of bindings from the JSP to the action bean: reading data and triggering an event handler, as illustrated in Figure 2.3, on page 21. That was simple, wasn't it? We have links that are bound to event handlers on HelloActionBean, which change the date and redisplay the page by returning a forward resolution back to hello.jsp. Let's talk a little more about these two key concepts: *event handlers* and *resolutions*.

 **Tim Says. . .**

JSP Schmay Ess Pee

That's the response a lot of people have to JSP these days. But the fact that most Stripes applications use JSP (as do the examples in this book) shouldn't put you off. I'll tell you now, JSP isn't nearly as bad as its haters would have you believe. It's true that JSP 1.0 was pretty darn awful and that it got only moderately better with version 1.1. At that point, many developers wrote JSP off entirely and stopped paying attention.

Modern JSP development is a different story. With the introduction of the JSP Expression Language (nowadays just "the Expression Language," or EL), the JSP Standard Tag Library (JSTL), and JSP tag files (essentially custom tags written as JSP fragments), JSP has moved past being painful and ugly to being a competent and usable view technology. It is now easy to develop pages without ever resorting to scriptlets!

A singular advantage of JSP over almost every other view technology out there today is by far and away better documentation, examples, and tool support. Every major IDE has a built-in JSP editor, and there are hundreds of articles and books about how to do JSP development. Chances are that developers on your team and developers you interview are already familiar with JSP—you won't find such a large pool of developers familiar with other templating systems.

And if you really, truly cannot stomach the thought of using JSP, Stripes works equally well with FreeMarker.*

---

*. http://www.freemarker.org. See http://www.stripesframework.org/display/stripes/
FreeMarker+with+Stripes for instructions on using FreeMarker with Stripes.

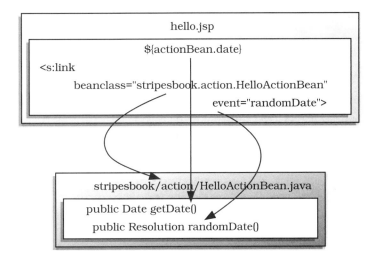

Figure 2.3: Binding a JSP to an action bean

Event Handlers

The currentDate() and randomDate() methods in the action bean are event handlers. But what makes Stripes recognize these methods? We didn't declare them in a configuration file. The method names don't have a special prefix or suffix. It's all in the method *signature*. An event handler is a method that does the following:

- Is declared as **public**
- Returns a Resolution
- Takes no parameters
- Is defined in an action bean

We choose the name of the method, and that becomes the name of the event handler. In HelloActionBean, the two event handlers are named currentDate and randomDate.

When we start the application and the initial request is made to HelloActionBean, how does Stripes know which event handler to execute? Here's where the notion of a *default event handler* comes in. When no event handler is specified (either because of a plain URL or with an <*s:link*> tag with no event= attribute), the default event handler is triggered. Stripes treats an event handler as the default when

- the event handler is annotated with @DefaultHandler, and
- the event handler is the only one defined in the action bean.

Joe Asks...

Where Does ${actionBean} Come From?

This is a feature that Stripes provides—it sets the action bean that has handled the current event as the "actionBean" request-scope attribute. This means that in your JSPs, you can always refer to the current action bean using ${actionBean}. From there, you can access the action bean's properties using standard EL expressions such as ${actionBean.date}. Because Stripes creates new instances of action beans for every request, it's quite appropriate to store request-related values in action bean properties.

With more than one event handler and no @DefaultHandler annotation, Stripes won't know which one is the default and will throw an exception. In the example, @DefaultHandler is on currentDate().

There's nothing wrong with using the @DefaultHandler annotation on an event handler that happens to be the only one defined in an action bean. In fact, consider it good practice, since it clearly marks the intent and saves us from forgetting to specify it if we decide later to add other event handlers to the action bean.

On the other hand, do *not* annotate more than one event handler with @DefaultHandler in the same action bean—you'll get an exception.

After an event handler has done its work, it returns a resolution. What's a resolution, besides something that people have at New Year's and abandon a few weeks later?

Resolutions

A *resolution* tells Stripes what to do next in response to the current request. An example of a resolution is to forward to a JSP, which is what the event handlers of HelloActionBean do by returning a ForwardResolution to /WEB-INF/jsp/hello.jsp.

In terms of actual code, Resolution is a one-method interface:

```
public interface Resolution {
    void execute(HttpServletRequest request,
                 HttpServletResponse response)
        throws Exception;
}
```

 **Tim Says...**

What's with These Resolution Classes and Hard-Coded Paths to Pages?

You might be wondering why we return instances of the Resolution interface directly instead of returning symbols or codes like "SUCCESS" and "FAILURE". Also, is it a bad idea to have paths to JSPs right there in the action bean? The simple answer is that we do things this way because it's simpler, it's easier, and it allows you to do more things without jumping through hoops.

If we were using result codes instead of Resolutions when writing action beans, we would also have to edit a configuration file to set up the result codes and the pages to which they map. That's another file that would have to be kept in sync with our beans; we'd have to be careful that our bean name and result codes always match between two places.

Returning instances of the Resolution interface avoids this and at the same time makes debugging and maintenance much simpler. When you observe a problem with a page, you can find the action bean class from the URL in your browser via the URL binding rules that we discuss in Section 2.3, *Binding to Action Beans*, on page 25. When you look at that class, you can see what it's doing and immediately see which page it forwards to without having to look in yet another file and match up a result code to a page name.

That's not all, though! The most important reason is that this provides a clean and cohesive interface for sending a response to the client that doesn't require the action bean to conform to an interface or put data onto a special stack just to pass it to the Resolution. If you want to add parameters to a forward or stream back a custom data type to the client, it's as easy as this:

```
// Send a forward with additional arbitrary parameters
return new ForwardResolution("/foo.jsp").addParameter("foo", bar);

// Send back a stream of an arbitrary content type
return new StreamingResolution("image/png", inputStream);
```

In my experience, most action beans deal with only one or two pages, and most pages are owned and forwarded to by a single action bean. As a result, even if you hard-code JSP names in your action bean, you're usually hard-coding them in only one place each and not scattering the same name in lots of places. If you still would prefer to centralize your JSP names, it's perfectly simple to move them into a page constants class and reference the constants instead—and since it's code, you'll still be able to click right through in your favorite IDE.

You usually don't need to implement the Resolution interface yourself; most of the time you'll find a ready-to-use Stripes implementation that does what you need:

ForwardResolution

Forwards to a path, such as a JSP, or to another action bean.

RedirectResolution

The same as a ForwardResolution but uses a client-side redirect instead of a forward.

StreamingResolution

Streams data directly back to the client, for example, to produce a binary file.

JavaScriptResolution

Converts a Java object to JavaScript code that is sent back to the client and is suitable for decoding using the JavaScript eval( ) function. This is particularly useful when using Ajax.

ErrorResolution

Sends an HTTP error message back to the client, using a status code and an optional error message.

That gives you an idea of what types of resolutions are provided by Stripes. We'll discuss them in more detail as we use them in examples.

Running the Example

To run the example, package the web application that you've so diligently created, and deploy it to your servlet container. Or, if you have just been reading along without typing anything, you can always take the easy way out and use the book's source code. Just go to the getting_started subdirectory of the source code bundle, and run ant. The example will be packaged into a WAR file, ready to be deployed. After starting your servlet container, use http://localhost:8080/getting_started to run this chapter's example.[4] You should see the page shown in Figure 2.2, on page 16. Try clicking the links to change the displayed date and time.

---

4. Open the index.html file in the root directory of source code bundle to get an index of all the examples.

When running the example, we used the <*welcome-file*> parameter in web.xml to set the default path to index.jsp. This file is a one-liner that forwards to /Hello.action:

`getting_started/web/index.jsp`

```
<jsp:forward page="/Hello.action"/>
```

This path targets HelloActionBean. Remember that we created links to HelloActionBean with the <*s:link*> tag. If you look at the generated HTML code for those links, you will see that they also point to /Hello.action.

So, the question is, how is the path, /Hello.action, connected to the class stripesbook.action.HelloActionBean?

2.3   Binding to Action Beans

Stripes doesn't bother you with URLs and instead lets you work with action bean class names. Behind the scenes, Stripes takes care of generating URLs and binding them with action beans. That's great, but there's no need to be left in the dark about how URLs and action beans are connected. So, let's discuss that briefly.

Remember that Stripes searches the class path at startup, looking for action beans. The fully qualified class name of each action bean that it finds is associated to a URL. Here are the steps involved to carry out this mapping, with the binding of stripesbook.action.HelloActionBean to /Hello.action as an example:

1. Start with the fully qualified class name of the action bean.
    - stripesbook.action.HelloActionBean

2. Remove the package prefix *up to and including* any of the following package names: action, stripes, web, or www.
    - HelloActionBean

3. If present, remove the class name suffix Action, Bean, or Action-Bean.
    - Hello

4. Convert the package and class name to a path by prefixing with a forward slash and changing all periods to forward slashes.
    - /Hello

5. Append the .action suffix.
    - /Hello.action

Action Bean Class	Default URL Binding
a.web.users.UserActionBean	/users/User.action
a.b.UserAction	/a/b/User.action
www.a.b.UserBean	/a/b/User.action
web.a.actions.User	/a/actions/User.action
theweb.ActionBeanImpl	/theweb/ActionBeanImpl.action
a.b.stripes.ActionBean	/.action

Figure 2.4: URL BINDING EXAMPLES

This mechanism is called *URL binding*. When a request arrives, Stripes looks at the URL and searches for the corresponding action bean in the mapping that was constructed during the binding process.

In Figure 2.4, we can see a few more examples of action bean class names and their corresponding URL bindings.

If you're not happy with default URL binding pattern, don't fret. We'll see how it can be changed in Section 13.2, *Customizing URL Bindings*, on page 277.

Using the href Attribute

When creating a link with *<s:link>*, we connected the link to an action bean by indicating the fully qualified class name of the action bean in the tag's beanclass= attribute:

```
<s:link beanclass="stripesbook.action.HelloActionBean"
  event="randomDate">
  Show a random date and time
</s:link>
```

We can also use URL bindings directly, such as /Hello.action, with the href= attribute. In this case, we would have created the link like this:

```
<s:link href="/Hello.action" event="randomDate">
  Show a random date and time
</s:link>
```

Notice that we did not need to put the context path at the beginning of the URL. The href= attribute of the *<s:link>* tag automatically does this for us. In most cases, using the beanclass= attribute is preferable:

- It clearly states which action bean is the target.
- It makes your code independent of URL binding details.

Mind the Context Path!

When you deploy web applications to a servlet container, the context path distinguishes one application from another. With Jetty and Tomcat, for example, an application deployed by placing the myapp.war file in the /webapps directory has a context path of /myapp. You can then access the root of the web application with http://localhost:8080/myapp.

Avoid using the same name for the context path of your web application and for the first part of the package name that contains your action beans—for example, a context path named /myapp and an action bean named myapp.mymodule.ui.MyActionBean. This will cause problems with the URL binding mechanism.

If you *must* use the same name for the context path and the first package name, place your action beans in a package that includes one of the names that are truncated by the URL binding strategy (action, stripes, web, or www), such as myapp.mymodule.ui.stripes.MyActionBean.

- If you decide to move or rename the action bean, modern IDEs will catch the beanclass= references in the refactoring process.

Nevertheless, it's useful to understand how URL binding works. For example, you might need to create links to action beans within non-Stripes tags or from an application that uses a different framework.

The Preaction Pattern

A good practice in a Stripes application is to use what is known as the *preaction* pattern. This consists of always having requests go to action beans rather than directly to JSPs. We did this in the example—both links target HelloActionBean using the beanclass= attribute of the <s:link> tag. There are no direct links to hello.jsp. In fact, we made sure of that by placing the JSP file in the /WEB-INF/jsp directory. In Java web applications, files anywhere under /WEB-INF cannot be accessed by the browser.

Using the preaction pattern has the following advantages:

- Ensures that the current action bean will be available in the JSP using ${actionBean}

- Routes requests through action beans, involving the full Stripes request-response life cycle and giving us more control over what happens between the stages of this life cycle
- Restricts the URLs used to access the application, making it easier to control security
- Targets action beans instead of JSPs, making our code refer to class names instead of URLs

2.4 Wrapping Up

You now have a working development environment and a Stripes application up and running. I hope you've gained a better understanding of the basics of Stripes by looking at the action bean and JSP code.

Here are a few things to notice after completing this exercise:

- Setting up a Stripes application does not stray from the standard procedure for a Java web application, and Stripes has very few dependencies.
- Stripes requires very little configuration. You just need to set up the Stripes modules in the standard web.xml file and indicate the root(s) of the packages that contain your action beans.
- You can add, remove, and rename action beans without having to make changes to the configuration. Stripes will automatically find and load your action beans, as long as they are in a package or subpackage of the roots you've configured.
- Day-to-day work involves action beans and JSPs, not configuration files.
- Your JSPs can link to action beans by class name, making the association crystal clear and shielding your code from the details of URL binding.
- The ${actionBean} expression allows you to generically refer to the current action bean and to its properties.
- You can trigger event handlers on action beans by writing a method that has the appropriate signature and referring to the name of the method in the JSP.

In the next chapter, we'll discover more about action beans, JSPs, and how they work together. We'll learn how to create HTML forms with Stripes. We'll also start the main sample application that we'll be working on for the remainder of the book.

Action is eloquence.
  ► William Shakespeare

Chapter 3

The Core:
Action Beans and JSPs

When you're developing a Stripes application, you will find that most of the work is done in action beans and view templates (JSPs in this book's examples). You use action beans to perform operations and JSPs to show the results.

JSPs also give the user an interface to submit requests, and action beans handle these requests and provide responses. Since action beans and JSPs play such important roles, we'll take a closer look at how they work and interact. We also begin building a "webmail" application in this chapter. This is the sample application that we'll use for the rest of the book.

Why a webmail application?

- It's a very familiar application (everyone uses email nowadays), so the features that we'll implement will feel intuitive.
- We can easily think of many ways to improve the application. Adding features is a great way to learn more about Stripes and gain practical experience.
- There are just too many shopping cart applications out there.
- The market for online pet stores is saturated.

We'll start with the contact list, which contains people with their names, email addresses, phone numbers, and birth dates. Three pages are involved: a Contact List page with a summary of all contacts in a table, a Contact View page that shows a contact's complete information, and a Contact Form page for creating and updating contacts. How you can navigate from one page to another is illustrated in Figure 3.1, on the following page.

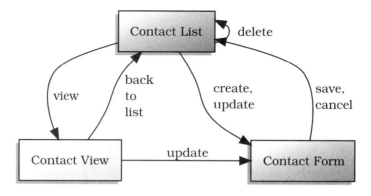

Figure 3.1: THE CONTACT LIST, VIEW, AND FORM PAGES

3.1 Let's CRUD

Just about every web application that does something useful is a CRUD application: it Creates, Reads, Updates, and Deletes data. Here, the data is the contact information. Implementing a CRUD application is a great way to learn more about how a framework works, and you'll see how easy it is to build this application with Stripes.

As we saw in Chapter 1, *Introduction*, Stripes is an MVC framework that provides support in the controller and view layers. But first, we need a model. This is not part of Stripes, but every application needs at least one class to represent the model—the contacts, in our case.

The Model Layer

We'll use a simple Contact class to represent a contact. This is a typical model class with properties for the contact's information. It also has an id property that uniquely identifies a contact object and makes it easy to write the equals() and hashCode() methods. These methods are important because Java uses them when comparing one object with another, adding objects to collections, and so on. Finally, Contact has a toString() method so that objects are displayed with the person's first and last names.

Here is the code for the Contact class:[1]

email_01/src/stripesbook/model/Contact.java

```java
package stripesbook.model;
public class Contact {
    private Integer id;
    private String firstName;
    private String lastName;
    private String email;
    private String phoneNumber;
    private Date birthDate;

    /* Getters and setters... */

    @Override
    public boolean equals(Object obj) {
        try { return id.equals(((Contact) obj).getId()); }
        catch (Exception exc) { return false; }
    }
    @Override
    public int hashCode() {
        return 31 + ((id == null) ? 0 : id.hashCode());
    }
    @Override
    public String toString() {
        return String.format("%s %s", firstName, lastName);
    }
}
```

The Data Access Layer

Now that we have a model, we need to make it easy for action beans (the controller) to work with this model. The approach I like to use is the Data Access Object (DAO). This is basically an object with methods to create, read, update, and delete model objects. Action beans don't need to know how objects get stored and retrieved, and the DAO hides these implementation details.

Since we might want to use different ways of managing model objects, we'll use an interface to define the DAO methods. Action beans call methods on this interface and do not need to change if we decide to swap implementations.

---

1. To reduce "noise," I leave out the import statements in code listings from this point on. Most of the time, I also omit getter and setter methods.

We'll call this interface ContactDao:

email_01/src/stripesbook/dao/ContactDao.java

```java
package stripesbook.dao;
public interface ContactDao {
    public List<Contact> read();
    public Contact read(Integer id);
    public void save(Contact contact);
    public void delete(Integer id);
}
```

You can retrieve all contacts in a list, or you can retrieve a single contact by ID. The save() method combines both creating and updating a contact. This way, you don't need to worry about whether a contact is new or existing. Just call save() and let the DAO figure it out. Finally, you can delete a contact by ID.

Now we need an implementation of ContactDao. I don't want to bog you down with the details of setting up a database, a JDBC abstraction layer, and so on. So to keep things simple, I wrote a MockContactDao class that manages objects in memory using plain Java data structures. The code is not important (you can always go check it out if you're curious). All you need to know here is that MockContactDao.getInstance() gives you a working implementation of ContactDao.[2]

We're done with the model and data access layers. Now it's time to return to Stripes and write some code that supports the action beans and JSPs that we'll be adding as we build the webmail application.

3.2   Writing a Base for a Stripes Application

In the "Hello, Stripes!" example from Chapter 2, *Stripes 101: Getting Started*, we wrote a very simple application just to get your feet wet. But when you write more complex Stripes applications with several action beans and JSPs, you'll want a base of reusable code: a base class for the action beans, a JSP for the tag libraries, and a JSP for a common page layout. You need to write this code only once, and it's worth the trouble: you'll benefit each time you add an action bean or a JSP, as well as when you need to add or modify behavior for the whole application.

---

2.   We'll look at using DAOs that connect to databases in Section 12.1, *Persistence with Stripersist, JPA, and Hibernate*, on page 239.

Support for Action Beans

A base class for action beans implements the ActionBean interface:

email_01/src/stripesbook/action/BaseActionBean.java

```java
package stripesbook.action;
public abstract class BaseActionBean implements ActionBean {
    private ActionBeanContext actionBeanContext;

    public ActionBeanContext getContext() {
        return actionBeanContext;
    }
    public void setContext(ActionBeanContext actionBeanContext) {
        this.actionBeanContext = actionBeanContext;
    }
}
```

When you add an action bean, you can just extend this class and get on with your business. BaseActionBean is also the place to put any other common code that you might want to reuse in all action beans.

Support for JSPs

For JSPs, it's nice to have all the tag library declarations in one place, such as in this taglibs.jsp file:

email_01/web/WEB-INF/jsp/common/taglibs.jsp

```jsp
<%@taglib prefix="s" uri="http://stripes.sourceforge.net/stripes.tld"%>

<%@taglib prefix="c" uri="http://java.sun.com/jsp/jstl/core"%>
<%@taglib prefix="fmt" uri="http://java.sun.com/jsp/jstl/fmt"%>

<c:set var="contextPath" value="${pageContext.request.contextPath}"/>
```

Besides importing the Stripes tag library and the JSTL, I've added a shortcut to the context path. Being a lazy typist, I prefer to use ${contextPath} whenever I need the context path, instead of ${pageContext.request.contextPath}.

Now, we get the tag libraries and the context path shortcut in a JSP with just one line:

```jsp
<%@include file="/WEB-INF/jsp/common/taglibs.jsp"%>
```

Finally, you'll appreciate having a JSP that provides a layout that's reused for every page of the application. It saves you from copying and pasting boilerplate HTML code and gives your pages a consistent look and feel.

In Chapter 7, *Reusable Layouts*, on page 131, we'll talk all about the Stripes layout mechanism, but here's a quick introduction. All we need is three tags:

- <s:layout-definition> in some.jsp

  This identifies some.jsp as a reusable layout.

- <s:layout-render name="/path/to/some.jsp"> in another.jsp

  This indicates that another.jsp uses the some.jsp layout to render a page.

- <s:layout-component name="*someName*">

  Within <*s:layout-definition*>, this tag says, "Put the contents of the *someName* component here." But within <*layout-render*>, it means this: "Here is the contents of the *someName* component." The renderer sends contents to the definition, and the definition decides where to place it within the layout. The other way for a renderer to send something to a definition is with arbitrary attributes. <*s:layout-render name="..." title="My Title"*> gives the definition a title attribute with a value of *My Title*. The definition can use ${title} to place this value in the layout.

That's a fair amount of theory, but it's really quite simple. Have a look at the code for layout_main.jsp, which we'll use for the webmail application:

email_01/web/WEB-INF/jsp/common/layout_main.jsp

```
<%@page contentType="text/html;charset=ISO-8859-1" language="java"%>
<%@include file="/WEB-INF/jsp/common/taglibs.jsp"%>

<s:layout-definition>
  <!DOCTYPE HTML PUBLIC "-//W3C//DTD HTML 4.01//EN"
    "http://www.w3.org/TR/html4/strict.dtd">
  <html>
    <head>
❶    <title>${title}</title>
      <link rel="stylesheet" type="text/css"
❷      href="${contextPath}/css/style.css">
    </head>
    <body>
      <div id="header">
❸        <span class="title">${title}</span>
      </div>
      <div id="body">
❹        <s:layout-component name="body"/>
      </div>
    </body>
  </html>
</s:layout-definition>
```

The <*s:layout-definition*> tag declares this JSP as a reusable layout.

Each page specifies a title, which the layout places at ❶ and ❸, and a body, which is placed at ❹. The layout provides a common HTML structure and imports style.css (a cascading style sheet) at ❷ using that convenient ${contextPath} shortcut I mentioned earlier.

With the layout_main.jsp file, we've created the page declaration, header, CSS file, and body structure for every page of the application. Instead of repeating all that code each time we add a JSP, we render the layout and need to specify only the title and the body contents. For example, this JSP:

```
<%@include file="/WEB-INF/jsp/common/taglibs.jsp"%>
<s:layout-render name="/WEB-INF/jsp/common/layout_main.jsp"
  title="My Title">
  <s:layout-component name="body">
    My page content
  </s:layout-component>
</s:layout-render>
```

produces the following result:

```
<html>
  <head>
    <title>My Title</title>
    <link rel="stylesheet" type="text/css"
      href="/myapp/css/style.css"/>
  </head>
  <body>
    <div id="header">
      <span class="title">My Title</span>
    </div>
    <div id="body">
      My page content
    </div>
  </body>
</html>
```

Pretty cool, no? Let's take a quick break here, and you can have a cold glass or hot cup of your favorite drink. Then we'll write the action bean and JSP for retrieving and displaying the contact list.

3.3 Displaying Data with Action Beans and JSPs

Let's display the list of contacts in a table. The best way to do this in Stripes is to write an action bean that obtains the list from the DAO and makes it available in a getter method. Then it's easy to write a JSP that retrieves the list from the action bean and renders it in an HTML table. That's all we need, clean and simple.

The Contact List Action Bean

We'll name the action bean that retrieves the list of contacts ContactList-ActionBean. The default event handler forwards to the JSP, and a getter method returns the list of contacts by calling read() on ContactDao (implemented by MockContactDao):

email_01/src/stripesbook/action/ContactListActionBean.java

```java
package stripesbook.action;
public class ContactListActionBean extends BaseActionBean {
    private static final String LIST="/WEB-INF/jsp/contact_list.jsp";
    private ContactDao contactDao = MockContactDao.getInstance();

    @DefaultHandler
    public Resolution list() {
        return new ForwardResolution(LIST);
    }
    public List<Contact> getContacts() {
        return contactDao.read();
    }
}
```

The Contact List JSP

ContactListActionBean forwards to contact_list.jsp, which renders an HTML table by iterating over the list of contacts and creating a table row for each contact:

email_01/web/WEB-INF/jsp/contact_list.jsp

```jsp
<%@include file="/WEB-INF/jsp/common/taglibs.jsp"%>

❶ <s:layout-render name="/WEB-INF/jsp/common/layout_main.jsp"
    title="Contact List">
    <s:layout-component name="body">
      <table>
        <tr>
          <th>First name</th>
          <th>Last name</th>
          <th>Email</th>
        </tr>
❷       <c:forEach var="contact" items="${actionBean.contacts}">
          <tr>
            <td>${contact.firstName}</td>
            <td>${contact.lastName}</td>
            <td>${contact.email}</td>
          </tr>
        </c:forEach>
      </table>
    </s:layout-component>
</s:layout-render>
```

At ❶ we're using the layout that we created earlier, with "Contact List" as the page's title. The page's body is the content between the <s:layout-component> tags.

After some standard table-rendering HTML, at ❷ we retrieve the list of contacts from the action bean with ${actionBean.contacts} and loop using the JSTL's <c:forEach> tag. Each individual contact is placed in the contact variable. We can then create rows of data and display the contact information by accessing the properties of contact.

Putting It All Together

Combining everything that we've created so far, we can obtain the contact list with the /ContactList.action URL. This triggers the default event handler of ContactListActionBean, which forwards to contact_list.jsp. In this JSP, the action bean is available via ${actionBean}, so ${action-Bean.contacts} calls getContacts() and obtains the list of contacts, which is then displayed in a table. This sequence is illustrated in Figure 3.2, on the next page, and the resulting table is shown in Figure 3.3, on page 39.

As you can see, the MockContactDao comes with batteries included—it is prepopulated with a list of ten contacts.[3]

So far so good. But you've probably noticed that the table looks rather bland. Let's pretty it up.

Using Display Tag

Display Tag (http://displaytag.sourceforge.net/) is a library for creating HTML tables. It is not part of Stripes, and it isn't required in order to use Stripes. But we'll use it as an example of how easy it is to integrate a third-party library that does what we want instead of having to write the code ourselves. Display Tag automatically makes the data sortable by clicking the column headers and adds CSS classes so that we can shade odd and even rows in different colors. The code in the JSP becomes even simpler—we get more for less.

To use Display Tag, add its required JAR files to the /WEB-INF/lib directory, and declare the library in taglibs.jsp:

email_02/web/WEB-INF/jsp/common/taglibs.jsp

```
<%@taglib prefix="d" uri="http://displaytag.sf.net"%>
```

---

3. The names are fictitious. They were obtained using the Random Name Generator (http://www.xtra-rant.com/gennames).

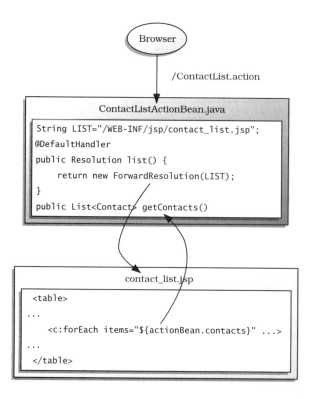

Figure 3.2: Displaying the contact list

In contact_list.jsp, we can now use <d:table> and <d:column> from Display Tag to render the table of contacts:

email_02/web/WEB-INF/jsp/contact_list.jsp

```
<%@include file="/WEB-INF/jsp/common/taglibs.jsp"%>

<s:layout-render name="/WEB-INF/jsp/common/layout_main.jsp"
  title="Contact List">
  <s:layout-component name="body">
    <d:table name="${actionBean.contacts}" id="contact" requestURI=""
      defaultsort="1">
    <d:column title="Last name" property="lastName"
      sortable="true"/>
    <d:column title="First name" property="firstName"
      sortable="true"/>
    <d:column title="Email" property="email" sortable="true"/>
    </d:table>
  </s:layout-component>
</s:layout-render>
```

Contact List

First name	Last name	Email
Sophie	Hunter	sh@stripesbook.org
Daniel	Greene	dg@stripesbook.org
Jen	Ballou	jb@stripesbook.org
Sammy	Blair	sb@stripesbook.org
Betty	Stocker	bs@stripesbook.org
Lou	Thompson	lt@stripesbook.org
Lexi	Hawk	lh@stripesbook.org
George	Wells	gw@stripesbook.org
Donna	McCallum	dm@stripesbook.org
Jason	Wilson	jw@stripesbook.org

Figure 3.3: THE LIST OF CONTACTS IN A BASIC TABLE

The code is more compact and more powerful. The <d:table> tag takes the list of objects from name= and places each object in the variable indicated in id=. The empty requestURI="" parameter is necessary so that the sorting URLs constructed by the Display Tag build on the Stripes URL. The table is now sortable by column and is sorted by the first column by default with defaultsort="1".

Each <d:column> tag adds a column to the table, with the given title= and the data coming from the property= of each object. Each column is made sortable by adding sortable="true".

Shading Alternate Rows

Display Tag adds class="odd" or class="even" to the <tr> tags that it generates. To shade these rows in different colors, you just have to style them in the CSS file.

For example:

email_02/web/css/style.css

```
tr.odd {
  background-color: #E5F5E5;
}
tr.even {
  background-color: #FFFFFF;
}
```

> ⋁⁄⁄ **Joe Asks...**
> ⤳⤳
> **Doesn't Stripes Have a Table Tag or Something?**
>
> Displaying HTML tables is a common task. Many libraries exist to make it a breeze to create tables with sophisticated features. In light of this, Stripes does not reinvent the wheel. Instead, it is designed for easy integration of third-party libraries.
>
> In that spirit, you can use Display Tag to jazz up your tables. There are other libraries, of course, such as *JMesa* (http://code. google.com/p/jmesa) and *ValueList* (http://valuelist.sourceforge. net), to name a few.

Highlighting the Sorted Column

Display Tag also adds classes to $<th>$ tags according to the currently sorted column and the sort direction. Let's highlight this column with a gradient shading, with the direction of the gradient indicating the sort direction. After creating the ascending and descending gradient images, this code styles the columns:

`email_02/web/css/style.css`

```css
th.sorted {
  background-color: #EECCAA;
}
th.order1 {
  background-image: url(../images/gradient_asc.png);
}
th.order2 {
  background-image: url(../images/gradient_desc.png);
}
```

Our Display Tag–powered table is now as shown in Figure 3.4, on the next page. We livened up the table with very little effort. Although there's nothing wrong with generating HTML tables yourself, it's nice to know that you can easily integrate your favorite library to do the work for you.

Contact List

Last name	First name	Email
Ballou	Jen	jb@stripesbook.org
Blair	Sammy	sb@stripesbook.org
Greene	Daniel	dg@stripesbook.org
Hawk	Lexi	lh@stripesbook.org
Hunter	Sophie	sh@stripesbook.org
McCallum	Donna	dm@stripesbook.org
Stocker	Betty	bs@stripesbook.org
Thompson	Lou	lt@stripesbook.org
Wells	George	gw@stripesbook.org
Wilson	Jason	jw@stripesbook.org

Figure 3.4: THE CONTACT LIST IN A DISPLAY TAG TABLE

3.4 Parameterized Links

Let's return to Stripes. We'll add the View and Delete links next to each contact in the last column of the table (Figure 3.5, on the following page).

Back on page 19, we saw how to create links with *<s:link>* and how to trigger an action bean's event handler with the beanclass= and event= attributes. Now, the links in each row of the table views or deletes the corresponding contact. How do we indicate the target contact for each link? With parameters.

Adding Parameters to Links

Parameterized links are powerful because they provide additional information that the action bean can then use. Stripes makes it easy to add parameters to links: add a property on the action bean and an *<s:param>* tag within *<s:link>* in the JSP. We can add as many parameters as we need; we indicate the name= and value= of each parameter in the *<s:param>* tag. When the user clicks the link, Stripes binds each parameter value to the corresponding property on the action bean

Contact List

Last name	First name	Email	Action
Ballou	Jen	jb@stripesbook.org	View | Delete
Blair	Sammy	sb@stripesbook.org	View | Delete
Greene	Daniel	dg@stripesbook.org	View | Delete
Hawk	Lexi	lh@stripesbook.org	View | Delete
Hunter	Sophie	sh@stripesbook.org	View | Delete
McCallum	Donna	dm@stripesbook.org	View | Delete
Stocker	Betty	bs@stripesbook.org	View | Delete
Thompson	Lou	lt@stripesbook.org	View | Delete
Wells	George	gw@stripesbook.org	View | Delete
Wilson	Jason	jw@stripesbook.org	View | Delete

Figure 3.5: ADDING VIEW AND DELETE LINKS

before invoking the event handler, as illustrated in Figure 3.6, on the facing page.

To send the contact ID as a parameter for the View and Delete links, add a column to the table like this:

```
email_03/web/WEB-INF/jsp/contact_list.jsp
<d:column title="Action">
  <s:link beanclass="stripesbook.action.ContactListActionBean"
    event="view">
    <s:param name="contactId" value="${contact.id}"/>
    View
  </s:link> |
  <s:link beanclass="stripesbook.action.ContactListActionBean"
    event="delete">
    <s:param name="contactId" value="${contact.id}"/>
    Delete
  </s:link>
</d:column>
```

Clicking either link first calls setContactId(Integer) on the action bean and supplies the contact ID as a parameter. It then calls the event handler.

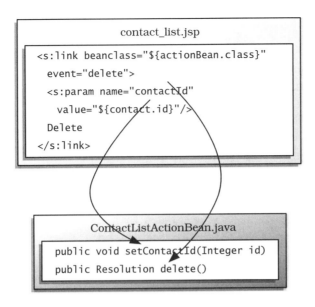

Figure 3.6: BINDING A LINK PARAMETER

Viewing Contact Information Details

Clicking the View link brings the user to a page that shows the contact information details, as shown in Figure 3.7, on page 45. We'll need to add code in ContactListActionBean to receive the parameter, retrieve the contact, and forward to the view:

email_03/src/stripesbook/action/ContactListActionBean.java

```
private static final String VIEW="/WEB-INF/jsp/contact_view.jsp";
public Resolution view() {
    return new ForwardResolution(VIEW);
}
private Integer contactId;

public void setContactId(Integer id) {
    contactId = id;
}
public Contact getContact() {
    return contactDao.read(contactId);
}
```

Notice that the contactId property is of type Integer, even though all parameters that come from an HTTP request are limited to the String type. Stripes automatically converts the parameter to an Integer for us.

The beanclass Attribute Also Accepts a Class

We're using a String value in the beanclass= attribute to indicate the fully qualified class name of the action bean. Another way is to use an expression that resolves to the actual Class of the action bean.

For example, you could use ${actionBean.class} to refer to the class of the current action bean:

```
<s:link beanclass="${actionBean.class}" .../>
```

This *dynamically* refers to the current action bean when triggering event handlers, opening the door to using the same JSP for more than one action bean. The JSP doesn't need to "know" which action bean is being used.

Dynamic magic is nice, but there is a drawback. When you are reading JSP code and you see beanclass="stripesbook. action.ContactListActionBean", you know exactly which action bean handles the request. But beanclass="${actionBean.class}" just tells you "the current action bean." It's not obvious which action bean is associated to the JSP—and there could even be more than one.

This is great—no need to manually convert String parameters to primitive types and their wrapper classes. Just declare the property using the desired type in the action bean, and Stripes uses a *type converter* to do the necessary conversion.

Now it's simple to retrieve the selected contact by using the DAO and the contact ID parameter. The JSP can now read the contact with ${actionBean.contact}.

The contact_view.jsp source is quite straightforward. It displays the information for the selected contact and adds a link at the bottom to return to the contact list:

email_03/web/WEB-INF/jsp/contact_view.jsp

```
<%@include file="/WEB-INF/jsp/common/taglibs.jsp"%>

<s:layout-render name="/WEB-INF/jsp/common/layout_main.jsp"
  title="Contact Information">
  <s:layout-component name="body">
    <table class="view">
```

Contact Information

First name: Jen
Last name: Ballou
Email: jb@stripesbook.org
Phone number: 555-555-6495
Birth date: Mon Aug 30 00:00:00 EDT 1982

Back to List

Figure 3.7: VIEWING THE FULL CONTACT INFORMATION

```
<tr>
  <td class="label">First name:</td>
  <td class="value">${actionBean.contact.firstName}</td>
</tr>
<tr>
  <td class="label">Last name:</td>
  <td class="value">${actionBean.contact.lastName}</td>
</tr>
<tr>
  <td class="label">Email:</td>
  <td class="value">${actionBean.contact.email}</td>
</tr>
<tr>
  <td class="label">Phone number:</td>
  <td class="value">${actionBean.contact.phoneNumber}</td>
</tr>
<tr>
  <td class="label">Birth date:</td>
  <td class="value">${actionBean.contact.birthDate}</td>
</tr>
</table>
<p>
  <s:link beanclass="stripesbook.action.ContactListActionBean">
    Back to List
  </s:link>
</p>
</s:layout-component>
</s:layout-render>
```

Excellent. Since the contact list and contact view pages are so closely
related, we were able to combine the code for both pages in the same
action bean and add the contact view page with just a JSP.

Deleting Contacts

To delete the contact when the user clicks the Delete link, we just need a delete() event handler in ContactListActionBean:

email_03/src/stripesbook/action/ContactListActionBean.java

```
public Resolution delete() {
    contactDao.delete(contactId);
    return new RedirectResolution(getClass());
}
```

After deleting the contact, we are using a RedirectResolution to the action bean instead of a ForwardResolution to the JSP. I'll explain this in Section 3.7, *The Redirect-After-Side-Effect Pattern*, on page 56.

3.5 Displaying Messages to the User

When the user clicks a Delete link, the contact is immediately deleted. This could be a little more forgiving. Since deleting a contact is such a drastic operation, we want the user to confirm before proceeding—just in case the user had a twitch and clicked the link by mistake.

"Are You Sure?" Messages

To ask for confirmation before proceeding, we can use the onclick= attribute in the link. This and other standard HTML attributes are accepted by Stripes tags as "pass-through," meaning that the attribute and its value are rendered as is. Clicking the link executes the Java-Script code provided in onclick=:

email_04/web/WEB-INF/jsp/contact_list.jsp

```
<s:link beanclass="stripesbook.action.ContactListActionBean"
    event="delete"
▶   onclick="return confirm('Delete ${contact}?');">
    <s:param name="contactId" value="${contact.id}"/>
    Delete
</s:link>
```

This asks the user to confirm the operation using the dialog box shown in Figure 3.8, on the next page. Notice that we used ${contact} to include the name of the contact in the message that appears in the dialog box. This is nicer than a catchall message such as "Delete the selected contact?" because we also confirm *which* contact to delete.

Contact List

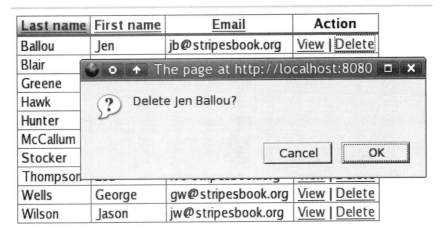

Last name	First name	Email	Action
Ballou	Jen	jb@stripesbook.org	View | Delete
Blair			
Greene			
Hawk			
Hunter			
McCallum			
Stocker			
Thompson			
Wells	George	gw@stripesbook.org	View | Delete
Wilson	Jason	jw@stripesbook.org	View | Delete

Figure 3.8: DIALOG BOX TO CONFIRM BEFORE DELETE

Information Messages

OK, so we've added a message *before* deleting a contact. It'd be nice to also add a message *after* deleting to inform the user that the operation was successful.

Stripes provides a simple mechanism for displaying information messages. It is a two-step process:

1. Add messages to the action bean context.
2. Display them in the view.

Adding Messages to the Context

The ActionBeanContext contains a list of information messages. We can retrieve the list via getMessages() and add messages with add(Message). Here's how we add a message to confirm that a contact was deleted:

`email_04/src/stripesbook/action/ContactListActionBean.java`

```java
public Resolution delete() {
    Contact deleted = contactDao.read(contactId);
    contactDao.delete(contactId);
    getContext().getMessages().add(
        new SimpleMessage("Deleted {0}.", deleted)
    );
    return new RedirectResolution(getClass());
}
```

Contact List

- Deleted Jen Ballou.

Last name	First name	Email	Action
Blair	Sammy	sb@stripesbook.org	View | Delete
Greene	Daniel	dg@stripesbook.org	View | Delete
Hawk	Lexi	lh@stripesbook.org	View | Delete
Hunter	Sophie	sh@stripesbook.org	View | Delete
McCallum	Donna	dm@stripesbook.org	View | Delete
Stocker	Betty	bs@stripesbook.org	View | Delete
Thompson	Lou	lt@stripesbook.org	View | Delete
Wells	George	gw@stripesbook.org	View | Delete
Wilson	Jason	jw@stripesbook.org	View | Delete

Figure 3.9: CONFIRMATION MESSAGE AFTER DELETING A CONTACT

The add() method requires an object that implements the Message interface. Stripes provides classes that fit most needs—we're using SimpleMessage, which provides a constructor that accepts parameters to be used when building the message. The parameters are replaced with values using the standard Java text-formatting syntax. Here we put the contact's name at the {0} placeholder in the message.

Displaying Messages in the View

Once we've added messages to the ActionBeanContext's list, we can display them in the view with the <s:messages/> tag. For example, we can place this tag before the table in contact_list.jsp:

```
...
<s:layout-component name="body">
  <s:messages/>
  <d:table ...>
...
```

Now, when the user deletes a contact, an information message is displayed as in Figure 3.9.

Not bad at all. We have the Contact List and Contact View pages working and linked together, and we're able to delete contacts directly in

---

⌇⌇ **Joe Asks...**
ʒʃ
~ **What If I Don't Like How Messages Are Displayed?**

By default, information messages are displayed in a plain unordered list (<*ul*> and <*li*> tags). We'll see how to customize this format in Chapter 6, *Customizing Stripes Messages*, on page 111.

---

the contact list. Let's see about creating new contacts and updating existing contacts with the Contact Form page.

3.6 Creating Forms

Forms are a breeze to create in Stripes. There is a Stripes tag for every type of input field (text field, radio button, and so on) and for submit buttons. Using these tags instead of plain HTML gives you extra features such as repopulating the inputs, highlighting them when they are in error, and supporting localization.

When the user submits a form, Stripes binds the values in the form fields to the corresponding properties in the action bean and triggers the event handler associated with the submit button. You can have multiple submit buttons without having to do anything special to figure out which button the user clicked: each button triggers its own event handler on the action bean.

Input fields have to be associated to properties of an action bean, but you don't have to copy the properties of a model object to the action bean. Instead, you put the model object directly in the action bean and use *nested* properties.

For example, you can add a Contact property in ContactListActionBean and create a text field associated with the contact's first name with <s:text name="contact.firstName"/>. To set the value, Stripes calls getContact().setFirstName() on the action bean. You don't even have to worry about a NullPointerException. If getContact() returns **null**, Stripes creates a new Contact object for you. This saves you a great deal of code because you don't have to copy each model property in the action bean and transfer information back and forth. If your model objects use other

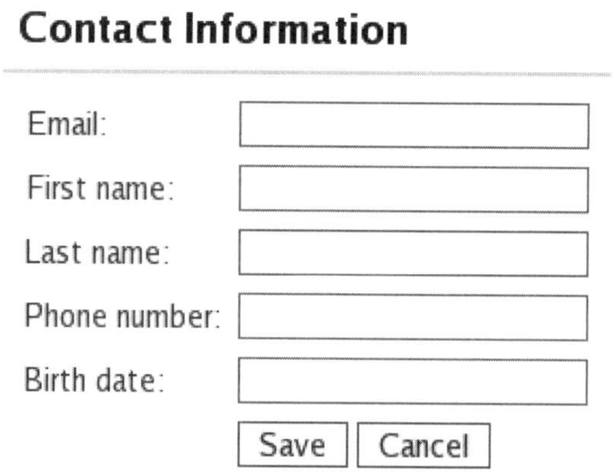

Contact Information

Email:	
First name:	
Last name:	
Phone number:	
Birth date:	

[Save] [Cancel]

Figure 3.10: THE CONTACT FORM

model objects, that's no problem either—Stripes happily uses deeply nested properties, such as "contact.address.street.name". Let's put all this to work and build a form for contacts.

Creating a Blank Form

The <s:form> tag creates a form associated with the action bean indicated in its beanclass= attribute. Within the tag, we add input fields with tags such as <s:text>, <s:radio>, and every other type of input. These tags all have a name= attribute in which we put the name of the action bean property that receives the user's input. To complete the form, we add one or more submit buttons with the <s:submit> tag and the name= of the event handler associated with the button.

Have a look at the following code. This creates the form shown in Figure 3.10:

email_05/web/WEB-INF/jsp/contact_form.jsp

```
❶   <s:form beanclass="stripesbook.action.ContactFormActionBean">
      <table class="form">
        <tr>
          <td>Email:</td>
❷         <td><s:text name="contact.email"/></td>
        </tr>
        <tr>
          <td>First name:</td>
          <td><s:text name="contact.firstName"/></td>
        </tr>
```

```
  <tr>
    <td>Last name:</td>
    <td><s:text name="contact.lastName"/></td>
  </tr>
  <tr>
    <td>Phone number:</td>
    <td><s:text name="contact.phoneNumber"/></td>
  </tr>
  <tr>
    <td>Birth date:</td>
    <td><s:text name="contact.birthDate"/></td>
  </tr>
  <tr>
    <td> </td>
    <td>
❸     <s:submit name="save" value="Save"/>
      <s:submit name="cancel" value="Cancel"/>
    </td>
  </tr>
</table>
</s:form>
```

At ❶, we're creating a form associated with the ContactFormActionBean class, which we'll be writing shortly. Starting at ❷, the text input fields for the contact's information are created with the <s:text> tag and name= attributes for the properties of the Contact class. The submit buttons (❸) call either save() or cancel() on the action bean according to which one the user clicked. The value= attribute is the button's label.

Notice how there is a very clean and clear relationship between the JSP and the action bean. The action bean's class name is indicated in the form tag's beanclass= attribute, each input's name= corresponds to an action bean property, and each submit button's name= is an action bean's event handler.

Let's create the ContactFormActionBean to handle the form submission. We'll need the following:

- A default event handler that forwards to contact_form.jsp
- The save() and cancel() event handlers
- The contactId and contact properties
- The ContactDao to save the contact

Looking at those last two points, you'll realize that the ContactListAction-Bean class already has the contact properties and DAO. You probably don't like copying and pasting code any more than I do, so let's do a little refactoring.

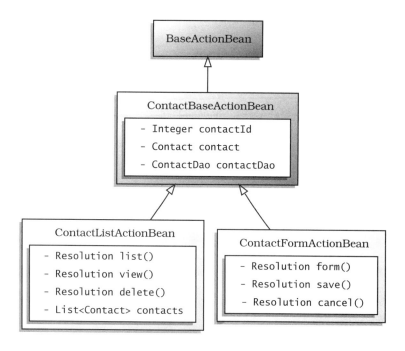

Figure 3.11: ACTION BEAN CLASS DIAGRAM

Check out Figure 3.11. We'll create the ContactBaseActionBean class and put the common code in there. Then, ContactListActionBean and Contact-FormActionBean can inherit from it.

Here is the ContactBaseActionBean class:

email_05/src/stripesbook/action/ContactBaseActionBean.java

```java
package stripesbook.action;
public abstract class ContactBaseActionBean extends BaseActionBean {
    private ContactDao contactDao = MockContactDao.getInstance();
    protected ContactDao getContactDao() {
        return contactDao;
    }
    private Integer contactId;
    public Integer getContactId() {
        return contactId;
    }
    public void setContactId(Integer id) {
        contactId = id;
    }
    private Contact contact;
```

```
        public Contact getContact() {
            if (contactId != null) {
                return contactDao.read(contactId);
            }
            return contact;
        }
        public void setContact(Contact contact) {
            this.contact = contact;
        }
    }
```

The code in the ContactFormActionBean class is now lean and mean:

email_05/src/stripesbook/action/ContactFormActionBean.java

```
package stripesbook.action;
public class ContactFormActionBean extends ContactBaseActionBean {
    private static final String FORM="/WEB-INF/jsp/contact_form.jsp";

    @DefaultHandler
❶   public Resolution form() {
        return new ForwardResolution(FORM);
    }
❷   public Resolution save() {
        Contact contact = getContact();
        getContactDao().save(contact);
        getContext().getMessages().add(
            new SimpleMessage("{0} has been saved.", contact)
        );
        return new RedirectResolution(ContactListActionBean.class);
    }
❸   public Resolution cancel() {
        getContext().getMessages().add(
            new SimpleMessage("Action cancelled.")
        );
        return new RedirectResolution(ContactListActionBean.class);
    }
}
```

The default event handler at ❶ forwards to contact_form.jsp. When the user clicks the $\boxed{\text{Save}}$ button, save() is called (❷) and uses the DAO to save the contact. It then adds an information message to the list and redirects to ContactListActionBean, which displays the messages and the table of contacts. The event handler for the $\boxed{\text{Cancel}}$ button (❸) just adds an information message and redirects to the contact list without saving the contact.

Contact List

- Kaylyn Shallenberger has been saved.

Create a New Contact

Last name	First name	Email	Action
Ballou	Jen	jb@stripesbook.org	View | Update | Delete
Blair	Sammy	sb@stripesbook.org	View | Update | Delete
Greene	Daniel	dg@stripesbook.org	View | Update | Delete
Hawk	Lexi	lh@stripesbook.org	View | Update | Delete
Hunter	Sophie	sh@stripesbook.org	View | Update | Delete
McCallum	Donna	dm@stripesbook.org	View | Update | Delete
Shallenberger	Kaylyn	ks@stripesbook.org	View | Update | Delete
Stocker	Betty	bs@stripesbook.org	View | Update | Delete
Thompson	Lou	lt@stripesbook.org	View | Update | Delete
Wells	George	gw@stripesbook.org	View | Update | Delete
Wilson	Jason	jw@stripesbook.org	View | Update | Delete

Figure 3.12: AFTER CREATING A CONTACT

To send the user from the contact list to the form, add a Create a New Contact link in contact_list.jsp:

`email_05/web/WEB-INF/jsp/contact_list.jsp`

```
<s:link beanclass="stripesbook.action.ContactFormActionBean">
  Create a New Contact
</s:link>
```

The result of using the form to create a new contact fictitiously named Kaylyn Shallenberger is shown in Figure 3.12.

There's only one more thing we need to do: add the Update links in the Action column.

Updating Information with a Prepopulated Form

Clicking the Update link should open the contact form prepopulated with the selected contact's information, as in Figure 3.13, on the next page. First, create the link with the selected contact's ID as a parameter:

`email_05/web/WEB-INF/jsp/contact_list.jsp`

```
<s:link beanclass="stripesbook.action.ContactFormActionBean">
  <s:param name="contactId" value="${contact.id}"/>
  Update
</s:link>
```

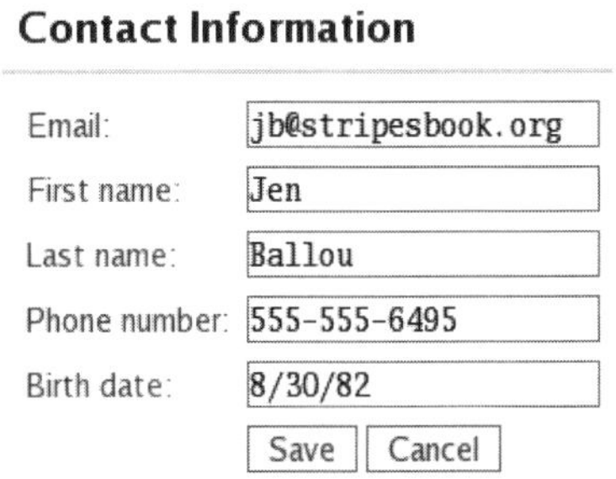

Contact Information

Email:	jb@stripesbook.org
First name:	Jen
Last name:	Ballou
Phone number:	555-555-6495
Birth date:	8/30/82

Save Cancel

Figure 3.13: PREPOPULATED FORM

Remember that the getContact() method in ContactBaseActionBean already retrieves the selected contact if the contact ID parameter was provided:

email_05/src/stripesbook/action/ContactBaseActionBean.java

```
public Contact getContact() {
    if (contactId != null) {
        return contactDao.read(contactId);
    }
    return contact;
}
```

The nice thing with the Stripes input tags is that they also *read* from the property in the name= attribute. So by making the selected contact available through getContact(), the inputs prepopulate themselves with the contact information such as *"contact.firstName"*, *"contact.lastName"*, and so on.

Just like that, we're almost there. To get the form to work for updating an existing contact, we need to resubmit the contact ID parameter that was sent with the Update link.

A hidden input does the trick:

email_05/web/WEB-INF/jsp/contact_form.jsp

```
    <s:form beanclass="stripesbook.action.ContactFormActionBean">
      <div><s:hidden name="contact.id"/></div>
      <table class="form">
```

The input obtains its value just like the other inputs and becomes a parameter when the form is submitted. It took very little code to add the

---

How Tags and Attributes Invoke Action Beans

We've used several tags and attributes to invoke methods on action beans. Here's a summary of what we've seen so far:

Tag and Attribute	Invocation on Action Bean
<s:link beanclass="*pkg.Name*">	pkg.Name's default event handler
<s:link event="*eventName*">	public Resolution eventName()
<s:link href="*URL*">	Action bean bound to *URL*
<s:param name="*property*">	setProperty(value)
<s:form beanclass="*pkg.Name*">	pkg.Name's default event handler
<s:form action="*URL*">	Action bean bound to *URL*
<s:hidden name="*property*">	setProperty(value)
<s:text name="*property*">	setProperty(value)
<s:submit name="*eventName*">	public Resolution eventName()

Update link and get inputs that autopopulate themselves, and before we know it, the contact form is complete.

3.7 Use a Forward or a Redirect?

After creating, updating, or deleting a contact, we're returning a RedirectResolution to ContactListActionBean instead of a ForwardResolution to contact_list.jsp. Why? Let's discuss the difference between the two resolutions and how to decide which one to use.

The Redirect-After-Side-Effect Pattern

The first thing to notice is the create, update, and delete operations all have *side effects*—they change the state of the data on the server.

Suppose that we returned a ForwardResolution to a contact_list.jsp after the user has deleted a contact. Looking at Figure 3.14, on the facing page, we see that the last request is "delete this contact." The problem is that if the user clicks the browser's Reload button, the "delete this contact" request will be sent *again*, causing an error because the contact has already been deleted.

In general, it is a bad idea to use a forward after any request that should not be resubmitted by hitting Reload. Imagine a request that makes a purchase with the user's credit card. You wouldn't want to repeatedly charge the credit card!

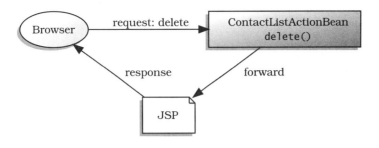

Figure 3.14: USING A FORWARD AFTER A DELETE REQUEST

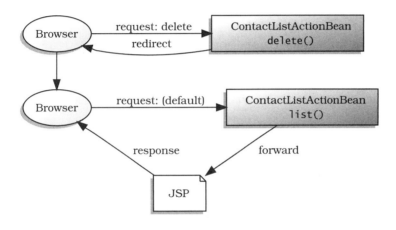

Figure 3.15: USING A REDIRECT AFTER A DELETE REQUEST

The "redirect after side effect" pattern comes to the rescue. Also known as "redirect after post" or "post/redirect/get," it involves sending a redirect—a response that instructs the browser to issue a *new request* that does not modify any data. According to Figure 3.15, we're redirecting to the default event handler of the action bean, which just displays the contact list. Clicking Reload is harmless: the request that is re-sent is the request to view the contact list, which has no side effect.

Using a redirect prevents unsafe behavior and eliminates those annoying "The page you are trying to view contains POSTDATA..." pop-up warnings. Get in the habit of using redirects to default event handlers of action beans at the end of event handlers that modify the state of the server. Of course, those default event handlers should do read-only operations.

\\// Joe Asks...
:
Why Can't I Redirect to a JSP?

A forward to a JSP is part of the response to the initial request, which was a request to an action bean. A redirect tells the browser to send a *new* request. Redirecting to a JSP is like linking directly to a JSP and breaks the pattern that we discussed in Section 2.3, *The Preaction Pattern*, on page 27.

The Flash Scope

Redirecting introduces a new problem. If you provide information to the view using attributes in the request scope, those attributes are kept only for that request. But because the response is a redirect, the browser issues a *second* request, for which those attributes are no longer available.

To solve this problem, Stripes provides what is called the *flash scope*. The flash scope stores attributes available for the current request *and* the following request. This mechanism provides a bridge for attributes when using a redirect.

Stripes uses the flash scope where appropriate. For example, the messages that you add to ActionBeanContext are stored in the flash scope. When you return a RedirectResolution from an event handler, you can display the messages in the view with the <s:messages/> tag because Stripes automatically makes them available for you in the flash scope.

The Story So Far

Using action beans and JSPs as building blocks, you can easily add features to a web application with parameterized links, forms, messages, reusable layouts, and even third-party JSP libraries.

We now have a good start to the webmail application, with a working contact list. In the next chapter, we'll improve it by adding some user input validation.

Freedom is not worth having if it does not include the freedom to make mistakes.

▶ Mahatma Gandhi

Chapter 4

Validating User Input

If you played around with the contact form that we created in the previous chapter, you probably realized that there is no validation on the input. The user can enter just about any data on the form, or no input at all, and submit it. The application will not complain about invalid or missing values.

Adding validation to your forms is essential to recovering gracefully from invalid input and keeping your model free of corrupted data. As you'll see, Stripes gives you easy-to-use built-in validations and a simple way to gain full control for those more complex validations.

4.1 Stripes Validation Concepts

In Stripes, validations are defined with *annotations* in an action bean. Using annotations gives you the advantage of being concise, compiled (so you know right away if there's a typo), and autocompleted by IDEs. Best of all, your validation rules are defined right there next to the property, not off in some separate template or configuration file.

To add validation to an action bean property, annotate it with @Validate. You can annotate either the field (even if it is private), the getter method, or the setter method associated to the property. Using attributes of @Validate, you specify the validation criteria.

@Validate annotations work only when used in an action bean.

Let's look at a simple example. Suppose we have an age property in an action bean and a corresponding text field in a form. We could make this field *required* and validate that the age entered by the user is *at least eighteen*, with this annotation:

```
@Validate(required=true, minvalue=18)
private Integer age;
```

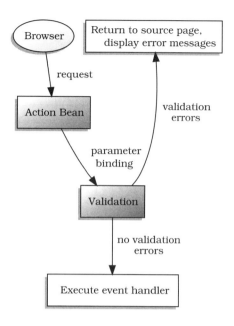

Figure 4.1: THE VALIDATION SEQUENCE

We now have a clearly defined validation for the age property. Submitting the form with the Age field left blank, or filled in with a value less than eighteen, produces a validation error. As illustrated in Figure 4.1, Stripes does *not* execute the intended event handler when a validation error occurs. Instead, the user is sent back to the form that was submitted. This way, we can safely save data in the event handler method because we know that Stripes won't call it if the data is invalid. All we need to do is to add the <s:errors> tag to our JSP to display error messages, and we're done!

Nested Properties

@Validate works only in an action bean. Annotating properties of a plain model class won't work, because Stripes doesn't go searching for annotations in model classes. Does this mean you have to copy properties from a model class to an action bean? Of course not—that wouldn't be very Stripesy! Just like forms, validations support *nested* properties.[1]

---

1. Remember that a nested property is a property of a property, such as getPerson().getAge().

Pick One Place for @Validate

For a given property, make sure to put the @Validate annotation on exactly *one* of either the field, the getter method, or the setter method. @Validate annotations in multiple places for the same property will cause a big ol' nasty exception to be thrown at you.

To make your code easier to read, be consistent. Once you've chosen where to put validations (say, on the setter method), use the same place for all properties if possible.

Suppose we have a Person property in an action bean, and suppose the Person class has an age property. As in the previous example, the age is a required field with a minimum of eighteen. We can't do this:

```
// This won't work
public class Person {
    @Validate(required=true, minvalue=18)
    private int age;
}
```

Instead, put @Validate inside a @ValidateNestedProperties annotation on the Person property of the action bean, like this:

```
public class MyActionBean implements ActionBean {
    @ValidateNestedProperties({
        @Validate(field="age", required=true, minvalue=18)
    })
    private Person person;
}
```

When @Validate is within @ValidateNestedProperties, indicate the field being validated with the field= attribute. You can add multiple @Validate annotations to @ValidateNestedProperties, one for each nested property being validated. Fields can be deeply nested, as in field="hair.color.rgb", so there's no limit to how far into your model you can go when you're adding validations.

Built-in Validations

Stripes offers several built-in validations with attributes of @Validate:

- Required field
- Length of the input

Tim Says...

Using Public Fields with Stripes Is Not a Bad Thing

Stripes can access action bean properties in two different ways. The most common way is through getter and setter methods, but Stripes will also work directly with public fields. These two ways are completely equivalent to Stripes. Using a public field is more compact—you don't need to write boilerplate getter and setter methods for each property. So, why wouldn't you use public fields?

Other than for constants, using public fields in Java has been looked down upon for a long time. The reason is encapsulation. Forcing client code to use methods to get and set properties allows you to change how the property is stored and retrieved without impacting client code. When a public field is used, you have to change all client code to use the getter method. Another benefit of using methods is that it allows you to do extra things when the value is read or set (increment a counter, log a message, and so on).

If method access is so good, why not just use methods? In my experience, most property accessors in action beans do nothing more than just get or set an instance field. If that's the case, then the argument that you can "do something extra" is pretty irrelevant! Most often, the only access to these properties is by methods in the declaring class and by Stripes. But Stripes doesn't need the encapsulation; if you use a public field today and then decide tomorrow that you want to use methods, you can simply make the field private, add the methods, and recompile. Stripes will immediately switch to using the methods instead of the field. You can even make some properties public and others private with methods in the same action bean.

If you can get over the mental hurdle of using public properties, you'll soon find it much more concise to write (and read) this:*

```java
public Date birthDate;
```

instead of:

```java
private Date birthDate;

public Date getBirthDate() {
    return birthDate;
}
public Date setBirthDate(Date birthDate) {
    this.birthDate = birthDate;
}
```

---

*. If you want to display the property in a JSP with an EL expression such as ${actionBean.birthDate}, you still have to provide a getter method to satisfy the JSP specification.

Attribute	Type	Description
field=	String	Name of nested field to validate.
required=	boolean	true indicates a required field.
on=	String[]	Event handlers for which to apply required=true.
minlength=	int	Minimum length of input.
maxlength=	int	Maximum length of input.
expression=	String	EL expression to validate the input.
mask=	String	Regular expression that the input must match.
minvalue=	double	Minimum numerical value of input
maxvalue=	double	Maximum numerical value of input.
converter=	Class	Type converter to use on the input.
trim=	boolean	Trim input before validating; true by default.
label=	String	Label to be displayed to the user.
ignore=	boolean	true indicates not to bind the parameter.
encrypted=	boolean	true encrypts the parameter to prevent injected values.

Figure 4.2: THE @VALIDATE ATTRIBUTES

- Validation with an EL expression
- Matching a regular expression mask
- Minimum and maximum numerical value

Other validations are implemented as "pseudo" type converters. Pseudo because the type conversion is from String to String, so the type is not really converted. But when any type conversion occurs, the input is validated. Stripes uses this trick to validate two String input formats:

- Email addresses
- Credit card numbers

In Figure 4.2, we can see the complete list of @Validate attributes. We'll use most of these attributes in the examples of this chapter. We'll see how to use the label= in Chapter 6, *Customizing Stripes Messages*, on page 111. The ignore= and encrypted= attributes are discussed in Chapter 14, *It's a Dangerous World: Adding Security*, on page 301.

Controlling Validation Execution

When a request arrives at an action bean, Stripes considers all validations you've added, no matter which event handler is the target. With event handlers that require different validations, you'll want to control for which event handlers the validations are executed. For example, an Age field might be required for the buyBeer() event handler, but not for buyMilk().

One way to control validations is by specifying, in the on= attribute, the event handlers for which to enforce required="*true*", such as @Validate(required="true", on="buyBeer") for the age property. The other way is to turn off *all* validations for an event handler by annotating it with @DontValidate. You'd want to do this for an event handler that doesn't do anything with the input, such as a cancel() method that just sends the user back to the previous page. With @DontValidate, the user is allowed to enter garbage in the fields and then cancel the form.

The subtleties of how on= and @DontValidate work have tripped up many Stripes users, including myself when I first started using the framework. But it's really not complicated; I have summed it up into two rules. Read them carefully, and you'll understand how Stripes decides whether to execute the validations for a given field:

- *Rule #1:* If the user has filled in a value for the field, it is validated *regardless* of the required= and on= attributes.
- *Rule #2:* If the user has left the field blank, the *only* validation that is executed, if present, is required=*true*.

The idea behind these rules is simple. If the user has entered a value for a field, it *must* be validated to prevent invalid values from corrupting the model. On the other hand, the user shouldn't be scolded for not filling out an *optional* field. So, the only possible error for a blank field is that the field is *required*.

Understanding this rationale is important to control the execution of validations. For example, ContactFormActionBean from the previous chapter had three event handlers:

- form(), which is called when the user arrives at the form
- save(), which handles the form submission and saves the contact information
- cancel(), which is also a form submission but for which no information is saved.

After adding validations in ContactFormActionBean, you need to control validation execution. For form(), the user is just arriving at the form, and no values have been entered yet. So, all fields are blank. The optional fields will not be validated, but the required fields will. It wouldn't be nice to welcome the user to the form with validation error messages! With on=*"save"*, required-field validations are restricted to save() and so do not cause errors in form().

Once in the form, the user may very well enter invalid values and then click the Cancel button. You need to turn off all validations by annotating cancel() with @DontValidate so that the user will be allowed to cancel the form even if the input is not valid.

Whew... enough theory. Let's look at some examples.

4.2 Using Built-in Validations

Let's get back to our webmail application. We have a form to enter a contact's information, displayed by contact_form.jsp:

email_06/web/WEB-INF/jsp/contact_form.jsp

```
<s:form beanclass="${actionBean.class}">
  <div><s:hidden name="contact.id"/></div>
  <table class="form">
    <tr>
      <td>Email:</td>
      <td>
        <s:text name="contact.email" class="required"/>
      </td>
    </tr>
    <!--Same for First and Last name, Phone number, Birth date-->
    <tr>
      <td> </td>
      <td>
        <s:submit name="save" value="Save"/>
        <s:submit name="cancel" value="Cancel"/>
      </td>
    </tr>
  </table>
</s:form>
```

ContactFormActionBean sends the user to the form and handles the form submission:

email_06/src/stripesbook/action/ContactFormActionBean.java

```
package stripesbook.action;
public class ContactFormActionBean extends ContactBaseActionBean {
    private static final String FORM="/WEB-INF/jsp/contact_form.jsp";

    @DefaultHandler
    public Resolution form() {
        return new ForwardResolution(FORM);
    }
}
```

```java
public Resolution save() {
    Contact contact = getContact();
    getContactDao().save(contact);
    getContext().getMessages().add(
        new SimpleMessage("{0} has been saved.", contact)
    );
    return new RedirectResolution(ContactListActionBean.class);
}
public Resolution cancel() {
    getContext().getMessages().add(
        new SimpleMessage("Action cancelled.")
    );
    return new RedirectResolution(ContactListActionBean.class);
}
}
```

We'll now add some validations to this form.

Making a Field Required

Let's begin by making the contact's email address a *required* field. First, it's better to let the user know up front about required fields. One way is to make the field border thicker by adding a *"required"* class and styling it in the CSS file:

email_06/web/WEB-INF/jsp/contact_form.jsp

```jsp
<s:text name="contact.email" class="required"/>
```

email_06/web/css/style.css

```css
input.required {
  border-width: 2px;
}
```

Next, adding @ValidateNestedProperties with @Validate(field="email") to contact validates the *"contact.email"* nested property. Remember that the contact property moved to the parent ContactBaseActionBean, so the validation must override either the getter or the setter method in Contact-FormActionBean:

email_06/src/stripesbook/action/ContactFormActionBean.java

```java
@ValidateNestedProperties({
    @Validate(field="email", required=true, on="save")
})
@Override
public void setContact(Contact contact) {
    super.setContact(contact);
}
```

Contact Information

Please fix the following errors:

1. Contact Email is a required field

Email: [   ]

First name: [   ]

Last name: [   ]

Phone number: [   ]

Birth date: [   ]

[Save] [Cancel]

Figure 4.3: A VALIDATION ERROR FOR A REQUIRED FIELD

As we discussed, the on=*"save"* restricts the validation to the *save()* event handler. Now, if the user saves the form with the email field left blank, a validation error occurs, and Stripes redisplays contact_form.jsp. To show the error message to the user as in Figure 4.3, add the <*s:errors/*> tag:

email_06/web/WEB-INF/jsp/contact_form.jsp

```
<s:form beanclass="${actionBean.class}">
  <s:errors/>
  <div><s:hidden name="contact.id"/></div>
  <table class="form">
```

Just like information messages, Stripes has a default way of displaying error messages: with a header message followed by the validation errors in a numbered list. A reasonable effort is made to construct error messages using the name of the field and the type of validation that failed, so we get something quite decent just by adding the <*s:errors/*> tag. In Chapter 6, *Customizing Stripes Messages*, on page 111, we'll talk about how to customize both the text and the presentation of error messages.

Email Addresses

We've made the email a required field, but this validates only that the user entered something in the field. It does not actually validate what the user entered. How about making sure that the email *format* is valid?

\\// Joe Asks. . .

Where Should I Put the <s:errors/> Tag?

Placing <s:errors/> within the <s:form> tag displays the error messages associated with that form. When you have more than one form in a single page, you can display the errors for each form or place the <s:errors/> outside the <s:form> tag to display the error messages that occurred in the current action bean.

I mentioned that in Stripes validations can be implemented as type converters. To use a type converter, you indicate its class in the converter= attribute of @Validate. The EmailTypeConverter validates that the input is of email address format, so we can use it with converter= to validate the contact email:

`email_06/src/stripesbook/action/ContactFormActionBean.java`

```
@ValidateNestedProperties({
    @Validate(field="email", required=true, on="save",
        converter=EmailTypeConverter.class)
})
@Override
public void setContact(Contact contact) {
    super.setContact(contact);
}
```

The EmailTypeConverter uses JavaMail to validate the email address, so we'll have to add the library to the WEB-INF/lib directory. Unless you are using Java 6, you will also have to add the JavaBeans Activation Framework:

```
WEB-INF/lib/javamail.jar
WEB-INF/lib/activation.jar
```

Now, entering an invalid email address such as "hello" displays this error message: "The value (hello) entered is not a valid email address."

Limiting the Length of Input

Let's add validation rules for the first and last name fields. These fields are optional, but if a value is entered, we'll enforce these restrictions:

- The first name cannot exceed twenty-five characters.
- The last name cannot exceed forty characters.
- The last name must be at least two characters.

> ### Required Fields and the on Parameter
>
> You can restrict the required=true validation to a *list* of event handlers, such as on={"save", "update"}. Another option is to specify the event handler(s) for which *not* to apply the validation using the ! negation symbol. For example, on="!save" executes the required=true validation for every event handler of the action bean except save(). You can also use a list with negations, as in on={"!save", "!update"}.
>
> Do not mix "positive" and "negative" event handler names in the on= attribute, such as on={"save", "!update"}, because logically it doesn't make sense. (Think about it.)

As we can see in the following code, it's very simple to add these validations with the minlength= and maxlength= attributes:

`email_06/src/stripesbook/action/ContactFormActionBean.java`

```java
@ValidateNestedProperties({
    /* previous validations... */
    @Validate(field="firstName", maxlength=25),
    @Validate(field="lastName",  minlength=2, maxlength=40)
})
```

Since the first and last name fields are optional, each validation is executed *only if the user enters a value for that field*. Now, entering a single character in the last name field produces the error shown in Figure 4.4, on the next page. Notice that Stripes used the value of minlength= to make the message more helpful.

As a bonus, Stripes automatically generates the maxlength= attribute in the form's HTML *<input>* tags to match the value in the maxlength= attribute of @Validate:

```html
<tr>
  <td>First name:</td>
  <td><input maxlength="25" type="text" name="contact.firstName"/></td>
</tr>
<tr>
  <td>Last name:</td>
  <td><input maxlength="40" type="text" name="contact.lastName"/></td>
</tr>
```

Any decent browser stops accepting characters in the text field after the maximum length has been reached.

Contact Information

Please fix the following errors:

1. Contact Email is a required field
2. Contact Last Name must be at least 2 characters long

Email:	
First name:	F
Last name:	D
Phone number:	
Birth date:	

Save Cancel

Figure 4.4: A validation error for minimum input length

Of course, the validation in the action bean is still executed—we can't rely only on client-side validation, because users could sent input in other ways than using the form. It's still nice to immediately let the well-intentioned user know when they've reached the limit as they are typing a value into the text field.

Another nice feature is that Stripes does not stop at the first encountered validation error. Instead, as many errors as possible are accumulated during the validation process to provide more information to the user.

Validating with EL Expressions

We can also validate user input by using an EL expression in the expression= attribute of @Validate. The **boolean** value of the expression determines whether the validation passed. This gives us an easy way to add a validation based on a conditional expression.

Within the expression, we can refer to the field that we are validating using the keyword **this** and to other properties of the action bean by their names. The action bean context, the request scope, and the session scopes are available with context, request, and session.

The birth date already benefits from the implicit validation of converting the input to a java.util.Date. Now that we've added the <s:errors/> tag to the JSP, the user sees an error message after entering an invalid date. Let's use an expression to also validate that the birth date in the contact form is *before the current date*. In other words, no unborn people in the contact list, please!

The key to this validation is that the current date is not a static value. So, we add a simple method in the action bean to provide it:

email_06/src/stripesbook/action/ContactFormActionBean.java

```
public Date getToday() {
    return new Date();
}
```

Now, using an expression makes it a cinch to validate that the birth date is in the past:

email_06/src/stripesbook/action/ContactFormActionBean.java

```
@ValidateNestedProperties({
    /* previous validations... */
    @Validate(field="birthDate", expression="${this < today}")
})
```

In the expression ${this < today}, **this** refers to the birthDate property, and today calls getToday() to obtain the current date.

Armed with this validation, submitting the form with a birth date in the future, such as 2040-01-27,[2] causes the action bean to return the error "The value supplied (Fri Jan 27 00:00:00 EST 2040) for field Contact Birth Date is invalid."

As you can see, using expressions gives you a concise and effective way of adding validations that are based on other fields or on values produced by any helper method.

Using Regular Expression Masks

Another way to validate user input is to use a regular expression mask.[3] To be considered valid, the entire input must match the mask. By placing the regular expression in the mask= attribute of @Validate, you can validate patterns that would otherwise require gobs of tedious code.

Consider the "Phone number" field in the contact form. For the sake of the example, let's say that the phone number should be in the format used in North America: a three-digit area code, followed by a three-digit

---

2. I'll be happy, but very surprised, if someone reads this book after 2040!
3. Refer to the java.util.regex.Pattern Javadocs for the regular expression syntax that Stripes uses.

> ### Using ${ } in Expressions
>
> Enclose the validation expression within ${ }, or don't—the choice is yours. Indeed, expression="this < today" and expression="${this < today}" are equivalent. Stripes automatically adds ${ } for you if you leave it out.
>
> Personally, I prefer using ${ } because I find it makes it clearer that an EL expression is being used. Whichever format you choose, being consistent will certainly make your code more readable.

prefix and a four-digit suffix, as in (654) 456-4567. To be lenient with our users, we'll allow some flexibility with the input format:

- The parentheses around the area code are optional.

- The separators between each part of the phone number can be hyphens, periods, or spaces, or they can be omitted altogether.

For example, all these phone numbers are acceptable:

```
(654) 456-4567    654-456-4567    654 456 4567    654.456.4567
(654)456 4567     6544564567      654 4564567     654.456-4567
```

Adding this validation is easy by building a regular expression mask with the following constructs:

- \(? and \)? to represent an optional opening and closing parenthesis

- [-.]? to accept an optional hyphen, period or space

- \d to represent a digit

- {N} to indicate the previous construct repeated N times

With these constructs, we can validate the phone number by adding the following mask. Since the regular expression is in a Java String, we have to use \\ to represent \.

email_06/src/stripesbook/action/ContactFormActionBean.java

```java
@ValidateNestedProperties({
    /* previous validations... */
    @Validate(field="phoneNumber",
        mask="\\(?\\d{3}\\)?[-. ]?\\d{3}[-. ]?\\d{4}")
})
```

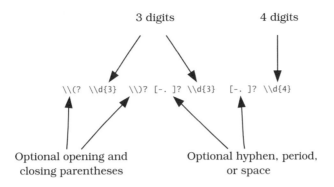

Figure 4.5: A REGULAR EXPRESSION TO VALIDATE A PHONE NUMBER

OK, regular expressions are rarely pleasing to the eye, so I've tried to make it clearer by breaking it down as shown in Figure 4.5.

The *entire* input must match the regular expression, so incomplete phone numbers are also rejected. An example of entering an invalid phone number is shown in Figure 4.6, on the next page.

We've added a fairly sophisticated validation for the phone number with a @Validate annotation and a regular expression mask. Think about how much more code we'd need to implement this validation by parsing the input string ourselves!

The Cancel Button

The last thing we need to do in the contact form is to turn all validations off for the Cancel button. Otherwise, canceling the form won't work if there are any invalid values that were entered by the user. We just need to add the @DontValidate annotation to the cancel() event handler:

```
email_06/src/stripesbook/action/ContactFormActionBean.java
@DontValidate
public Resolution cancel() {
    getContext().getMessages().add(
        new SimpleMessage("Action cancelled.")
    );
    return new RedirectResolution(ContactListActionBean.class);
}
```

Contact Information

Please fix the following errors:

1. *(654) 343-2* is not a valid Contact Phone Number

Email: fd@stripesbook.org

First name: Fred

Last name: Daoud

Phone number: (654) 343-2

Birth date:

Save Cancel

Figure 4.6: A VALIDATION ERROR USING A REGULAR EXPRESSION MASK

Pretty good. We've added validation to the contact form, and all we needed were annotations in the action bean and a single <s:errors/> tag in the JSP.

We didn't use the minimum/maximum numerical value and credit card validations in the contact form because we don't have any fields that are relevant to those validations. Nevertheless, let's look at them briefly before continuing.

Minimum and Maximum Numerical Values

Stripes provides validation of minimum and maximum numerical values with the minvalue= and maxvalue= attributes of @Validate. These attributes accept values of type **double**, and they work for properties of any primitive numerical type as well as all subclasses of Number.

Suppose you wanted to restrict some field to a value between 0 and 7, inclusive. You would use this:

```
@Validate(minvalue=0, maxvalue=7)
private int someField;
```

Now, entering an invalid value for this field would give an error message such as this:

- "The minimum allowed value for Some Field is 0."
- "The maximum allowed value for Some Field is 7."

Again, Stripes is smart enough to use the values that we specify in the minvalue= and maxvalue= attributes to construct the error messages.

> ### A Note About Trimming Input
>
> After some discussion, the Stripes community agreed that user input should be trimmed before validating. This makes validations such as required fields, minimum length, and so on, behave as most developers expect: entering two spaces in a required field should not be valid, and it shouldn't pass a min-length=2 validation.
>
> Because trimming the input is so often desirable, it is the default behavior in Stripes. You can disable trimming for a field by annotating it with @Validate(trim=false).

Credit Card Numbers

CreditCardTypeConverter checks that the input *could* be a valid credit card number, without actually connecting to anything to check whether an account with that number actually exists. Here's what the type converter does:

- Starts by removing all nondigit characters from the input
- Checks that the card corresponds to AMEX, Diners Club, Discover Card, enRoute, JCB, MasterCard, or Visa, based on the prefixes and the number of digits that these cards use
- Validates the Luhn algorithm[4] on the number

CreditCardTypeConverter is similar to EmailTypeConverter in that it validates the input without converting it to a different type. To use it, just add @Validate(converter=CreditCardTypeConverter.class) on the "Credit card number" field.

How Stripes Processes Built-in Validations

Now that we've seen examples of each built-in validation, let's take a closer look at how Stripes executes these validations. I've illustrated the process in Figure 4.7, on the following page. Validations are run on a list of fields, which initially contains every field. After performing a validation, only the fields that are valid are kept in the list for the next validation. The validations are arranged in order such that later validations are worth running only if previous validations have passed. Validation errors are accumulated and made available for the JSP to display with <s:errors/>.

---

4. See http://en.wikipedia.org/wiki/Luhn if you really want to know how that works.

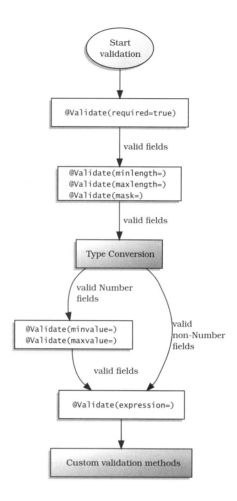

Figure 4.7: PROCESSING VALIDATIONS IN ORDER OF PRIORITY

In the middle of the diagram, notice the box labeled "Type Conversion." I've briefly touched on the subject that Stripes performs type conversion for all basic data types. If the type conversion passes and the property type extends Number, then the minimum and maximum numerical value validations are executed. We'll talk about type conversion in more detail in Chapter 5, *There's More to Life Than Strings: Working with Data Types*, on page 87.

After processing all built-in validations, Stripes moves on to *custom validation methods*. This is where you get to do pretty much anything you need to do to validate the input.

4.3 When You Need More: Custom Validation Methods

Sometimes you want to perform validations other than those provided by the attributes of @Validate. Perhaps the validation is a complex multistep process that is best implemented in code. Perhaps the validation requires accessing a database. Whatever the reason, you can implement a validation using an arbitrary block of code called a *validation method.*

By annotating a method *in an action bean* with @ValidationMethod, you tell Stripes to invoke it during the validation process. Stripes is pretty flexible about the signature of the method—you can use any name, return any type, and throw any exception. The only requirements are that the method be **public** and accept either no parameters or one parameter of type ValidationErrors.

In a validation method, you signal errors by adding them to ValidationErrors. You can use the object passed to the method if you have included it as a parameter or obtain it from the action bean context:

```
@ValidationMethod
public void validateSomething(ValidationErrors errors) {
    // Perform validation
    // If validation errors occur, add them to 'errors'
}

@ValidationMethod
public void validateSomethingElse() {
    // Perform validation

    ValidationErrors errors =
        getContext().getValidationErrors();

    // If validation errors occur, add them to 'errors'
}
```

To add an error to ValidationErrors, create an object that implements the ValidationError interface. Stripes offers some ready-to-use implementations, such as the SimpleError class, which works much like the SimpleMessage class that we've used to display information messages. The constructor accepts the message string and an optional list of parameters. These parameters replace standard Java MessageFormat tokens, starting at {2}. Indeed, the {0} and {1} tokens are reserved for the name of the field and the value entered by the user. What's nice is that you can use {0} and {1} in the message without having to provide those parameters yourself.

For example:

```
new SimpleError("Invalid input");
new SimpleError("For field {0}, the value {1} is not valid");
new SimpleError("{1} is not valid because {2}", someText);
```

Once you've created a validation error, you can associate it to a specific field using the field name such as *"age"* or *"contact.firstName"*, or you can make it a global error. Add the error to ValidationErrors with the appropriate method:

- void add(String field, ValidationError error)

- void addGlobalError(ValidationError error)

After adding errors to the list, you can display them in the JSP with the <s:errors/> tag just like built-in validation error messages. As we'll see in Chapter 6, *Customizing Stripes Messages*, on page 111, you can also display errors next to their associated fields and display global errors at the top.

Restricting Validation Methods to Specific Event Handlers

@ValidationMethod accepts the on= attribute to restrict the validation to specific event handlers:

```
// on the "save" and "update" event handlers
@ValidationMethod(on={"save", "update"})

// on every event handler except "save"
@ValidationMethod(on="!save")
```

Just like the on= attribute of @Validate, this lets you control the event handlers for which your validation methods are executed.

Continue or Stop Validation When There Are Previous Errors?

Stripes invokes validation methods after all @Validates have been processed and the inputs have been bound to the action bean's properties. By default, Stripes does *not* invoke a validation method if errors occurred during the execution of previous validations, including @Validates as well as @ValidationMethods of higher priority. The idea is that you know every previous validation has passed when executing a given validation method.

You can control this behavior with the when= attribute of @Validation-Method. This indicates whether to execute the validation method when there are previous validation errors. The value must be a ValidationState, which is an **enum** with these possible values:

- ALWAYS: Executes the validation method even if there are previous validation errors

- NO_ERRORS: Executes the validation method only if there are no previous validation errors

- DEFAULT: Uses the default behavior of the application

For example, this validation method will be executed regardless of previous errors:

```
@ValidationMethod(when=ValidationState.ALWAYS)
public void validateSomething(ValidationErrors errors) {
    // ...
}
```

The default value of when= is, not surprisingly, ValidationState.DEFAULT. This means "use the application's default," and *that* default is Validation-State.NO_ERRORS. You can change the "application default" to Validation-State.ALWAYS by adding an initialization parameter to the Stripes filter in web.xml:

```
<filter>
  <filter-name>StripesFilter</filter-name>
  <filter-class>
    net.sourceforge.stripes.controller.StripesFilter
  </filter-class>
  <!-- ... -->
  <init-param>
    <param-name>Validation.InvokeValidateWhenErrorsExist</param-name>
    <param-value>true</param-value>
  </init-param>
</filter>
```

With this configuration, validation methods will always be executed by default. To execute a validation method only if there are no previous errors, you'd have to explicitly add when=ValidationState.NO_ERRORS to @ValidationMethod.

Whether you are changing the default or using the when= attribute, when you execute a validation method even if previous errors have occurred, the fields could contain invalid values or even be **null**. Keep that in mind when writing the code for a validation method that will always be executed.

Executing Validation Methods in a Specific Order

When you define two or more validation methods in an action bean, you may need to execute them in a specific order. The priority= attribute of @ValidationMethod lets you indicate an **int** value that determines the method's priority. Stripes executes the validation methods in numerical order of priority, as in -1, 0, 1, 2. The default value of priority= is 0. If two or more methods have the same priority, the tiebreaker is the alphabetical order of the methods' names.

Let's look at an example using the following validation methods:

```
@ValidationMethod(priority=0)
public void extraValidation()

@ValidationMethod
public void checkAge()

@ValidationMethod(priority=1)
public void anotherValidation()

@ValidationMethod(priority=-1)
public void youMustValidateThis()
```

During the validation process, Stripes executes these methods in the following order:

1. youMustValidateThis() (priority of -1)

2. checkAge() (priority of 0 by default, first in alphabetical order)

3. extraValidation() (priority of 0, second in alphabetical order)

4. anotherValidation() (priority of 1)

Knowing that the default Stripes behavior is to stop executing validation methods when a validation error has occurred, you can use priorities to simplify your validation methods. Strategically order your methods so that later methods rely on earlier methods having passed validation. That way, you can structure your validation code in a logical sequence and avoid having to do **null** checks and other such prevalidations.

Example: A Validation Method to Ensure Unique Email Addresses

Let's return to the contact form for an example of a validation method. In the form, the email address is a required field, and we've validated the format of the user's input. Let's take it one step further by validating that the email address is not already used by another contact.

Tim Says...

Use the Minimum Number of Validation Methods Necessary to Get the Job Done

Stripes will happily invoke any number of validation methods in a single Action Bean. As Freddy has shown, there are mechanisms for coordinating the ordering of the validation methods and whether they should be executed when errors already exist. So, you might be thinking that the best thing to do is to have a method for each custom validation you want to write and then let Stripes execute them in order. In my experience, though, it's often easier to write and maintain action beans where custom validations are grouped into as few methods as possible—often only one.

The main reason is that, for Java developers, it's always going to be more natural to understand the flow of code in a single method than to understand the rules used by a framework for ordering the execution of a set of methods. For example, it is fairly obvious when the following pseudo-code executes and what it does:

```
@ValidationMethod
public void validateUniqueFields(ValidationErrors errors) {
    if (username != null && userDao.exists(username)) // add error
    if (email != null && userDao.emailExists(email)) // add error
    if (username != null && password != null
        && password.indexOf(userName) >= 0)) // add error
}
```

The preceding code is reasonably compact, and anyone familiar with Java will be able to tell what it does: all three validations are run, in order, regardless of whether preceding checks in the same method failed. By contrast, the following code requires much deeper knowledge of Stripes to determine the same information:

```
@ValidationMethod public void validateUniqueUsername() {...}
@ValidationMethod public void validateUniqueEmail() {...}
@ValidationMethod public void validateUsernameNotInPassword() {...}
```

The previous code, with method bodies filled out, will also be much less compact. The one time it does make sense to start splitting custom validations into multiple methods is when you have multiple events that require either overlapping or completely different validations. In these cases, you will find it best to split the validations into methods that can be shared across events without duplicating the code.

First, pull out the ContactDao interface, and add a method to search for a contact by email address:

email_06/src/stripesbook/dao/ContactDao.java

```java
package stripesbook.dao;
public interface ContactDao {
    public List<Contact> read();
    public Contact read(Integer id);
    public void save(Contact contact);
    public void delete(Integer id);
    public Contact findByEmail(String email);
}
```

Next, assume that the code for this method is in the MockContactDao class. Again, don't bother with the implementation details.

Now, since we need to query the DAO to perform the unique email validation, implement a validation method in ContactFormActionBean:

email_06/src/stripesbook/action/ContactFormActionBean.java

```java
@ValidationMethod(on="save")
public void validateEmailUnique(ValidationErrors errors) {
    String email = getContact().getEmail();
    Contact other = getContactDao().findByEmail(email);
    if (other != null && !other.equals(getContact())) {
        errors.add("contact.email", new SimpleError(
            "{1} is already used by {2}.", other));
    }
}
```

We'll want to use on="save" so that the validation method will be executed only for the save() event handler of ContactFormActionBean.

This method is executed only if there are no previous errors. This is handy because there's no point in checking whether the email is already in use if the email input is omitted or if the format is invalid.

Using the contact DAO to find the contact that has the entered email address, the code flags a validation error if a contact was found and is different from the one being updated in the form. Using {1} and {2}, the email address and the name of the other contact are included in the error message.

Now, if the user enters an email that is already in use by another contact, we'll get the result shown in Figure 4.8, on the next page.

Contact Information

Please fix the following errors:

1. sb@stripesbook.org is already used by Sammy Blair.

Email: `sb@stripesbook.org`

First name: `Sonny`

Last name: `Braddock`

Phone number:

Birth date:

Save Cancel

Figure 4.8: AN ERROR DETECTED BY A VALIDATION METHOD

The Final Step: What to Do About Validation Errors?

When there are errors at the end of the validation process, the default behavior is to send the user back where they came from instead of executing the event handler. The list of errors is made available to the view page.

We can gain control of what happens in the presence of validation errors by having the action bean implement the ValidationErrorHandler interface, which has one method:

```
public interface ValidationErrorHandler {
    Resolution handleValidationErrors(ValidationErrors errors)
        throws Exception;
}
```

This method is called after the validation process if at least one validation error occurred and the list of errors is passed as a parameter. In the method, we can do pretty much anything, including the following:

- Change the list by adding, modifying, or deleting errors
- Change properties in the action bean
- Make calls to a DAO, and so on

We can also decide what happens next:

- If we return a Resolution, it is executed directly instead of returning to the source page.
- If we return **null** and the list of errors is not empty, the user is returned to the source page.

> **Source Page Resolution**
>
> To determine the page from which a request came from, Stripes calls the getSourcePageResolution() method of the Action-BeanContext class. This method uses the _sourcePage request parameter, which is automatically generated by Stripes.

- If we delete all errors from the list and return **null**, it's as if those errors never happened. Only in this case is the event handler executed.

For example:

```
public class MyActionBean extends BaseActionBean
    implements ValidationErrorHandler
{
    Resolution handleValidationErrors(ValidationErrors errors) {
        if (specialSituation) {
            return new ForwardResolution("/WEB-INF/jsp/special.jsp");
        }
        if (bypassErrors) {
            errors.clear();
        }
        return null;
    }
}
```

If the specialSituation flag is **true**, the user is sent directly to special.jsp. If the bypassErrors flag is **true**, the event handler is executed because the list of errors is emptied before returning **null**. If neither flag is **true**, the user is sent back to the source page because the method returns **null** but the list still contains errors.

The custom methods part of the validation process is summarized in Figure 4.9, on the facing page. With validation methods and the handleValidationErrors() method of the ValidationErrorHandler interface, we have full control over what happens after the built-in validations have been executed. We can run custom validation methods and control what happens when errors have occurred.

Validation in the Event Handler

Finally, we may encounter situations where the validation that we want to perform just doesn't fit anywhere in the validation process.

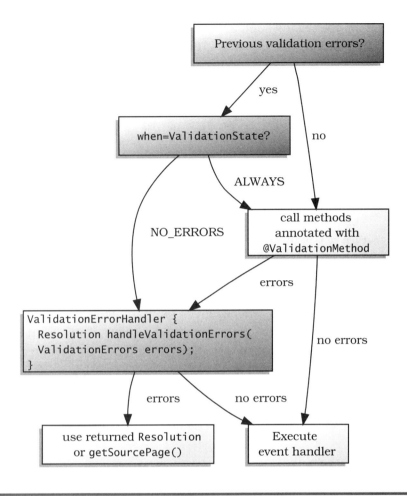

Figure 4.9: CUSTOM VALIDATION METHODS

For example, we might be adding a record in a database and we won't know whether there is a duplication error until the operation returns or throws an exception:

```
try {
    database.add(record);
    // all is well
}
catch (DuplicateRecordException) {
    // validation error: duplicate record
}
```

Validation for operations such as adding a record to a database belongs in an event handler, not in a validation method. Since event handlers return a Resolution, it's up to us to send the user back where they came from in case of a validation error. As we can see, it's quite straightforward with the action bean context:

```java
public Resolution add() {
    try {
        database.add(record);
        return new RedirectResolution(ListActionBean.class);
    }
    catch (DuplicateRecordException) {
        getContext().getValidationErrors().addGlobalError(
            new SimpleError("Add error: duplicate record"));
        return getContext().getSourcePageResolution();
    }
}
```

With built-in validations, validation methods, error handlers, and validation in event handlers, Stripes gives us many tools to validate user input. We can use them to keep your model clean of invalid data, let our users know about the errors that occurred, and give them a chance to fix the input and resubmit the form.

Think like a wise man, but communicate in the language of the people.
▶ William Butler Yeats

Chapter 5

There's More to Life Than Strings: Working with Data Types

When a client submits an HTTP request, all parameters are limited to the String type. We certainly don't want our action bean properties to suffer from this limitation; we want properties that can be of any type. When request parameters are bound to action bean properties, some work has to be done to convert the String parameter to the property's data type. This is what Stripes calls *type conversion*.

Going the other way, the information that action beans provide are of any data type but must be converted to a String to be displayed to the client. Stripes refers to this as *formatting*.

When developing applications, we want to use the data types that are best suited to our business model. We also want to let our users express their input in a format that is most natural to them. With type conversion and formatting, we can bridge the gap between these two requirements. Stripes makes it easy to work with any data type, including adding support for our own custom types.

5.1 Type Conversion Concepts

Look at Figure 5.1, on the next page. When the name=value request parameter is bound to the name property of type T in the action bean, Stripes needs to know how to convert "value" from String to T. This is where a *type converter* is used. A type converter is simply an implementation of the TypeConverter<T> interface:

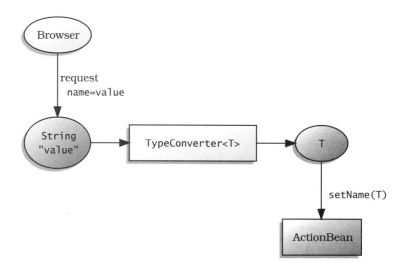

Figure 5.1: TYPE CONVERSION

```
public interface TypeConverter<T> {
  void setLocale(Locale locale);
  T convert(String input, Class<? extends T> targetType,
      Collection<ValidationError> errors);
}
```

Stripes gives type converters the user's locale so that the type conversion can be done in a locale-sensitive manner, if necessary. Then, Stripes calls the convert() method with the String input parameter from the request, the action bean property type, and a list of validation errors. If the type conversion fails, the converter adds an error message to the list and returns **null**. If all goes well, the method returns the value converted to the T type, and Stripes sets the action bean property with this value.

Out of the box, Stripes automatically uses built-in type converters for basic data types:

- **byte**, Byte, **short**, Short, **int**, Integer, **long**, Long, java.math.BigInteger
- **float**, Float, **double**, Double, java.math.BigDecimal
- java.util.Date
- **boolean**, Boolean
- **char**, Character
- **enum**

We get type conversion for action bean properties of these types, including nested properties, without having to do anything special. We just declare the action bean property with its type, and Stripes does the conversion for us. Let's take a closer look at how these built-in type converters work.

5.2 Built-in Type Converters

The types for which Stripes does automatic conversion boil down to these: numbers, dates, booleans, characters, and enumerations. Learning how these type converters work will help you understand why certain inputs are successfully converted while others cause a validation error.

Working with Numbers

For the numerical types—**byte, short, int, long, float, double**, their wrapper classes, BigDecimal, and BigInteger—the type converters use a common strategy for improving their chances of parsing the String input into a number:

1. Remove the currency symbol, if present. The currency symbol is the current locale's if available and otherwise the dollar sign ($).

2. If parentheses surround the input, such as (42), replace them with a leading negation sign as in -42.

After performing these operations, the number type converters then use Java's built-in NumberFormat with the user's locale to attempt parsing the input into a Number. If parsing fails, a validation error occurs, the user is sent back to the form, and we can display the error message with the <s:errors/> tag.

Byte, Short, Integer, Long, BigInteger

The type converters for whole number types accept valid numerical values within the accepted range of the target type, as shown in Figure 5.2, on the following page. These type converters do not accept decimals in the input.

Float, Double, BigDecimal

The type converters for the decimal number types follow the same rules as their whole number cousins, except that they accept decimals. If the number of decimals exceeds the precision of the target type, rounding is

Primitive Type	Wrapper Class	Minimum	Maximum
byte	Byte	−128	127
short	Short	−32768	32767
int	Integer	$−2^{31}$	$2^{31} − 1$
long	Long	$−2^{63}$	$2^{63} − 1$
float	Float	2^{-149}	$(2–2^{-23}) \times 2^{127}$
double	Double	2^{-1074}	$(2–2^{-52}) \times 2^{1023}$

Figure 5.2: MIN AND MAX VALUES FOR NUMBER TYPES

done at the last accepted decimal position. The input must also respect the minimum and maximum values from Figure 5.2.

Working with Dates

The date type converter attempts to parse the input to obtain a Date, with help from Java's DateFormat and a series of locale-sensitive format patterns.

Just like the number type converters, the date type converter does some preprocessing operations before trying to parse the input:

1. Replace all dashes (-), slashes (/), periods (.), and commas (,) with spaces.

2. Collapse any sequences of two or more spaces to a single space.

3. If the result at this point is a string that contains two parts separated by a space, assume that these are the day and month (or the month and day). Since the year is required for any of the format patterns to succeed, append a space and the current year to at least give the input a chance of being parsed successfully.

By accepting any of - / . , as a separator but preprocessing the input to replace the separators with spaces, the converter knows that at this point the input is a date with the fields separated by a single space. It becomes easy to match different date format patterns that also use a space character as a separator, while allowing other separators in the input.

Now that the date type converter is ready to parse the input, it tries these date formats in order, using the first one that works.

Format	Example (Varies According to Locale)
DateFormat.SHORT	1 27 07
DateFormat.MEDIUM	Jan 27 2007
DateFormat.LONG	January 27 2007
d MMM yy	27 Jan 07
yyyy M d	2007 01 27
yyyy MMM d	2007 Jan 27
EEE MMM dd HH:mm:ss zzz yyyy	Sat Jan 27 07:27:00 EST 2007

If all formats fail, the converter produces a validation error.

Using Different Date Format Patterns

It's easy to configure the date type converter to use different date format patterns. For example, we might want to use a pattern that reads the date *and* the time. Looking at the default date formats, the only one that includes the time is EEE MMM dd HH:mm:ss zzz yyyy, which is quite tedious for the user to type!

To configure a list of date format patterns that will replace the defaults for the date type converter—and for all date fields of the application—add a line to the StripesResources.properties file. Using the stripes.dateTypeConverter.formatStrings key, define a comma-separated list of date format patterns in order of priority. For example:

```
stripes.dateTypeConverter.formatStrings=yyyy M d HH:mm, yyyy M d
```

Use a space to separate the date parts when defining a format pattern.

The first pattern parses both the date and the time, while the second pattern parses just the date. This makes it easy for the user to enter the date and the time, while also allowing only the date to be entered.

Enumerated Types

Stripes also provides a type converter for working with enumerated types (types defined with **enum**). The converter takes a String input and produces an **enum** of type T using Enum.valueOf(T, input). For this to work, the input must *exactly* match the identifier used to declare the **enum** constant in the type T.

For example, given an enumerated type:

```
public enum Gender {
  Female,
  Male
}
```

the input would have to be either "Female" or "Male" (case sensitive) to be converted to the Gender type.

 **Joe Asks. . .**

What If I Want a Specific Separator in a Date Pattern?

The default behavior of the date type converter is to allow any of - / . , as separators. You can change this if you prefer to require a specific separator in a date pattern, as in yyyy-MM-dd.

When the date type converter preprocesses the input, it uses a regular expression pattern and replaces all matches by a single space. The default pattern matches the - / . , characters. You can change this pattern by adding a line in the StripesResources.properties file with the stripes.dateTypeConverter.preProcessPattern key:

```
stripes.dateTypeConverter.preProcessPattern=\\s+
```

With this pattern, sequences of one or more spaces are matched and replaced by a single space, but other characters are left intact, and you can use a specific separator in the date pattern:

```
stripes.dateTypeConverter.formatStrings=yyyy-M-d
```

Boolean Values

Boolean properties are also supported. The type converter accepts certain values to mean **true**, and any other input produces **false**. So, this type converter never causes a validation error—any input is accepted and will produce either **true** or **false**.

The following values (case insensitive) are recognized as meaning **true**:

- true
- t
- yes
- y
- on
- 1, or any other whole number greater than zero

Anything else will be converted to **false**.

Single Characters

Last (and perhaps least) of the built-in type converters is the character type converter. It just takes the first character in the input String to produce a **char** or a Character. So, "Hello" will be converted to 'H'.

Other Provided Type Converters

The type converters we've seen so far are used automatically. Stripes also provides a few other type converters that do the conversion only if we specifically tell Stripes to use them. These additional type converters are as follows:

- EmailTypeConverter
- CreditCardTypeConverter
- PercentageTypeConverter
- OneToManyTypeConverter

To indicate we want one of these type converters to convert the input for a given property, we annotate the property with @Validate(converter= *TheTypeConverter*.class). For example:

```
// Use EmailTypeConverter for this property
@Validate(converter=EmailTypeConverter.class)
public String email;
```

We saw EmailTypeConverter in Section 4.2, *Email Addresses*, on page 67 and CreditCardTypeConverter in Section 4.2, *Credit Card Numbers*, on page 75. Let us now look at PercentageTypeConverter and OneToMany-TypeConverter.

PercentageTypeConverter

PercentageTypeConverter works on a property of decimal type: **float**, Float, **double**, Double, or BigDecimal. The input string is considered as a *percentage*, with or without a percent symbol (%). The numerical result is the value of the input divided by 100.

PercentageTypeConverter preprocesses the input just like the other decimal type converters. For example, it accepts all these inputs to produce the corresponding results, as we can see in the table on the next page.

Input	Result
"72%"	0.72
"72 %"	0.72
"-84"	-0.84
"0.5"	0.005
"(45%)"	-0.45
"(45)"	-0.45

The One-to-Many Type Converter

The OneToManyTypeConverter is a nifty type converter that accepts a list of values in one String input and converts them into a Collection<T>, converting each individual value to T. For example, if you declare the property to be a Collection<Long>, each value will be converted to a Long and added to the collection. If you just use Collection without declaring the type <T> of the individual items, Stripes uses String by default.

Each value in the input string has to be separated by either of the following:

- One or more spaces

- A comma followed by one or more spaces

Note that a comma alone is *not* treated as a separator by OneToMany-TypeConverter, because a comma could be used within a single value, such as a thousands separator in a numerical value.

Instead of type converting the input string, OneToManyTypeConverter extracts the values and passes each individual value to the type converter for the type inside the collection. For example, using OneToMany-TypeConverter on a List<Long> property will use the LongTypeConverter to convert each value to a Long and will put all the values in List.

Although OneToManyTypeConverter does not produce any validation errors, it does transmit any errors that occur when converting the individual values.

Here are some examples of inputs and results:

Input	Property Type	Result
"a b c d"	List<String>	["a", "b", "c", "d"]
"a, b, c"	List<String>	["a", "b", "c"]
"a,b,c d, e"	List<String>	["a,b,c", "d", "e"]
"1, 2.5, -3 4"	List<Double>	[1.0, 2.5, -3.0, 4.0]

Tim Says...

Type Converters Can Return More Than One Type!

When you implement a TypeConverter, you implement it for a specific type T. You may have noticed that the main method you implement has a slightly different signature, though:

```
T convert(String in, Class<? extends T> targetType, ...);
```

Providing the target type at invocation time allows Stripes to ask TypeConverter for instances of T, any subclasses of T, or, if T is an interface, implementations of T. When performing type conversion, Stripes will identify the declared type of a property and supply it to the type converter.

This is how both PercentageTypeConverter and OneToManyType-Converter know what type to return. PercentageTypeConverter implements TypeConverter<Number>, but it can return, when asked, **float**s, **double**s, and BigDecimals. Since it returns a number between 0 and 1, it throws an exception if requested to convert to any other numeric type. Similarly, the OneToMany-TypeConverter class implements TypeConverter<Object> and can return collections of any type for which the system has a registered TypeConverter.

Stripes will ask converters for subtypes only if you use a property in your action bean for which Stripes doesn't have a Type-Converter registered but can find a TypeConverter for a superclass. Using this approach you can develop some pretty powerful type converters. For example, if your domain objects all extend from a base class or implement a common interface, you can write a single TypeConverter to look them up from an ID property.

Stripes offers solid built-in type conversion support. Let's discuss how to convert data types to Strings: formatting.

5.3 Formatting

Formatting is type conversion in the opposite direction. An object of type T must be converted to a String to be displayed to the user. There's always the toString() method, but Stripes gives us a more powerful way. With formatters, the value can easily be displayed in different ways and can do so in a locale-sensitive manner as well.

As shown in Figure 5.3, on the facing page, a formatter is an implementation of the Formatter<T> interface and returns a String for a given object of type T. Formatters are called upon when we use Stripes tags that support formatted values, such as <s:format> and <s:text>. When the tag refers to a property of type T, Stripes uses a Formatter<T> implementation to convert the property's value to a String, which is returned to the tag.

Here is the Formatter<T> interface:

```
public interface Formatter<T> {
    void setLocale(Locale locale);
    void setFormatType(String formatType);
    void setFormatPattern(String formatPattern);
    void init();
    String format(T input);
}
```

Along with the user's locale, a formatter is given a *type* and a *pattern* with the formatType= and formatPattern= attributes of format-aware Stripes tags. The type indicates what to display, as in "date", "time", and "datetime" for the Stripes Date formatter. The pattern describes how to display the value, such as "short", "medium", "long", and "full".

Let's look at the formatters provided by Stripes.

Built-in Formatters

Stripes comes with built-in formatters for Dates, all Number types, and enumerated types. The date and number formatters support different format types, named patterns, and arbitrary patterns using the Java SimpleDateFormat and DecimalFormat syntax. The result is formatted according to the user's locale.

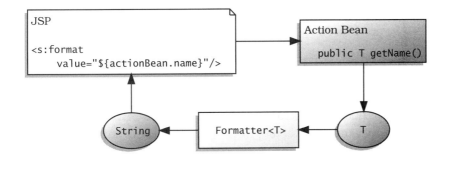

Figure 5.3: FORMATTING

Dates

Examples are sometimes worth 1,000 explanations. Here are the different combinations of the format types and format patterns understood by the date formatter, with the results of formatting a value of March 2, 2008 at 2:42 PM EST:

Pattern/Type	"date"	"time"
"short"	3/2/08	2:42 PM
"medium"	Mar 2, 2008	2:42:00 PM
"long"	March 2, 2008	2:42:00 PM EST
"full"	Sunday, March 2, 2008	2:42:00 PM EST

Pattern/Type	"datetime"
"short"	3/2/08 2:42 PM
"medium"	Mar 2, 2008 2:42:00 PM
"long"	March 2, 2008 2:42:00 PM EST
"full"	Sunday, March 2, 2008 2:42:00 PM EST

The formatPattern= may also be any pattern that is understood by Simple-DateFormat, such as "yyyy-MM-dd HH:mm", which would return "2008-03-02 14:42" in the previous example.

Numbers

The following are the different format types and patterns understood by the number formatter, with the results of formatting a value of 2468.24682468:

Pattern/Type	"number"	"percentage"	"currency"
"plain"	2468.247	246825%	$2468.25
"integer"	2,468	246,825%	$2,468
"decimal"	2,468.246825	246,824.682468%	$2,468.246825

You can also use a DecimalFormat-compatible format pattern, such as "#,##0.0" to produce "2,468.2".

Enumerated Types

Stripes also has a formatter for enumerated types, EnumFormatter, which simply uses Enum.name() to return a result. This is always the name of the **enum** constant—the locale, format type, and format pattern are not used by this formatter.

Objects

Finally, when Stripes has no specific formatter for a type T, the fallback is to just call the toString() method. This way, formatting always produces a String even if Stripes doesn't know anything about the type T, because toString() is defined on Object, the parent of all Java classes.

Using Formatters

The Stripes tags that accept the formatType= and formatPattern= attributes, such as <s:format> and <s:text>, use formatters to display values. Both formatType= and formatPattern= are optional attributes, so formatters either have a default value or do not use these attributes. Let's look at an example of using a formatter.

In the contact form of the webmail application, the user can enter the contact's birth date. This date is displayed in the contact view and also redisplayed in the form when updating an existing contact.

Without formatting, a birth date entered by the user as 1982-08-30 is displayed in the contact view as Mon Aug 30 00:00:00 EDT 1982 and in the contact form's text field as 8/30/82.

Let's use the date formatter to display the contact birth date in the yyyy-MM-dd format, both in the contact view and in the contact form. In the contact view, we can do this with the <s:format> tag:

email_07/web/WEB-INF/jsp/contact_view.jsp

```
<td class="label">Birth date:</td>
<td class="value">
  <s:format value="${actionBean.contact.birthDate}"
    formatPattern="yyyy-MM-dd"/>
</td>
```

The date is displayed in the contact form using the same formatPattern= in the <s:text> tag:

email_07/web/WEB-INF/jsp/contact_form.jsp

```
<td>Birth date:</td>
<td>
  <s:text name="contact.birthDate"
    formatPattern="yyyy-MM-dd"/>
</td>
```

The birth date is now displayed in a consistent format.

We can still let the user enter the birth date using the default patterns accepted by the date type converter. If we wanted to enforce the Year-Month-Day pattern for user input, we'd just add one line to the StripesResource.properties file:

email_07/res/StripesResources.properties

```
stripes.dateTypeConverter.formatStrings=yyyy M d
```

That's all well and good for built-in type conversion and formatting, but what about using our own data types? That's coming up next, after this word from your local station. (That's your cue to get up, stretch, and go grab something from the refrigerator.)

5.4 Working with Custom Data Types

The Stripes type conversion and formatting mechanisms make it easy to add support for custom data types. Let's see how this works by adding a PhoneNumber data type in the contact information of the webmail application.

Implementing a Type Converter

The contact form supports many variations of input for the contact's phone number. The value is stored in a String exactly as entered by the user. We might end up with values such as 654-456-4567, (654) 567-5678, 654 234.2345, and so on. It'd be nice to continue accepting these different input formats but store the value in the model in a format-independent way. A phone number has an area code, a prefix, and a suffix. We can use a simple PhoneNumber class.

```
email_07/src/stripesbook/model/PhoneNumber.java
```

```java
package stripesbook.model;
public class PhoneNumber {
    private String areaCode;
    private String prefix;
    private String suffix;

    public PhoneNumber() {
    }
    public PhoneNumber(String areaCode, String prefix, String suffix) {
        this.areaCode = areaCode;
        this.prefix = prefix;
        this.suffix = suffix;
    }
    /* Getters and setters... */
}
```

This makes it a lot easier to work with phone numbers, such as finding all contacts that are in a given area code. We can just look at the areaCode property and not worry about the format in which the user entered the phone number.

The first thing to do is to change the phone number property in the Contact class from String to PhoneNumber:

```
email_07/src/stripesbook/model/Contact.java
```

```java
private PhoneNumber phoneNumber;
public PhoneNumber getPhoneNumber() {
    return phoneNumber;
}
public void setPhoneNumber(PhoneNumber phoneNumber) {
    this.phoneNumber = phoneNumber;
}
```

A type converter must create a PhoneNumber object from an input String. This calls for an implementation of TypeConverter<PhoneNumber>:

```
email_07/src/stripesbook/ext/PhoneNumberTypeConverter.java
```

```java
package stripesbook.ext;
public class PhoneNumberTypeConverter
    implements TypeConverter<PhoneNumber>
{
    private static final Pattern pattern = Pattern.compile(
        "\\(?(\\d{3})\\)?[-. ]?(\\d{3})[-. ]?(\\d{4})");

    public PhoneNumber convert(String input,
        Class<? extends PhoneNumber> type,
        Collection<ValidationError> errors)
    {
        PhoneNumber result = null;
```

```
            Matcher matcher = pattern.matcher(input);
            if (matcher.matches()) {
                result = new PhoneNumber(
                    matcher.group(1), matcher.group(2), matcher.group(3));
            }
            else {
                errors.add(new SimpleError("{1} is not a valid {0}"));
            }
            return result;
        }
        public void setLocale(Locale locale) {
        }
}
```

The regular expression pattern is from the mask= attribute of the phone number validation in Section 4.2, *Using Regular Expression Masks*, on page 71. Grouping with parentheses around the digits for the area code, prefix, and suffix (see Figure 5.4, on the following page) makes it easy to extract those parts of the phone number and construct a PhoneNumber object. If the input does not match the regular expression, a validation error is added to the list of errors.

We're using SimpleError here, which is fine for our purposes at this point. However, we can create validation errors without hard-coding the message in the code but rather by having the message in a resource bundle. We'll see how it's done in Chapter 6, *Customizing Stripes Messages*, on page 111.

Now that we have a type converter for phone numbers, how do we use it? First, remove the mask= attribute from @Validate since the phone number validation has been moved to the type converter. Next, use the converter= attribute.

```
@ValidateNestedProperties({
    @Validate(field="phoneNumber",
      converter=PhoneNumberTypeConverter.class)
    // (removed mask="...")
    // (other validations...)
})
@Override
public void setContact(Contact contact) {
    super.setContact(contact);
}
```

We can also tell Stripes to use PhoneNumberTypeConverter by default for every PhoneNumber property. All we have to do is configure a package for *extensions* (see the sidebar on page 104) and put the PhoneNumberTypeConverter class in that package. Now we can use PhoneNumber

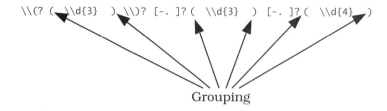

Figure 5.4: USING GROUPING IN A REGULAR EXPRESSION

properties, and Stripes will automatically use the phone number type converter. We can still override the default for a given property by using the converter= attribute.

Implementing a Formatter

With a type converter for the PhoneNumber data type, we're halfway there. Let's implement a formatter, with two format types:

- "dashes": NNN-NNN-NNNN

- "parens": (NNN) NNN-NNNN

With a default value for the format type (say, "dashes"), the formatType= attribute will be optional. The formatPattern= attribute will not be used. Here is the resulting PhoneNumberFormatter:

`email_07/src/stripesbook/ext/PhoneNumberFormatter.java`

```java
package stripesbook.ext;
public class PhoneNumberFormatter implements Formatter<PhoneNumber> {
    private String formatType = "dashes";

    public void setFormatType(String formatType) {
        this.formatType = formatType;
    }
    public void setLocale(Locale locale) { }
    public void setFormatPattern(String formatPattern) { }
    public void init() { }

    public String format(PhoneNumber phoneNumber) {
        String format = null;
        if ("dashes".equalsIgnoreCase(formatType)) {
            format = "%s-%s-%s";
        }
```

```
        else if ("parens".equalsIgnoreCase(formatType)) {
            format = "(%s) %s-%s";
        }
        else {
            throw new StripesRuntimeException(String.format(
                "Invalid phone number formatType: %s. Valid values "
                + "are 'dashes' and 'parens'.", formatType));
        }
        return String.format(format, phoneNumber.getAreaCode(),
            phoneNumber.getPrefix(), phoneNumber.getSuffix());
    }
}
```

PhoneNumber objects can now be formatted with <s:format>, using formatType="dashes" or formatType="parens". Since the formatter is in an extension package, it will be loaded by Stripes. We can display phone numbers in the contact view and in the text field of the contact form in a consistent format, no matter how the phone number was entered by the user. For example:

email_07/web/WEB-INF/jsp/contact_view.jsp

```
<td class="label">Phone number:</td>
<td class="value">
  <s:format formatType="dashes"
      value="${actionBean.contact.phoneNumber}"/>
</td>
```

email_07/web/WEB-INF/jsp/contact_form.jsp

```
<td>Phone number:</td>
<td>
  <s:text name="contact.phoneNumber" formatType="dashes"/>
</td>
```

The formatType= attribute could also have been omitted to use the formatter's default.

Using a Different Date Pattern Just for One Field

Back on page 91, we discussed changing the patterns for the date type converter, which affects all date input fields in the application. But what if we want to use a different pattern just for one field? For example, we might have a field where we expect the user to enter a time with no date, such as "10:30". We want to use the "HH:mm" pattern for that field without changing the patterns used for other date fields.

In a case like this, we're better off creating a separate type converter that parses the time only and *not* configuring it as an automatically loaded extension so that it doesn't replace the default type converter.

Stripes Extensions

Custom type converters, custom formatters, and many other custom components are collectively known in Stripes as *extensions*. To minimize configuration, Stripes gives you a way to set, once and for all, the packages that contain your extensions. Stripes automatically loads all extensions found in these packages and their subpackages. So, you can add, remove, and rename your extensions without changing the configuration, as long as the packages still correspond to the ones you configured.

To indicate the packages for your extensions, give the Stripes filter a value for the Extension.Packages parameter in web.xml:

email_07/web/WEB-INF/web.xml

```
<filter>
  <filter-name>StripesFilter</filter-name>
  <filter-class>
    net.sourceforge.stripes.controller.StripesFilter
  </filter-class>
  <!-- ... -->
  <init-param>
    <param-name>Extension.Packages</param-name>
    <param-value>stripesbook.ext</param-value>
  </init-param>
</filter>
```

The Extension.Packages parameter works much like the ActionResolver.Packages, except that the package roots are for extensions instead of action beans. With the previous configuration, all extensions found in stripesbook.ext or any subpackage will automatically be loaded. You can specify several packages by separating them with commas.

In the packages you have configured as extension packages, you can still have nonextension classes. Stripes simply ignores those classes during the extension autoloading process. On the other hand, if you have an extension class in one of the extension packages and you'd like to tell Stripes *not* to load it, changing its package is not the only way to do that—you can also annotate the class with @DontAutoLoad.

Stripes defines key functionalities with interfaces so that you can easily provide custom behavior by plugging in your own extensions. We'll discover the other extensible parts of Stripes throughout the rest of the book.

Tim Says...

One Class Can Implement Both TypeConverter and Formatter

It is possible, and often desirable, to have a single class implement both the TypeConverter and Formatter interfaces. Type conversion and formatting are really two sides of the same coin—the processes of going from String to something more strongly typed and back again.

Keeping all the code in one place can cut down on clutter (fewer classes) and make maintenance simpler—if you modify the target type, you can review a single class instead of two to see whether changes are required. In addition, since you will be dealing with the same classes, there may be common code that can be more easily shared between the methods doing type conversion and formatting. Lastly, since both interfaces share the same setLocale(Locale) method, writing one class that implements both means you have one less method to write!

Creating a custom type converter for Date is easily done by extending DateTypeConverter. Earlier we saw that this converter does some preprocessing and uses a series of formats to parse the input. These operations are implemented as **protected** methods so that subclasses can easily make changes to the behavior:

```
protected Pattern getPreProcessPattern()
protected String preProcessInput(String input)
protected String checkAndAppendYear(String input)
protected String[] getFormatStrings()
protected DateFormat[] getDateFormats()
```

A TimeTypeConverter only has to override getFormatStrings() to return the "HH:mm" format:

`data_types/src/stripesbook/opt/TimeTypeConverter.java`

```java
package stripesbook.opt;
public class TimeTypeConverter extends DateTypeConverter {
    private static final String[] TIME_FORMAT = { "HH:mm" };
    @Override
    protected String[] getFormatStrings() {
        return TIME_FORMAT;
    }
}
```

To make sure TimeTypeConverter is not an automatically loaded extension, either it can be in a different package than an extension package, such as the stripesbook.opt package used earlier, or it can be in an extension package and annotated with @DontAutoLoad. We can now use Time-TypeConverter only on demand by annotating the property associated with the time field:

`data_types/src/stripesbook/action/DataTypesActionBean.java`

```
@Validate(converter=TimeTypeConverter.class)
private Date time;
```

Using a Type Converter and Formatter to Load Model Objects

A great way of using type converters and formatters is to load model objects. Right now Contact objects are loaded from the contact DAO using the contact's ID. This works fine but requires separate contactId and contact properties in the action bean.

The contactId property can be removed by implementing a type converter that takes the contact ID as an input and returns the corresponding Contact object with help from the contact DAO. With a formatter that does the opposite—takes a Contact object and returns the contact ID—the Contact type can then be used directly, and JSPs can use a contact parameter as follows:

`email_07/web/WEB-INF/jsp/contact_list.jsp`

```
<s:param name="contact" value="${contact}"/>
```

The ContactTypeConverter uses the String input as a contact ID and calls ContactDao to return the corresponding Contact object:

`email_07/src/stripesbook/ext/ContactTypeConverter.java`

```java
package stripesbook.ext;
public class ContactTypeConverter implements TypeConverter<Contact> {
    private ContactDao contactDao = MockContactDao.getInstance();

    public Contact convert(String string,
        Class<? extends Contact> type,
        Collection<ValidationError> errors)
    {
        try {
            return contactDao.read(new Integer(string));
        }
        catch (Exception exc) {
            errors.add(new SimpleError(
                "The contact ID {1} is not valid."));
            return null;
        }
    }
}
```

```
    public void setLocale(Locale locale) { }
}
```

Being in an extension package, the type converter will automatically be loaded. Just like that, we have support for the Contact class, as shown in Figure 5.5, on the following page.

The ContactFormatter's task of returning a String from a Contact is very simple:

email_07/src/stripesbook/ext/ContactFormatter.java

```
package stripesbook.ext;
public class ContactFormatter implements Formatter<Contact> {
    public String format(Contact contact) {
        return String.valueOf(contact.getId());
    }
    public void init() { }
    public void setLocale(Locale locale) { }
    public void setFormatType(String type) { }
    public void setFormatPattern(String pattern) { }
}
```

We can now work directly with Contact objects in action beans and JSPs, with the logic of going from String to Contact and back to String being encapsulated in the type converter and formatter.

Using Constructor and toString

We've seen how Stripes type converters and formatters give us a place for the code that converts a String to T and back to String. Using type converters keeps the logic separate from the T class and enables us to use Stripes validation errors. Formatters are powerful because we can define different format types and patterns and easily format according to the user's locale.

Despite all these advantages, sometimes we need only the bare minimum for a data type.

I'll let you in on a dirty little secret. If Stripes doesn't find a type converter for a type T—either built-in, specified in @Validate(converter=), or located in an extension package—it tries one last resort. If a T(String) constructor is defined in the class T, Stripes uses it to create an instance of T, passing the input as a parameter to the constructor.

So, to get type conversion and formatting with the least amount of code, we can use a constructor that accepts one argument of type String for type conversion and the toString() method for formatting, both directly in the model class.

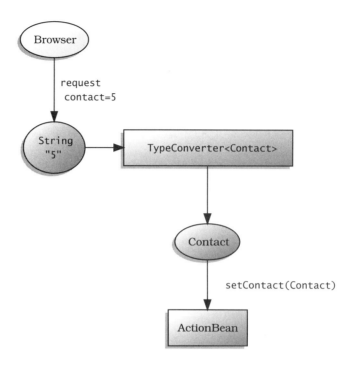

Figure 5.5: USING A TYPE CONVERTER TO LOAD A CONTACT

Here is an example with the PhoneNumber class:

```
package stripesbook.model;
public class PhoneNumber {
    private int areaCode;
    private int prefix;
    private int suffix;

    private static final Pattern pattern = Pattern.compile(
        "\\(?(\\d{3})\\)?[-. ]?(\\d{3})[-. ]?(\\d{4})");

    public PhoneNumber() {
    }
    public PhoneNumber(int areaCode, int prefix, int suffix) {
        this.areaCode = areaCode;
        this.prefix = prefix;
        this.suffix = suffix;
    }
    // Stripes will use this for String -> PhoneNumber type conversion
    public PhoneNumber(String input) {
        if (input != null) {
            Matcher matcher = pattern.matcher(input);
```

```
        if (matcher.matches()) {
            areaCode = Integer.parseInt(matcher.group(1));
            prefix   = Integer.parseInt(matcher.group(2));
            suffix   = Integer.parseInt(matcher.group(3));
        }
        else {
            // This exception will only get logged
            throw new IllegalArgumentException(input +
                " is not a valid phone number.");
        }
    }
}
/* Getters and setters... */

// Stripes will use this for PhoneNumber -> String formatting
public String toString() {
    // Only one format can be supported
    return String.format("%s-%s-%s", areaCode, prefix, suffix);
}
}
```

That's all we need to support the PhoneNumber data type. Although quick, this strategy is also limited: we can't signal validation errors in the constructor, and any exception we throw will not be propagated by Stripes. Invalid input will just leave the target property unbound. We can't use different format types and patterns in the toString() method, and it's more tedious to obtain the user's locale if the formatting should be locale-sensitive.

Most of the time you'll want to use type converters and formatters, but it's nice to know that for basic requirements, you can get it all done directly in the data type class.

When I'm working on a problem, I never think about beauty. I think only how to solve the problem. But when I have finished, if the solution is not beautiful, I know it is wrong.

▶ R. Buckminster Fuller

Chapter 6

Customizing Stripes Messages

When displaying information messages to the user, you decide on the text and show the messages with the *<s:messages/>* tag. Stripes has a default way of displaying these messages.

For error messages, Stripes not only has a default display but also takes care of constructing the text.

Although that's pretty good bang for your buck, you can also change these defaults to display messages exactly like you want by doing the following:

- Customizing the appearance of information and error messages
- Displaying error messages in a group or individually next to corresponding fields
- Customizing how fields that are in error are highlighted
- Changing the text of error messages

Let's start with the customization of information messages.

6.1 Customizing Information Messages

When you add the *<s:messages/>* tag to a JSP, Stripes follows these steps to render information messages:

1. Display a *header*.
2. Render something *before* the message.
3. Write the message text.
4. Render something *after* the message.
5. Repeat steps 2 to 4 for each message.
6. Display a *footer*.

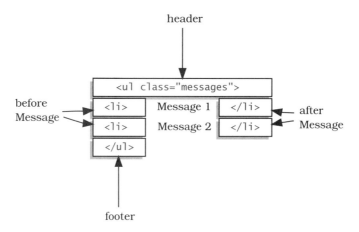

Figure 6.1: CONSTRUCTING THE DISPLAY OF INFORMATION MESSAGES

The default is to display the messages in a bulleted list, using the HTML code shown in Figure 6.1. An example of the result is illustrated in Figure 6.2, on the facing page. This is the message that we created in Section 3.5, *Information Messages*, on page 47. After the user deletes a contact, the message confirms that the operation was successful.

If you like the bulleted list but just want to change its look, you can use the *"messages"* class that Stripes adds to the <*ul*> tag to style the list with CSS code.

You can also change the HTML code for each part of the information message display by modifying the following entries in the Stripes-Resources.properties file:

- stripes.messages.header
- stripes.messages.beforeMessage
- stripes.messages.afterMessage
- stripes.messages.footer

For example, let's display information messages in a box with an icon and a shaded background, as in Figure 6.3, on page 114.

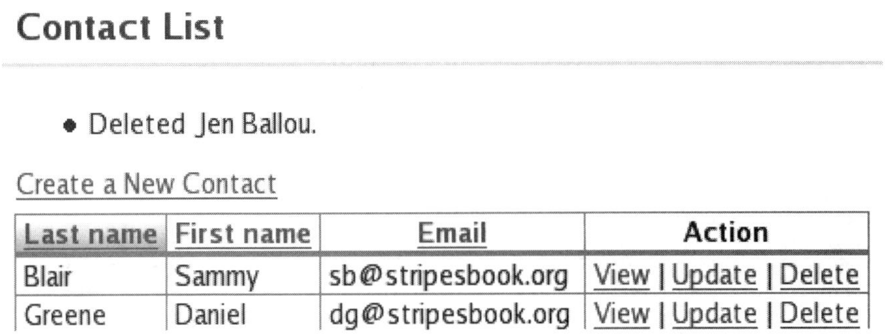

Contact List

- Deleted Jen Ballou.

Create a New Contact

Last name	First name	Email	Action
Blair	Sammy	sb@stripesbook.org	View | Update | Delete
Greene	Daniel	dg@stripesbook.org	View | Update | Delete

Figure 6.2: THE DEFAULT DISPLAY OF INFORMATION MESSAGES

With the icon image file in images/info.gif, the following code will generate the message box:

`email_08/res/StripesResources.properties`

```
stripes.messages.header=<div class="messages">\
  <img src="images/info.gif"/>
stripes.messages.beforeMessage=<p>
stripes.messages.afterMessage=</p>
stripes.messages.footer=</div>
```

The following CSS code displays the box with a border, a shaded background, and the message text in bold:

`email_08/web/css/style.css`

```
div.messages {
  display: block;
  border: 2px solid #008800;
  margin-bottom: 8px;
  background-color: #CCFFCC;
}
div.messages p {
  font-weight: bold;
  color: #008800;
  margin: 0;
}
```

As we can see, customizing the display of messages is just a matter of changing a few entries in the properties file. We can also use style classes and customize the appearance with CSS code.

Any part that Stripes uses to construct the code (header, beforeMessage, afterMessage, and footer) can be left blank. For example, we could use stripes.messages.footer= if we don't need a footer.

Contact List

Create a New Contact

Last name	First name	Email	Action
Blair	Sammy	sb@stripesbook.org	View | Update | Delete
Greene	Daniel	dg@stripesbook.org	View | Update | Delete

Figure 6.3: CUSTOMIZING THE DISPLAY OF INFORMATION MESSAGES

6.2 Customizing Error Messages

Error messages can be customized in the same way as information messages, but they also support additional features. They can be displayed in a group or individually next to the input field associated with the error. The labels and input fields that are in error can be highlighted. The message text can be modified. With all these features, we can display error messages so that they fit in well with the look and feel of our web application.

Error Messages in a Group

Much like the *<s:messages/>* tag, the *<s:errors/>* tag generates HTML code using the values defined in StripesResources.properties. The keys start with stripes.errors and have the default values shown in the following code. This displays error messages as in the example shown in Figure 6.4, on the next page.

```
email_07/res/StripesResources.properties
stripes.errors.header=<div style="color:#b72222; font-weight: bold">\
  Please fix the following errors:</div><ol>
stripes.errors.beforeError=<li style="color: #b72222;">
stripes.errors.afterError=</li>
stripes.errors.footer=</ol>
```

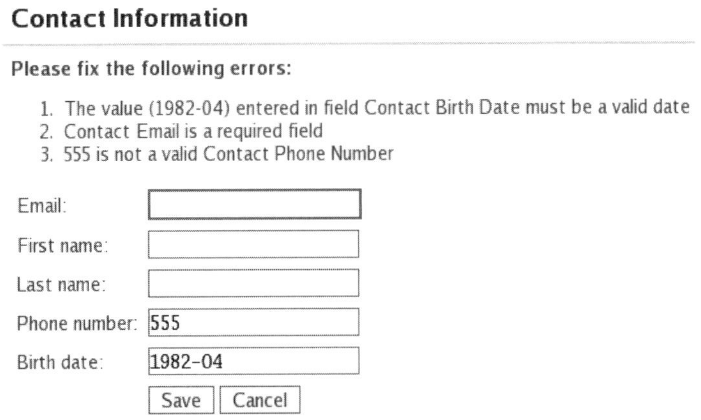

Contact Information

Please fix the following errors:

1. The value (1982-04) entered in field Contact Birth Date must be a valid date
2. Contact Email is a required field
3. 555 is not a valid Contact Phone Number

Email:	
First name:	
Last name:	
Phone number:	555
Birth date:	1982-04

Save Cancel

Figure 6.4: The default display of error messages

Let's modify these values to display error messages in a box with an error icon, as illustrated in Figure 6.5, on the following page:

email_08/res/StripesResources.properties

```
stripes.errors.header=<div class="errors">\
  <img src="images/error.gif"/>
stripes.errors.beforeError=<p>
stripes.errors.afterError=</p>
stripes.errors.footer=</div>
```

email_08/web/css/style.css

```
div.errors {
  display: block;
  border: 2px solid #880000;
  margin-bottom: 8px;
  background-color: #FFDDDD;
}
div.errors p {
  font-weight: bold;
  color: #880000;
  margin: 0;
}
```

As we can see, we did that much in the same manner as we changed the display of information messages.

Contact Information

⊗
The value (1982-04) entered in field Contact Birth Date must be a valid date
Contact Email is a required field
555 is not a valid Contact Phone Number

Email:	
First name:	
Last name:	
Phone number:	555
Birth date:	1982-04

Save   Cancel

Figure 6.5: CUSTOMIZING THE DISPLAY OF ERROR MESSAGES

Error Messages Next to Fields

Stripes makes it easy to display error messages individually, next to each corresponding field, as in Figure 6.6, on the next page. This is nice because the user doesn't have to read the error messages at the top and then scan down the form to figure out to which field each message refers.

If you indicate the name of a field in the field= attribute of the <s:errors> tag, only the error messages for that field will be displayed. The value for field= must match the name= attribute of the corresponding input field. For example, this would display error messages concerning the contact's email next to the email field:

```
<td>Email:</td>
<td><s:text name="contact.email"/></td>
<td><s:errors field="contact.email"/></td>
```

After adding <s:errors> tags with the field= attribute next to each input field, we can remove the <s:errors/> tag at the top. Now, to display the messages with the error icon, the entries that start with stripes.fieldErrors must be modified:

email_09/res/StripesResources.properties

```
stripes.fieldErrors.header=
stripes.fieldErrors.beforeError=<img src="images/error.gif"/>\
  <span class="error">
stripes.fieldErrors.afterError=</span><br/>
stripes.fieldErrors.footer=
```

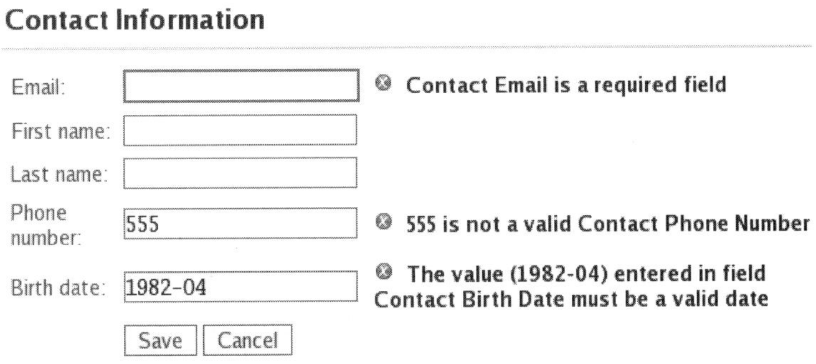

Contact Information

Email:	[ ]	⊗ **Contact Email is a required field**
First name:	[ ]	
Last name:	[ ]	
Phone number:	[555]	⊗ **555 is not a valid Contact Phone Number**
Birth date:	[1982-04]	⊗ **The value (1982-04) entered in field Contact Birth Date must be a valid date**

[Save] [Cancel]

Figure 6.6: DISPLAYING ERROR MESSAGES NEXT TO INPUT FIELDS

We can use the error class on the *<span>* tag to display the error text in bold and red:

`email_09/web/css/style.css`

```
span.error {
  font-weight: bold;
  color: #880000;
  padding: 8px;
}
```

This will display error messages as in Figure 6.6.

Highlighting Errors

Stripes automatically adds class="*error*" to labels and input fields that are in error, as long as they are created with Stripes tags. We're already using the *<s:text>* tag for the text fields; we need to use an *<s:label>* tag to take advantage of this feature for labels. To associate a label to an input field, place the name of the field in the for= attribute of *<s:label>*. For example:

`email_10/web/WEB-INF/jsp/contact_form.jsp`

```
<tr>
  <td><s:label for="contact.email">Email:</s:label></td>
  <td>
    <s:text name="contact.email" class="required"/>
  </td>
  <td><s:errors field="contact.email"/></td>
</tr>
<%-- same for other fields --%>
```

⫶⫶⫷ Joe Asks...

How Can I Display Error Messages in More Than One Way?

Changing the values in the StripesResources.properties file sets the display of error messages for the whole application. We can override these settings in a page by nesting the *<s:errors-header>*, *<s:individual-error>*, and *<s:errors-footer>* tags within *<s:errors>*:

```
<s:errors>
  <s:errors-header>code for header goes here</s:errors-header>
  code before each message goes here
  <s:individual-error/>
  code after each message goes here
  <s:errors-footer>code for footer goes here</s:errors-footer>
</s:errors>
```

For example, if we wanted to keep the Stripes defaults in Stripes-Resources.properties and use the error box just for the contact form, we would have replaced the *<s:errors/>* tag in contact_form.jsp with this:

```
<s:errors>
  <s:errors-header>
    <div class="errors">
      <img src="images/error.gif"/>
  </s:errors-header>
  <p>
    <s:individual-error/>
  </p>
  <s:errors-footer>
    </div>
  </s:errors-footer>
</s:errors>
```

We can customize field-specific error messages in the same way—just specify the field= attribute in the *<s:errors>* tag.

This gives us the possibility of having the most-often used error message display configured in StripesResources.properties and still have as many different ways of displaying error messages as we need.

CUSTOMIZING ERROR MESSAGES ◀ 119

Combining Global and Field-Specific Errors

You can create error messages that are not associated with a specific field with the addGlobalError() method of the Validation-Errors class. These global errors will not be displayed if you have only <s:errors field="..."/> tags. Adding the plain *<s:errors/>* tag displays global errors but duplicates the field-specific error messages. To combine the display of global and field errors, add the globalErrorsOnly=*"true"* attribute to the *<s:errors/>* tag. This way, you can display global errors in a group and field-specific errors next to fields:

```
<s:form ...>
  <s:errors globalErrorsOnly="true"/>
  ...
  <td>Email:</td>
  <td><s:text name="contact.email"/></td>
  <td><s:errors field="contact.email"/></td>
  ...
</s:form>
```

Highlighting the labels and text fields that are in error is now a simple matter of some CSS code:

email_10/web/css/style.css

```
input.error {
  border: 2px solid #880000;
  background-color: #FFDDDD;
}
label.error {
  color: #880000;
  font-weight: bold;
  text-decoration: underline;
}
```

This will highlight errors as shown in Figure 6.7, on the next page. Notice that both the labels and the fields that are in error are highlighted.

If the error class is not enough to highlight tags as we require, we can take full control of how tags are rendered when they are in error by implementing the TagErrorRenderer interface:

```
public interface TagErrorRenderer {
    void init(InputTagSupport tag);
    void doBeforeStartTag();
    void doAfterEndTag();
}
```

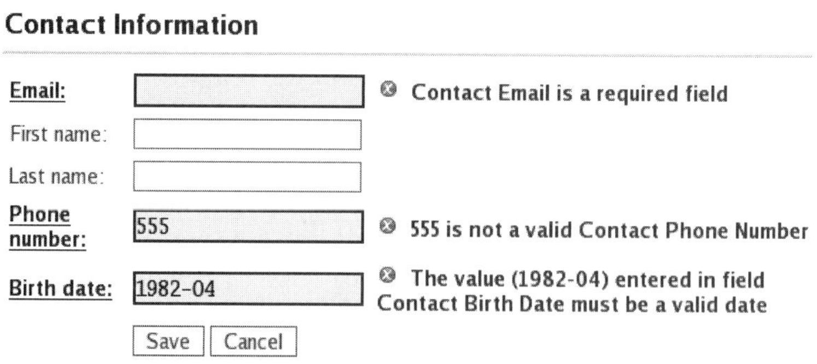

Contact Information

Email: [   ] ⊗ Contact Email is a required field

First name: [   ]

Last name: [   ]

**Phone
number:** [555   ] ⊗ 555 is not a valid Contact Phone Number

Birth date: [1982-04   ] ⊗ The value (1982-04) entered in field
                                          Contact Birth Date must be a valid date

[Save] [Cancel]

Figure 6.7: HIGHLIGHTING LABELS AND INPUT FIELDS FOR ERRORS

The DefaultTagErrorRenderer adds the class="*error*" attribute to tags that
are in error. If the tag already had another class= defined, such as
"myClass", the renderer produces class="error myClass" to preserve any
previously specified CSS classes.

Suppose we want to display ** after tags that are in error, as illustrated
in Figure 6.8, on the facing page. We can do this with a simple implementation of TagErrorRenderer:

```
email_11/src/stripesbook/ext/MyTagErrorRenderer.java
package stripesbook.ext;
public class MyTagErrorRenderer implements TagErrorRenderer {
    private InputTagSupport tag;
    public void init(InputTagSupport atag) { tag = atag; }
    public void doBeforeStartTag() { }
    public void doAfterEndTag() {
        try { tag.getPageContext().getOut().write("**"); }
        catch (IOException exc)
            { throw new StripesRuntimeException(exc); }
    }
}
```

TagErrorRenderer implementations are Stripes extensions, so having the
MyTagErrorRenderer class in the stripesbook.ext package is enough to have
it automatically loaded by Stripes. Remember that on page 104 we configured stripesbook.ext in web.xml as an extension package with the Exten-
sion.Packages parameter.

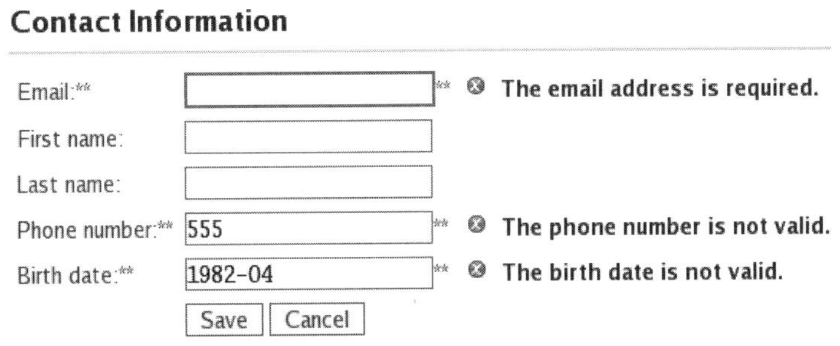

Contact Information

Email:** [   ] ** ⊗ The email address is required.

First name: [   ]

Last name: [   ]

Phone number:** [555   ] ** ⊗ The phone number is not valid.

Birth date:** [1982–04   ] ** ⊗ The birth date is not valid.

[Save] [Cancel]

Figure 6.8: USING A TAG ERROR RENDERER

6.3 Changing the Text of Error Messages

When a validation error occurs, Stripes constructs an error message based on the type of validation that failed, the name of the field, and the value entered by the user. Although this gives messages that are quite reasonable, we can change the text in two ways: by changing the field label and keeping the rest of the text or by changing the text completely. Let's start with using different field labels.

Changing Field Labels

Stripes constructs a field label by taking the name of the field and separating words based on dots (.) and uppercase letters. For example, "contact.phoneNumber" becomes "Contact Phone Number". This label replaces the {0} token in an error message, while {1} is replaced by the value entered by the user. So if the user enters 555 in the contact.phoneNumber field, the following message:

{1} is not a valid {0}

becomes the following:

555 is not a valid Contact Phone Number.

The label you want to appear in an error message may not correspond to the name of the property. I'm sure you don't want to change property names just for labeling purposes. Instead, you can use the label= attribute of @Validate, or you can define the label in the StripesResources.properties file. Let's see how each technique works by changing the labels for the fields of the Contact class.

> ### Accessing the List of Messages
>
> The <s:messages> and <s:errors> tags take care of displaying messages for you. However, nothing stops you from accessing the list of messages directly and doing whatever you want with it. Messages are stored in ActionBeanContext and are available with getMessages() for information messages and getValidation-Errors() for error messages, so you can easily access them in a JSP with an expression. For example:
>
> ```
> <c:if test="${not empty actionBean.context.messages}">
>    There are ${fn:length(actionBean.context.messages)}
>    information messages.
> </c:if>
>
> <c:if test="${not empty actionBean.context.validationErrors}">
>    There are ${fn:length(actionBean.context.validationErrors)}
>    error messages.
> </c:if>
> ```

The first way is to add label= attributes to @Validate annotations:

`email_12/src/stripesbook/action/ContactFormActionBean.java`

```
@ValidateNestedProperties({
    @Validate(field="firstName", maxlength=25, label="Given name"),
    @Validate(field="lastName",  minlength=2, maxlength=40,
      label="Surname"),
    @Validate(field="email", required=true, on="save",
        converter=EmailTypeConverter.class, label="E-mail"),
    @Validate(field="birthDate", expression="${this < today}",
        label="Date of birth"),
    @Validate(field="phoneNumber", label="Telephone number")
})
@Override
public void setContact(Contact contact) {
    super.setContact(contact);
}
```

These labels will be used for {0} tokens in error messages. Now, the following:

{1} is not a valid {0}

will be displayed as this:

555 is not a valid Telephone number.

Field labels are also used in the <s:label> tag. Back on page 117, we discussed using <*s:label*> for labels so that Stripes would automatically highlight them when the corresponding field was in error. Now that the text is in @Validate(label=), there's no need to repeat it in the body of the <*s:label*> tag. We can remove the text from the body and use empty <*s:label/*> tags:

email_12/web/WEB-INF/jsp/contact_form.jsp

```
<td><s:label for="contact.phoneNumber"/>:</td>
<td>
  <s:text name="contact.phoneNumber" formatType="dashes"/>
</td>
<td><s:errors field="contact.phoneNumber"/></td>
```

Stripes automatically uses the label that we defined in @Validate(label=) as the text of the <*s:label/*> tag. In the previous example, *Telephone number:* will appear in front of the text field. The label will be displayed normally when all is well and will be highlighted when the field is in error.

Using the label= attribute is quick and easy but limited. The text is not localizable, and the labels are limited to the form linked to the action bean—the contact form, in this example.

The second way of changing field labels that are used in error messages and the <*s:label/*> tag is with the resource bundle. This method, which overrides any existing @Validate(label="...") definitions, allows you to use the labels everywhere in the application. They also make the labels localizable, as we'll see in Chapter 11, *Parlez-Vous Français? Making It Multilingual*, on page 211. We define a field label by using the field name as a key in StripesResources.properties:

email_13/res/StripesResources.properties

```
contact.firstName=FIRST NAME
contact.lastName=LAST NAME
contact.email=EMAIL
contact.phoneNumber=PHONE NUMBER
contact.birthDate=BIRTH DATE
```

This would display field labels in uppercase letters. We can now use these labels everywhere—for example, in the contact view with empty <*s:label/*> tags:

email_13/web/WEB-INF/jsp/contact_view.jsp

```
<tr>
  <td class="label"><s:label for="contact.firstName"/>:</td>
  <td class="value">${actionBean.contact.firstName}</td>
</tr>
```

Now, field labels are defined in one place and reused in the contact view, in the contact form, and in error messages. Nice!

With labels in resource bundles, we can still use different labels for fields that are in different forms but have the same name. Just put the package and class name of the action bean in front of the field name, as in the following:

`email_14/res/StripesResources.properties`

```
stripesbook.action.ContactFormActionBean.contact.firstName=FIRST NAME
stripesbook.action.ContactFormActionBean.contact.lastName=LAST NAME
stripesbook.action.ContactFormActionBean.contact.email=EMAIL
stripesbook.action.ContactFormActionBean.contact.phoneNumber=PHONE NUMBER
stripesbook.action.ContactFormActionBean.contact.birthDate=BIRTH DATE

contact.firstName=first name
contact.lastName=last name
contact.email=email
contact.phoneNumber=phone number
contact.birthDate=birth date
```

This would use uppercase labels in the contact form and lowercase labels everywhere else.

Changing the Error Message Text

If changing field labels is not enough to get the error messages that we want, we can change the text completely. By default, Stripes looks for an error message in the StripesResources.properties file. When a validation error occurs, Stripes uses several keys to search for the corresponding message. The keys go from more specific to more general, making it possible to have very specific messages as well as general-purpose messages. The StripesResources.properties file you copied over from the Stripes distribution contains messages for all possible errors that Stripes produces, using the most general key.

We can change the text either by overriding the Stripes default or by providing a message using a more specific key. Let's talk a bit more about these keys.

To build the list of search keys, Stripes uses different combinations of the following values:

actionBeanFullName: The fully qualified name of the action bean class, as in stripesbook.action.ContactFormActionBean.

fieldName: The name of the field that is in error. This name corresponds to the name= attribute of the form control, such as contact.firstName.

errorName: The name associated with the type of validation that caused the error. Each built-in validation has a specific *errorName*. For example, the *errorName* for @Validate(required=true) is valueNotPresent.

defaultScope: Like *errorName*, the *defaultScope* is associated with a type of validation, such as validation.required for @Validate(required=true).

Here are the combinations of these values that Stripes uses when it searches through the resource bundle:

actionBeanFullName.*fieldName*.*errorName*
actionBeanFullName.*fieldName*.errorMessage
fieldName.*errorName*
fieldName.errorMessage
actionBeanFullName.*errorName*
actionBeanFullName.errorMessage
defaultScope.*errorName*

For example, when a @Validate(required=true) validation fails for the contact.email field in stripesbook.action.ContactFormActionBean, Stripes searches for the following keys:

stripesbook.action.ContactFormActionBean.contact.email.valueNotPresent
stripesbook.action.ContactFormActionBean.contact.email.errorMessage
contact.email.valueNotPresent
contact.email.errorMessage
stripesbook.action.ContactFormActionBean.valueNotPresent
stripesbook.action.ContactFormActionBean.errorMessage
validation.required.valueNotPresent

Stripes uses the first matching key or throws an exception if no key is found. As mentioned earlier, StripesResources.properties comes with messages for every built-in validation using the last key in the search list, *defaultScope*.*errorName*.

The following table shows the *defaultScope* and *errorName* for each built-in validation and type converter:

Validation	defaultScope	errorName
required=true	validation.required	valueNotPresent
minlength=*N*	validation.minlength	valueTooShort
maxlength=*N*	validation.maxlength	valueTooLong
minvalue=*N*	validation.minvalue	valueBelowMinimum
maxvalue=*N*	validation.maxvalue	valueAboveMaximum
mask=*"M"*	validation.mask	valueDoesNotMatch
expression=*"E"*	validation.expression	valueFailedExpression
Type Converter		
DateTypeConverter	converter.date	invalidDate
EmailTypeConverter	converter.email	invalidEmail
EnumeratedTypeConverter	converter.enum	notAnEnumeratedValue
*Number*TypeConverter[1]	converter.number	invalidNumber
*Number*TypeConverter	converter.*type*[2]	outOfRange
PercentageTypeConverter	converter.number	invalidNumber
PercentageTypeConverter	converter.*type*	outOfRange

To change the text of an error message, change the corresponding entry in the StripesResources.properties file, or add a new entry. We can use a key that is as specific or as general as we want. For example, the following

```
stripesbook.action.ContactFormActionBean.contact.email.valueNotPresent
```

is most specific, while the following

```
validation.required.valueNotPresent
```

is most general. We can use the {0} and {1} tokens to include the field label and the value entered by the user in the error message text.

Certain validators and type converters provide additional parameters, starting at {2}, as shown here in the table on the next page.

---

1. *Number* refers to each number type converter: ByteTypeConverter, IntegerTypeConverter, and so on.
2. *type* refers to the number type, as in converter.byte, converter.integer, and so on.

Validator/Type Converter	{2}	{3}
minlength=N	N	
maxlength=N	N	
minvalue=N	N	
maxvalue=N	N	
NumberTypeConverter[3]	range minimum	range maximum

For example, the @Validate(minvalue=N) validation provides the value for N. If the user enters 15 in an Age field for which you have @Validate(minvalue=18), we could use this:

{1} is below the minimum {0} of {2}

to produce the following error message:

15 is below the minimum age of 18

Let's change the error messages in the contact form. For example, if the user enters a date in the future, such as 2040-01-27, the error message is currently as follows:

The value supplied (Fri Jan 27 00:00:00 EST 2040) for field Birth date is invalid.

This message is quite long and doesn't say *why* the birth date is invalid. The *errorName* for an expression= validation is valueFailedExpression. Using the contact.birthDate.valueFailedExpression key, the message can be changed to a less intimidating and more informative message:

email_15/res/StripesResources.properties

```
contact.birthDate.valueFailedExpression=The birth date is in the future.
```

Using the field names and error names, we can customize the text for the other error messages as well:

email_15/res/StripesResources.properties

```
contact.firstName.valueTooLong=The first name cannot exceed {2} characters.
contact.lastName.valueTooShort=The last name must be at least {2} characters.
contact.lastName.valueTooLong=The last name cannot exceed {2} characters.
contact.email.valueNotPresent=The email address is required.
contact.birthDate.invalidDate=The birth date is not valid.
```

---

3. Provided when an outOfRange error occurs.

6.4 Creating Messages for Custom Errors

Back on page 100, we created a PhoneNumberTypeConverter class to convert an input String to a PhoneNumber. If the input was not valid, we created an error. The error message was directly in the code:

email_12/src/stripesbook/ext/PhoneNumberTypeConverter.java

```
errors.add(new SimpleError("{1} is not a valid {0}"));
```

With all other error messages in the StripesResources.properties file, it'd be a shame not to have messages for custom errors in there as well. Say we wanted to use the following key:

```
contact.phoneNumber.invalid
```

To use the message defined with this key, we can simply use the LocalizableError class. This class allows us to specify a resource bundle key instead of a hard-coded message. For example:

```
errors.add(
  new LocalizableError("contact.phoneNumber.invalid");
```

Now we can define the error message in StripesResources.properties with all the other error messages:

email_15/res/StripesResources.properties

```
contact.phoneNumber.invalid=The phone number is not valid.
```

That's fine when you are creating errors that are specific to our application. But PhoneNumberTypeConverter is useful for any phone number field, not just the one in the contact form. In fact, word of your phone number type converter has spread around the office, and people from other departments have asked us whether they could use it in their applications.

The problem right now is that we're limited to the same error message for every phone number field. What if other developers use PhoneNumberTypeConverter in more than one form and need different error messages in each form?

The ScopedLocalizableError class is specifically designed for use in type converters such as PhoneNumberTypeConverter. It takes advantage of the key lookup mechanism, just like the type converters provided by Stripes.

Tim Says...

Make Judicious Use of ScopedLocalizableError

At first glance, the ScopedLocalizableError class might look rather complicated. That's because ScopedLocalizableError is designed exclusively for use in TypeConverters. Of course, like any class, you can use it elsewhere if you need to—I've just never found it useful outside of writing TypeConverters.

But when you write your own TypeConverters, you should always use ScopedLocalizableError, never SimpleError or LocalizableError. Doing so ensures that your custom TypeConverter will work just like Stripes' built-in ones and make it easy to customize the error message as appropriate when you use your new converter. At first this might not seem like a big deal—"I'm using my custom converter on only one page," you say. Doing it right from the beginning will mean that when you do need to use your type converter somewhere else—or better yet someone else on your team needs to—it'll be ready to go, and there'll be no temptation to replicate code or do something quick and dirty.

To get our custom error messages to be part of that mechanism, we specify the *defaultScope* and *errorName* for our type converter in the constructor of the ScopedLocalizableError class:

email_15/src/stripesbook/ext/PhoneNumberTypeConverter.java

```java
errors.add(
    new ScopedLocalizableError("converter.phoneNumber", "invalid"));
```

Now Stripes will search all the different key combinations that we saw on page 125. We can define a different error message for a specific form by using a key that includes the action bean name or field name.

The best part is that the error message we added earlier with the contact.phoneNumber.invalid key still works. Indeed, *fieldName.errorName* is among the list of keys that Stripes uses in the search. Since *fieldName* is contact.phoneNumber in the contact form and we defined *errorName* to be invalid when we created the ScopedLocalizableError, contact.phoneNumber.invalid will match.

Finally, to make PhoneNumberTypeConverter easy to reuse, we would provide a general error message with the converter.phoneNumber.invalid key in the StripesResources.properties file. That's the last key in the search, and defining a message with that key would make sure that Stripes uses it by default. Our type converter now works right out of the box!

Wrapping Up

Stripes gives you a reasonable display of information and error messages with minimal effort. If the defaults do not suit you, you can customize just about everything about how you present messages to your users. Using entries in the StripesResources.properties file and a touch of CSS goes a long way.

So, what's next? When we started building the sample application in Chapter 3, *The Core: Action Beans and JSPs*, we touched on the topic of reusable layouts. It's time to discuss them in more detail.

I don't think necessity is the mother of invention—invention,
in my opinion, arises directly from idleness, possibly also
from laziness. To save oneself trouble.
▶ Agatha Christie

Chapter 7

Reusable Layouts

Web applications are typically composed of several pages. As soon as you have more than one page in your application, you'll notice that some parts are the same for every page: the HTML header code, the title, the footer, and so on. You certainly don't want to copy and paste those parts in every page and then have the nightmare of maintaining all that duplicated code. Reusable layouts to the rescue: you put the common parts in one place and reuse them in as many pages as you like. Then, when you want to make a change to the header, for example, you have only one file to edit. All pages that use this file will automatically inherit the change. This makes it easier to maintain consistency in your application—no more "Oops, how come the new header appears only in some pages but not others?"

Having one place for static code is only half the story. You also want to be able to assemble your pages with dynamic content that comes from each page. You need a way of saying "The title goes here, the body of the page goes there... whatever they may be." Each page specifies its own content for the title, body, and so on, and the layout assembles all the parts together to produce the final result.

Stripes gives you a simple and powerful reusable layout system. You don't need to install any additional libraries to use it, and you won't have to create and maintain any configuration files either!

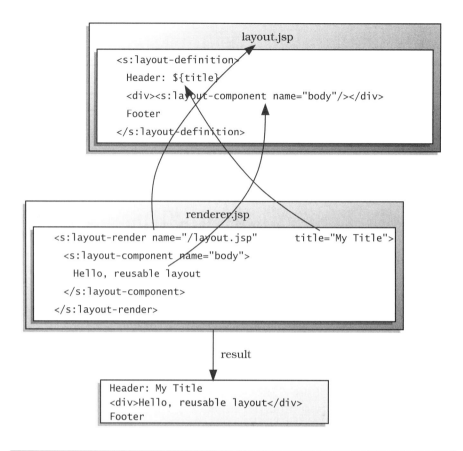

Figure 7.1: THE STRIPES REUSABLE LAYOUT TAGS

7.1 Basic Stripes Layout Concepts

Look at the example illustrated in Figure 7.1. Stripes reusable layouts
come down to three tags and four concepts:

Layout: A template that can be reused for multiple pages. To indicate
that a JSP defines a layout, just wrap the contents with opening
and closing <*s:layout-definition*> tags.

Renderer: A page that uses a layout to produce a result. Use the
<*s:layout-render*> tag with the path to the layout JSP in the
name= attribute to render the layout. Starting with a forward slash
(/), write the path relative to the web application's root directory.

Component: A building block for layouts and renderers. In a layout, add a component to indicate *where* to put a block of content. In a renderer, use a component to say *what* goes in that block. In both cases, use the <s:layout-component> tag with matching name= attributes.[1]

Attribute: You can optionally add arbitrary attributes to the <s:layout-render> tag and place their values in the layout with the name of the attribute within ${ }. If you have something=*somevalue* in the <s:layout-render> tag, using ${something} in the layout produces *somevalue.*

That's it! Everything gets done with three tags. When you look at a JSP, you can tell right away whether it is a layout by the <s:layout-definition> tag. You also know that a JSP is rendering a layout when you see the <s:layout-render> tag, and the path to the layout JSP is right there in the name= attribute. The <s:layout-component> tags determine the layout-related content. It's all there. No need to go fishing around in configuration files to figure out what's going on.

You can think of layouts as abstract classes. They contain code that can be reused, and components are like abstract methods. Renderers are concrete subclasses that implement these methods by providing content for components.

Just like abstract classes cannot be instantiated, layouts cannot be used on their own to produce a result. Indeed, if you forward to a <s:layout-definition> JSP, you'll get an exception. To produce a result, you must use a renderer—a concrete implementation.

Providing Default Content

Sometimes you might find you're using the same content for a component in most (but not all) pages. Instead of copying and pasting the same content in those pages, you can use that content as a *default* for the component in the layout. This is like having a default implementation of a method in an abstract class, which can optionally be overridden by a subclass. To do this, put the default content in the

---

1. Get in the habit of using valid Java identifiers as component names—no dashes, no spaces. . . you get the picture. Although the name "body-content" will work in a basic layout, it can cause errors that are difficult to track down when using the more advanced layout techniques that we'll talk about later in the chapter. Save yourself trouble, and use either underscores or CamelCase to separate words in the names of your layout components.

body of the *<s:layout-component>* tag used in the layout. You can still override the content in a renderer, but you can omit the component altogether in all those pages that use the default content.

For example, this layout has three components: part1, part2, and part3:

reusable_layouts/web/default_content/layout.jsp

```
<s:layout-definition>
  Header
  <div>
    <s:layout-component name="part1">
      Default Part 1
    </s:layout-component>
  </div>
  <div>
    <s:layout-component name="part2">
      Default Part 2
    </s:layout-component>
  </div>
  <div><s:layout-component name="part3"/></div>
  Footer
</s:layout-definition>
```

The following renderer renders the layout:

reusable_layouts/web/default_content/renderer.jsp

```
<s:layout-render name="/default_content/layout.jsp">
  <s:layout-component name="part2">
    My Part 2
  </s:layout-component>
</s:layout-render>
```

And produces the following:

```
Header
Default Part 1
My Part 2
Footer
```

The renderer does not provide content for part1, so the layout's default is used. The renderer's content overrides the layout's default for part2. For the part3 component, neither the layout nor the renderer provides content. Layouts are more forgiving than abstract classes here: empty components don't cause errors; they are just left blank.

Using Attributes

Besides the *<s:layout-component>* tag, a renderer can also send content to a layout with dynamic attributes of the *<s:layout-render>* tag.

For example, look at the following layout and renderer:

`reusable_layouts/web/attributes/layout.jsp`

```
<s:layout-definition>
❶   Header: ${title}
    <div><s:layout-component name="body"/></div>
    <div>
      Objects:
      <ul>
❷       <c:forEach var="object" items="${objects}">
          <li>${object}</li>
        </c:forEach>
      </ul>
    </div>
    Footer
</s:layout-definition>
```

`reusable_layouts/web/attributes/renderer.jsp`

```
❶  <s:layout-render name="/attributes/layout.jsp" title="My Title"
❷     objects="${pageContext.request.parameterMap}">
     <s:layout-component name="body">
       Hello, reusable layout
     </s:layout-component>
   </s:layout-render>
```

At ❶ in renderer.jsp, the title attribute has the value "My Title". The layout can put this value in the page using the attribute name within ${ }, as in ${title} at ❶ in layout.jsp. Attributes are *not* components, so <s:layout-component name="title"/> won't work in the layout to display "My Title".

As you can see, attributes are more concise and are good for short content. They also give you a way to send types other than String from a renderer to a layout. At ❷ in renderer.jsp, the objects attribute is a Map<String,String[]>, and the layout receives a value of that type. In this example, the layout iterates over the values of the list in ❷ of layout.jsp and outputs each item. With these request parameters:

```
dir=example&files=one&files=two
```

renderer.jsp produces the following:

```
Header: My Title
Hello, reusable layout
Objects:

    o dir=[example]
    o files=[one, two]


Footer
```

> ### Joe Asks...
> #### Should I Use Components or Attributes?
>
> You can use either components or attributes in renderers. Choosing between them depends on the content you are sending to the layout:
>
> - For multiple lines of content, you must use a component.
> - For non-String content, you must use an attribute.
>
> It also depends on how you place the content in the layout:
>
> - If the content is placed in the layout with a component, the renderer must use a component to provide the content.
> - If the renderer specifies content with an attribute, the layout must use ${ } to place the content.
> - Whether the renderer uses a component or an attribute, the layout can use ${ } to place the content.
>
> You'll find that using components for blocks of content, and attributes for short content or parameter-like values, generally works out well.

The *<s:layout-render>* tag does not know in advance the names of the attributes you will use, so it actually supports *dynamic* attributes. This allows you to choose whatever attribute names you want to send parameters from a renderer to a layout.

7.2 Putting Layouts to Work: Decorators

Now that we've seen the building blocks of Stripes reusable layouts, let's put them to work beyond the "Hello, reusable layout" examples. With layout decorators, we can create a rich set of layouts for the pages of your applications.

A powerful way of using layouts is to build a layout "hierarchy," where we start with a base layout at the top that contains what's common to all pages and add more layouts that contain parts that are used in subsets of pages. Each additional layout is a *decorator*, because it uses another layout higher up in the hierarchy and "decorates" it by adding more parts.

Take the layout.jsp file from Figure 7.1, on page 132, for example. Say we are using this layout in many pages of our application, but now we need to add several new pages that will have ads and a menu. We want to create a layout for this without changing the original layout because not all pages should have the ads and the menu. You don't want to copy and paste the original layout either, because that would give us an unpleasant WET feeling.[2]

A great way to solve this problem is to define a new layout that uses the original layout.jsp as a base and adds sections on the left and right for the ads and adds the menu on the left of the body, as shown here:

`reusable_layouts/web/ads_and_menu/layout_decorator.jsp`

```
<s:layout-definition>
  <table>
    <tr>
      <td>Ads Left</td>
      <td>
        <s:layout-render name="/ads_and_menu/layout.jsp">
          <s:layout-component name="body">
            <table>
              <tr>
                <td>Menu</td>
                <td>${body}</td>
              </tr>
            </table>
          </s:layout-component>
        </s:layout-render>
      </td>
      <td>Ads Right</td>
    </tr>
  </table>
</s:layout-definition>
```

Here, layout_decorator.jsp is both a layout and a renderer: it is a layout with sections for the ads, and it is a renderer of layout.jsp. The "body" component is decorated by adding a menu on the left.

Now, the only difference in renderer.jsp is that it renders layout_decorator. jsp instead of layout.jsp.

---

2. Write Everything Twice! Write Everything Twice! WET is the opposite of the better-known DRY, which stands for Don't Repeat Yourself. Thomas and Hunt's *The Pragmatic Programmer: From Journeyman to Master* [HT00] discusses the importance of DRY in detail.

> reusable_layouts/web/ads_and_menu/renderer.jsp

```
<s:layout-render name="/ads_and_menu/layout_decorator.jsp">
  <s:layout-component name="body">
    Hello, reusable layout
  </s:layout-component>
</s:layout-render>
```

which produces a page with ads and a menu:

Ads Left	Header		Ads Right
	Menu	Hello, reusable layout	
	Footer		

The thing to watch for in a layout decorator is the role of the <s:layout-component> tag. Look at the nearest parent layout tag to determine the role. Within <s:layout-render>, the component provides content to the layout being rendered; within <s:layout-definition>, the component is a placeholder for content provided by a renderer.

In layout_decorator.jsp, the <s:layout-component> tag is nested in <s:layout-render>, so it sends content to layout.jsp. The question is this then: how do we render the content provided by renderer.jsp for the "body" component? A-ha—with ${body}. This is how we can both provide content to the layout *and* render content received from the renderer for the same component.

Adding Components

Layout decorators are not limited to adding static content and decorating the components of the parent layout. You can also add components to the layout decorator so that renderers can provide different content for those new components.

Taking the previous example, say you wanted to turn the menu part into a "menu" component so that pages can have different menus. You cannot use the <s:layout-component> tag because it is nested within <s:layout-render> and will send content for the "menu" component to layout.jsp (which will cheerfully ignore it).

Again, the solution is to use ${menu}:

reusable_layouts/web/ads_and_menu_component/layout_decorator.jsp

```
<s:layout-definition>
  <table>
    <tr>
      <td><s:layout-component name="adsLeft"/></td>
      <td>
        <s:layout-render name="/ads_and_menu_component/layout.jsp">
          <s:layout-component name="body">
            <table>
              <tr>
                <td>${menu}</td>
                <td>${body}</td>
              </tr>
            </table>
          </s:layout-component>
        </s:layout-render>
      </td>
      <td><s:layout-component name="adsRight"/></td>
    </tr>
  </table>
</s:layout-definition>
```

Now, the renderer can provide its own menu with the "menu" component. Looking again at the previous listing, you see that you can also turn the ads on the left and right into components. In this case, the parent layout tag is *<s:layout-definition>*, so you can use the *<s:layout-component>* tag for these components—"adsLeft" and "adsRight".[3] The content for these components is now also provided by each renderer. For example, the following:

reusable_layouts/web/ads_and_menu_component/renderer.jsp

```
<s:layout-render name="/ads_and_menu_component/layout_decorator.jsp">
  <s:layout-component name="body">
    Hello, reusable layout
  </s:layout-component>
  <s:layout-component name="menu">
    My Menu
  </s:layout-component>
  <s:layout-component name="adsLeft">
    My Ads Left
  </s:layout-component>
  <s:layout-component name="adsRight">
    My Ads Right
  </s:layout-component>
</s:layout-render>
```

---

3. Note that you could still use ${adsLeft} and ${adsRight} here—in this case, it would be up to you to choose the notation that you prefer.

produces this:

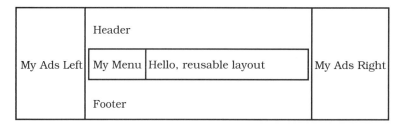

Notice that the order in which we specify components in a renderer does not matter—what matters is where the layout places the components within the template.

Default Content in Layout Decorators

The components in the last layout_decorator.jsp are "adsLeft", "menu", "body", and "adsRight". We can also provide default content for these components. It's straightforward for "adsLeft" and "adsRight": just add the default in the body of the *<s:layout-component>* tag. But how do we provide a default for "menu" and "body", where we can't use the *<s:layout-component>* tag?

Remember a component can also be placed in the layout using the component name within ${ }, such as ${menu} and ${body}. That's because components are in the JSP's context. We can set a value in the same context with the JSTL's *<c:set>* tag, as shown here:

`reusable_layouts/web/default_content_in_decorators/layout_decorator.jsp`

```
► <c:set var="menu">Default Menu</c:set>
► <c:set var="body">Default Body</c:set>
  <s:layout-definition>
    <table>
      <tr><td>
        <s:layout-component name="adsLeft">
          Default Ads left
        </s:layout-component>
      </td><td>
        <s:layout-render name="/default_content_in_decorators/layout.jsp">
          <s:layout-component name="body">
            <table><tr>
              <td>${menu}</td>
              <td>${body}</td>
            </tr></table>
          </s:layout-component>
        </s:layout-render>
      </td><td>
```

```
      <s:layout-component name="adsRight">
        Default Ads right
      </s:layout-component>
    </td></tr>
  </table>
</s:layout-definition>
```

By placing the *<c:set>* tags **before** the *<s:layout-definition>* tag, we are setting values that act as defaults. Indeed, these values are used unless they are overridden by the renderer's own values.

Now, this renderer:

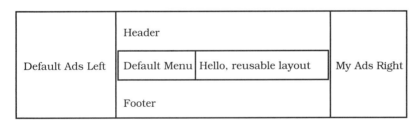

reusable_layouts/web/default_content_in_decorators/renderer.jsp

```
<s:layout-render name="/default_content_in_decorators/layout_decorator.jsp">
  <s:layout-component name="body">
    Hello, reusable layout
  </s:layout-component>
  <s:layout-component name="adsRight">
    My Ads Right
  </s:layout-component>
</s:layout-render>
```

produces the following:

Default Ads Left	Header		My Ads Right
	Default Menu	Hello, reusable layout	
	Footer		

As we can see, setting default values with *<c:set>* gives us the same behavior as with *<s:layout-component>*: defaults are used unless overridden by the renderer. It's also with *<c:set>* that we can have defaults for values provided by renderers in attributes, as in <s:layout-render name="/layout.jsp" title="My Title">. We would use <c:set var="title">Default title</c:set> to have a default title in layout.jsp.

Adding Pages to the Webmail Application

Let's use layout decorators to add pages to the webmail application. Skeletons of these pages are shown in Figure 7.2, on page 143. We'll start adding content to the pages in the next chapter—for now, let's focus on the layouts.

Layouts Are Flexible

The name of the layout in the *<s:layout-render>* tag does not have to be a static value. For example, you might like to render different layouts according to the user's preference or depending on whether the user has guest or administrator access rights. You can use a runtime value as the name of the layout, as follows:

```
<s:layout-render name="${someValue}">...</s:layout-render>
```

You can now write code that uses whatever criteria that you need to dynamically set the value of the someValue variable to the path and name of the layout file.

Another nice layout feature is that you can specify a component only once in a renderer but use that component multiple times in the layout. For example, you might want to have the list of links that a renderer provides both at the top and at the bottom of a layout. There's no problem with placing the same component in more than one location in the layout.

When the user arrives at the application, the Login page appears. If the user doesn't already have an account, the Registration page is available to create one.

Once inside the application, a menu at the top divides the pages into three sections: Messages, Contact List (which we've already implemented), and Compose. Notice that the Login and Registration pages just have a welcome message in place of the menu.

The pages of the Message List section, which include the list of messages and the detailed view of a message, have an additional feature: the list of folders is shown on the left part of the page.

To support these variants of what's included in a page, we will use a structure of three layouts: layout_main.jsp, layout_menu.jsp, and layout_folders.jsp. As you can see in Figure 7.3, on page 144, each layout builds on the previous layout. The base layout is layout_main.jsp. It shows the page title on the top-left corner of the page and has a menu component to show a menu next to the title. By default, the text *Welcome to Stripes Webmail* is displayed in place of the menu. The main part of the page is the body component.

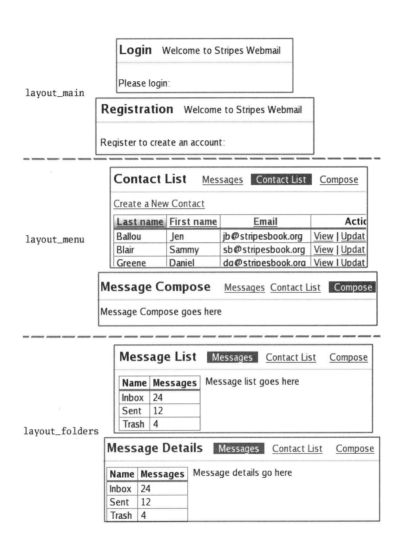

Figure 7.2: ADDING PAGES TO THE WEBMAIL APPLICATION

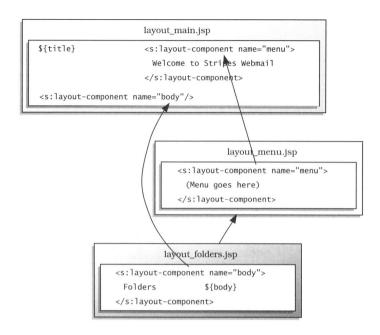

Figure 7.3: USING THREE LAYOUTS FOR THE WEBMAIL APPLICATION

Next, layout_menu.jsp decorates layout_main.jsp to add the menu. The menu component contains the real menu that is shown to the user once they have logged in.

Finally, layout_folders.jsp decorates layout_menu.jsp to add the list of folders on the left side of the body content.

First, here's what the interesting part of layout_main.jsp looks like:

```
email_16/web/WEB-INF/jsp/common/layout_main.jsp
```

```
<div id="header">
  <span class="title">${title}</span>
  <span class="menu">
    <s:layout-component name="menu">
      Welcome to Stripes Webmail
    </s:layout-component>
  </span>
</div>
<div id="body">
  <s:layout-component name="body"/>
</div>
```

Each renderer provides a page title and a body. The "menu" component is placed next to the page title and contains *Welcome to Stripes WebMail*

as a default. The Login and Registration pages can use layout_main.jsp
without providing the "menu" component.

Next, the layout_menu.jsp file uses layout_main.jsp and provides the "menu"
component:

email_16/web/WEB-INF/jsp/common/layout_menu.jsp

```
<s:layout-definition>
  <s:layout-render name="/WEB-INF/jsp/common/layout_main.jsp"
    title="${title}">
    <s:layout-component name="menu">
      (menu will go here)
    </s:layout-component>
    <s:layout-component name="body">${body}</s:layout-component>
  </s:layout-render>
</s:layout-definition>
```

Notice that the content for the "title" attribute and "body" component
must be taken from the renderer and sent to the layout even if they are
not modified; otherwise, the content from the renderer would be lost.
Indeed, when a JSP "A" renders a layout "B" and "B" renders another
layout "C," content is not automatically transmitted from "A" to "C"—it
is the responsibility of "B" to do so.

Finally, layout_folders.jsp uses layout_menu.jsp and decorates the "body"
component to add the folders on the left:

email_16/web/WEB-INF/jsp/common/layout_folders.jsp

```
<s:layout-definition>
  <s:layout-render name="/WEB-INF/jsp/common/layout_menu.jsp"
    title="${title}" currentSection="${currentSection}">
    <s:layout-component name="body">
      <div id="folders">
        (folders go here)
      </div>
      <div id="main">
        ${body}
      </div>
    </s:layout-component>
  </s:layout-render>
</s:layout-definition>
```

This brings us to another interesting feature that we want in sophisticated reusable layouts. The menu and folders are in layouts and used
in multiple pages, but their content is not static. It changes constantly:
the menu switches the highlighted section according to what the user
selects, and the folders are updated as messages are added, moved,
and deleted.

View helpers are awesome for dynamic content in reusable layouts. Let's break for a short walk and some fresh air before looking at view helpers.

7.3 Using View Helpers

When you're creating a view by writing a JSP, you have access to the current action bean with ${actionBean} and can use the information it provides to build the view. However, sometimes you'll find that the code to provide the data you need doesn't belong in the current action bean. This is often the case when working with layouts, because you're creating a view that will be reused across several pages. The current action bean will be different on each page. In these situations, you'll want to use a view helper.

Using a Simple Bean as a View Helper

A *view helper* is a block of Java code that is independent of the current action bean and makes your life easier when you're building dynamic parts of a view. You write the Java code that does the work and then use the results in the JSP to create the view. Let's look at a simple example of how it's done.

At the bottom of Figure 7.2, on page 143, we see that both the Message List and Message Details pages have a table on the left. The table shows the folders with the number of messages in each folder. We need the list of folders in layout_folders.jsp to create the table.

Say we have a Folder class to represent a folder:

email_16/src/stripesbook/model/Folder.java

```
package stripesbook.model;
public class Folder extends ModelBase {
    private String name;
    private int numberOfMessages;

    /* getters and setters... */
}
```

Suppose we have a FolderDao implementation that provides the list of folders with its read() method. We need a block of code that retrieves the list and makes it available to the JSP. That doesn't belong in any specific action bean, so we write a view helper.

```
email_16/src/stripesbook/view/FoldersViewHelper.java
```

```java
package stripesbook.view;
public class FoldersViewHelper {
    private FolderDao folderDao = MockFolderDao.getInstance();

    public List<Folder> getFolders() {
        return folderDao.read();
    }
}
```

This is similar to providing the list of contacts with the getContacts() method in ContactListActionBean, as we did back in Section 3.3, *The Contact List Action Bean*, on page 36. So, what's the difference? Although the contact list is displayed in a page, the list of folders is shown in a layout and used across multiple pages. No specific action bean is associated with displaying the list of folders. In fact, you don't need an action bean—just the previous FoldersViewHelper class is enough.

To use FoldersViewHelper in layout_folders.jsp, create an instance with the *<jsp:useBean>* tag, and assign it to a variable with the id= attribute:

```
email_16/web/WEB-INF/jsp/common/layout_folders.jsp
```

```
<jsp:useBean class="stripesbook.view.FoldersViewHelper" id="folders"/>
```

We can now use ${folders} to refer to FoldersViewHelper. Creating the list of folders in a table becomes a simple task:

```
email_16/web/WEB-INF/jsp/common/layout_folders.jsp
```

```
<div id="folders">
  <d:table name="${folders.folders}">
    <d:column property="name"/>
    <d:column property="numberOfMessages" title="Messages"/>
  </d:table>
</div>
```

Voilà. That was easy. Using view helpers can help us modularize functionality in self-contained blocks of code that we can use to keep JSP code simple and concise.

This works well for simple beans such as FoldersViewHelper, but if we need the added benefits of action beans, such as having the action bean context, access to event handlers, and so on, we can use the *<s:useActionBean>* as a replacement for *<jsp:useBean>*. Specify the class name in the beanclass= attribute instead of class=, and make sure the bean implements ActionBean, of course. If we want to execute an event, we add the event= attribute with the name of the event handler.

We can even execute the resolution returned by the event handler with executeResolution=*"true"*.

Using an Action Bean-JSP Combination as a View Helper

Sometimes you'll find that after you've modularized the Java code in a view helper class, you'd like to do the same for the block of JSP code that uses it. The code that we used earlier to create the table of folders was only a few lines long. But if you're doing a significant amount of work, you may prefer to extract that block of code into a separate JSP and keep the original JSP from getting too lengthy.

To accomplish this, you can write a view helper as an action bean–JSP combination. The action bean is a view helper class and has a default event handler that forwards to a JSP. The JSP contains the block of view code that uses the information provided by the action bean to produce the desired portion of the view. You can then "embed" the result in the original JSP.

Let's see how that technique works by using it to implement the menu that appears at the top of each page:

We'll start with the MenuViewHelper action bean. It defines the sections of the application (Messages, Contact List, and Compose) and makes them available in a getter method. It also has a property to hold the currently selected section:

`email_16/src/stripesbook/action/MenuViewHelper.java`

```
package stripesbook.action;
public class MenuViewHelper extends BaseActionBean {
    public Section[] getSections() {
        return Section.values();
    }
    private Section currentSection;
    public Section getCurrentSection() {
        return currentSection;
    }
    public void setCurrentSection(Section currentSection) {
        this.currentSection = currentSection;
    }
    @DefaultHandler
    public Resolution view() {
        return new ForwardResolution("/WEB-INF/jsp/common/menu.jsp");
    }
```

```
    public enum Section {
        MessageList("Messages", MessageListActionBean.class),
        ContactList("Contact List", ContactListActionBean.class),
        Compose("Compose", MessageComposeActionBean.class);

        private String text, beanclass;
        Section(String text, Class<? extends ActionBean> beanclass) {
            this.text = text;
            this.beanclass = beanclass.getName();
        }
        public String getText() { return text; }
        public String getBeanclass() { return beanclass; }
    }
}
```

The default event handler forwards to menu.jsp. This is where we display the menu:

email_16/web/WEB-INF/jsp/common/menu.jsp

```
<c:forEach var="section" items="${actionBean.sections}">
  <c:choose>
❶    <c:when test="${section eq actionBean.currentSection}">
      <span class="currentSection">${section.text}</span>
    </c:when>
    <c:otherwise>
❷      <s:link beanclass="${section.beanclass}" class="sectionLink">
        ${section.text}
      </s:link>
    </c:otherwise>
  </c:choose>
</c:forEach>
```

The JSP goes through the sections provided by MenuViewHelper. The test at ❶ determines whether the section is currently selected and displays a highlighted label in that case. Otherwise, a link to the section is created at ❷, using the action bean class name and text. With the event omitted, the link uses the default event handler of the action bean.

The menu view helper is now ready to use. How do we embed it in the "menu" component of layout_menu.jsp? The standard JSP tag <jsp:include> issues a request and includes the response within the original JSP.

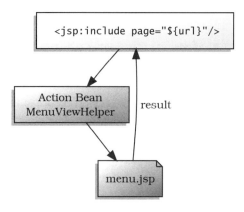

Figure 7.4: USING A VIEW HELPER

That's exactly what we need:

```
email_16/web/WEB-INF/jsp/common/layout_menu.jsp
```

```
<s:layout-component name="menu">
  <s:url var="url" beanclass="stripesbook.action.MenuViewHelper"
    prependContext="false">
    <s:param name="currentSection" value="${currentSection}"/>
  </s:url>
  <jsp:include page="${url}"/>
</s:layout-component>
```

The URL is bound to the MenuViewHelper action bean. Its default event handler forwards to menu.jsp, which displays the menu. The result is put back in place of the *<jsp:include>* tag, as illustrated in Figure 7.4.

Notice that we have to use a URL in the *<jsp:include>* tag because it's a JSP tag, not a Stripes tag. But we can still continue to use action bean class names instead of URLs. The *<s:url>* tag constructs the URL for an action bean and stores it in a variable. We can then pass the value to the *<jsp:include>* tag.

The prependContext=*"false"* attribute is necessary because *<s:url>* prepends the application context to the URL by default, and the URL passed to the *<jsp:include>* tag should not include the application context.

With *<jsp:useBean>*, *<s:useActionBean>*, and the *<s:url>*/*<jsp:include>*/action bean/JSP combination, we have powerful ways of providing view helpers and building dynamic reusable layouts.

Now that all the layouts are ready, each page of the application can use the appropriate layout (layout_main.jsp, layout_menu.jsp, or layout_folders. jsp), providing a title, the section to which it belongs, and a body. For example, the Message List page would be as follows:

email_16/web/WEB-INF/jsp/message_list.jsp

```
<s:layout-render name="/WEB-INF/jsp/common/layout_folders.jsp"
  title="Message List" currentSection="MessageList">
  <s:layout-component name="body">
    Message list goes here
  </s:layout-component>
</s:layout-render>
```

to produce the following:

As we can see, layouts give us a way to organize the reusable parts of our view code and concentrate on the specific content of each page.

7.4 If You're Used to Tiles or SiteMesh

Stripes comes with an easy-to-use, full-featured reusable layout mechanism. But if you're already using Tiles or SiteMesh and you're not ready to switch, you can still use one of those frameworks for your layouts within a Stripes application. Although I won't go into the details of using either of these frameworks, I'll tell you what you need to do to integrate them with Stripes.

Tiles

Apache Tiles[4] became popular as part of the Struts web application framework and has since been extracted into a stand-alone framework. Configuring Tiles for use with Stripes doesn't involve any special tricks.

---

4. http://tiles.apache.org/

Just add TilesListener to web.xml as you would do to use Tiles with any other Java web application:

```
email_17/web/WEB-INF/web.xml

<listener>
  <listener-class>
    org.apache.tiles.web.startup.TilesListener
  </listener-class>
</listener>
```

Of course, you'll need to add the Tiles JARs and dependencies to /WEB-INF/lib:

```
commons-beanutils-1.7.0.jar
commons-digester-1.8.jar
commons-logging-api-1.1.jar
tiles-api-2.0.5.jar
tiles-core-2.0.5.jar
tiles-jsp-2.0.5.jar
```

Optionally, you can add the TilesDispatch servlet:

```
email_17/web/WEB-INF/web.xml

<servlet>
  <servlet-name>TilesDispatch</servlet-name>
  <servlet-class>
    org.apache.tiles.web.util.TilesDispatchServlet
  </servlet-class>
</servlet>
<servlet-mapping>
  <servlet-name>TilesDispatch</servlet-name>
  <url-pattern>*.tiles</url-pattern>
</servlet-mapping>
```

This allows you to use URLs that end in .tiles, and they will automatically be resolved to the names of the definitions that you use in the tiles.xml file. For example, in ContactListActionBean, you would return a path such as "/contact_list.tiles" instead of "/WEB-INF/jsp/contact_list.jsp":

```
email_17/src/stripesbook/action/ContactListActionBean.java

package stripesbook.action;
public class ContactListActionBean extends ContactBaseActionBean {
    private static final String LIST="/contact_list.tiles";
    private static final String VIEW="/contact_view.tiles";

    @DefaultHandler
    public Resolution list() {
        return new ForwardResolution(LIST);
    }
```

```
    public Resolution view() {
        return new ForwardResolution(VIEW);
    }
    /* ... */
}
```

You then define the contact_list and contact_view layouts in tiles.xml:

email_17/web/WEB-INF/tiles.xml

```
<!DOCTYPE tiles-definitions PUBLIC
  "-//Apache Software Foundation//DTD Tiles Configuration 2.0//EN"
  "http://tiles.apache.org/dtds/tiles-config_2_0.dtd">
<tiles-definitions>
  <definition name="layout_main"
    template="/WEB-INF/jsp/common/layout_main.jsp"/>

  <definition name="contact_list" extends="layout_main">
    <put-attribute name="title" value="Contact List"/>
    <put-attribute name="currentSection" value="ContactList"/>
    <put-attribute name="body" value="/WEB-INF/jsp/contact_list.jsp"/>
  </definition>

  <definition name="contact_view" extends="layout_main">
    <put-attribute name="title" value="Contact Information"/>
    <put-attribute name="currentSection" value="ContactList"/>
    <put-attribute name="body" value="/WEB-INF/jsp/contact_view.jsp"/>
  </definition>
</tiles-definitions>
```

Tiles will take care of mapping the URL to the definition and assembling layout to construct the page.

Like I said earlier, I won't go into any more detail about using Tiles. The point here is that its integration with Stripes is easy and straightforward. You'll find a complete working example in the book's sample code.

SiteMesh

OpenSymphony SiteMesh[5] is another layout framework that has its share of users. Because of the way it works, its integration with Stripes is not quite as straightforward as Tiles. After adding the sitemesh.jar file to /WEB-INF/lib, you'll need to do some configuration in web.xml.

---

5.   http://www.opensymphony.com/sitemesh/

First, add the SiteMesh filter *at the top* of the file, before all other elements:

`email_18/web/WEB-INF/web.xml`

```xml
<web-app version="2.4" xmlns="http://java.sun.com/xml/ns/j2ee"
  xmlns:xsi="http://www.w3.org/2001/XMLSchema-instance"
  xsi:schemaLocation="http://java.sun.com/xml/ns/j2ee
  http://java.sun.com/xml/ns/j2ee/web-app_2_4.xsd"
>
  <filter>
    <filter-name>SiteMesh</filter-name>
    <filter-class>
      com.opensymphony.module.sitemesh.filter.PageFilter
    </filter-class>
  </filter>
  <filter-mapping>
    <filter-name>SiteMesh</filter-name>
    <url-pattern>/*</url-pattern>
  </filter-mapping>
  <!-- ... -->
```

Next, add the INCLUDE and ERROR dispatchers to the Stripes filter:

`email_18/web/WEB-INF/web.xml`

```xml
<filter-mapping>
    <filter-name>StripesFilter</filter-name>
    <servlet-name>DispatcherServlet</servlet-name>
    <dispatcher>REQUEST</dispatcher>
    <dispatcher>FORWARD</dispatcher>
▶   <dispatcher>INCLUDE</dispatcher>
▶   <dispatcher>ERROR</dispatcher>
</filter-mapping>
```

Finally, add a mapping for *.jsp to the Stripes filter:

`email_18/web/WEB-INF/web.xml`

```xml
<filter-mapping>
    <filter-name>StripesFilter</filter-name>
    <url-pattern>*.jsp</url-pattern>
    <dispatcher>REQUEST</dispatcher>
    <dispatcher>FORWARD</dispatcher>
    <dispatcher>INCLUDE</dispatcher>
    <dispatcher>ERROR</dispatcher>
</filter-mapping>
```

SiteMesh is now ready. Discussing how SiteMesh works is outside the scope of this book (had to use that "outside the scope" phrase, didn't I?), but, again, you'll find a working example in the book's sample code.

Part II

Revving Up

I do not fear computers. I fear the lack of them.
    ▶ Isaac Asimov

Chapter 8

Adding Form Input Controls

Fasten your seat belt, because the next few chapters will be fast-paced. We're going to crank up the webmail application by giving life to the pages that we laid out in the previous chapter and using all kinds of nifty Stripes features. We'll start with the three pages that deal with email messages: the Message List, Message Details, and Message Compose pages.

The Message List page shows the messages that are in a folder. Each message has a link that displays the text of the message in the Message Details page. The user can write and send emails in the Message Compose page.

There's a lot going on in these pages. In this chapter, we'll concentrate on using the different types of form input controls—checkboxes, radio buttons, and so on. In the next chapter, we'll discuss the other features that we need to finish implementing the three message pages.

A few supporting classes—model classes, a DAO, and type converters—are involved here, but I don't want to spend too much time and space discussing the details because they don't involve anything we haven't seen before. So, let's briefly discuss the essentials. The classes involved in supplying information about folders and messages are illustrated in Figure 8.1, on the next page.

- The Folder model class represents a folder and contains a List of Message objects, which contain the information concerning an individual message: who it's from, the subject, the message text, and so on.

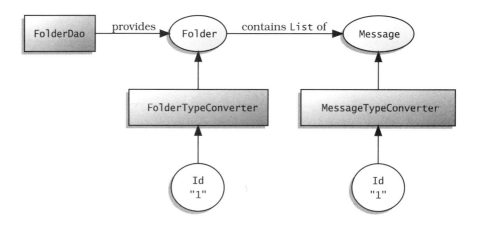

Figure 8.1: Folders and messages

- The FolderDao interface defines methods to manage folders and the messages they contain. MockFolderDao is an implementation that contains a few fictitious messages so that we see something when trying the example.

- FolderTypeConverter converts a String ID to a Folder, while Message-TypeConverter does the same for a Message. With these type converters, we can use ID parameters in forms and the Folder and Message property types in action beans. We discussed this technique in Section 5.4, *Using a Type Converter and Formatter to Load Model Objects*, on page 106.

Let's get to using form input controls, starting with checkboxes.

8.1 Checkboxes

The Message List page, shown in Figure 8.2, on the next page, allows the user to select a folder on the left and view the messages that are in that folder. The list of messages includes links to view the details of a message. There's also a column of checkboxes on the left, allowing the user to select messages. With the controls at the bottom, the user can delete the selected messages or move them to a different folder.

The MessageListActionBean class is the action bean associated to this page, with a default event handler that forwards to message_list.jsp. This JSP renders the page.

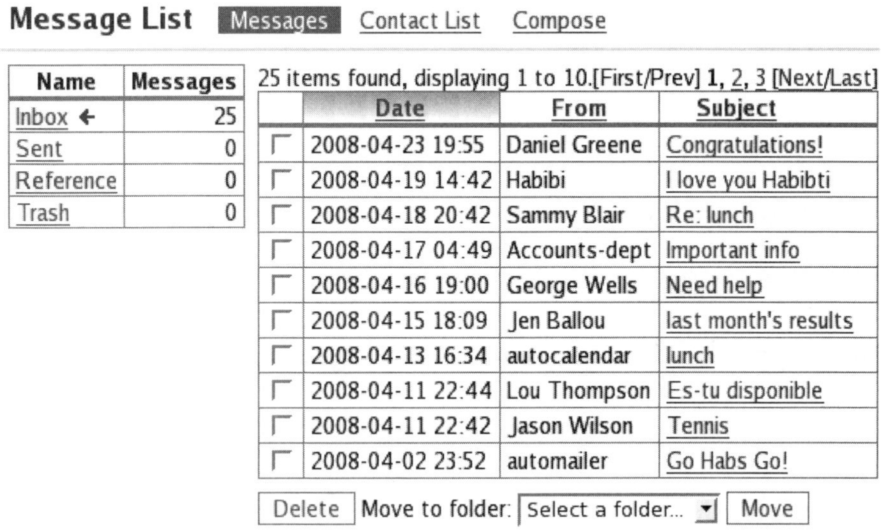

Figure 8.2: THE MESSAGE LIST PAGE

To create the column of checkboxes in the message list, we'll use the
<s:checkbox> tag:

email_19/web/WEB-INF/jsp/message_list.jsp

```
<s:form beanclass="stripesbook.action.MessageListActionBean">
  <d:table name="${folder.messages}" requestURI="" id="message"
    pagesize="10" defaultsort="2" defaultorder="descending">
    <d:column>
      <s:checkbox name="selectedMessages" value="${message.id}"/>
    </d:column>
    <!-- ... -->
  </d:table>
</s:form>
```

The checkboxes are bound to the selectedMessages property of Message-
ListActionBean. For every checkbox that the user checks, the value that's
in the value= attribute will be sent as input—in this case, the ID of the
corresponding message.

Stripes Form Input Tags

All Stripes form input tags use the name= attribute to bind the value of the input to an action bean property. Also note that these tags must always be nested within an <s:form> tag.

Using Stripes form input tags gives Stripes a chance to do several things for you, such as automatically populating the fields with existing data. This works both for updating the properties of an existing object and for redisplaying a form when validation errors have occurred. Other goodies include adding the maxlength= attribute to a text field when the corresponding property has a maxlength= validation, using model objects to generate options in a select box (as we'll see in this chapter), and looking up labels in resource bundles (explored in Chapter 11, *Parlez-Vous Français? Making It Multilingual.*)

Finally, the Stripes input tags also support all HTML attributes. The attributes for which Stripes has no use are passed through without modification. Yes, this includes the class= attribute—you don't have to use styleClass=, cssClass=, or any other renamed attribute like some other frameworks require you to do.

We can use a List<Message> property in order to receive all the selected messages:[1]

`email_19/src/stripesbook/action/MessageListActionBean.java`

```
private List<Message> selectedMessages;
public List<Message> getSelectedMessages() {
    return selectedMessages;
}
public void setSelectedMessages(List<Message> selectedMessages) {
    this.selectedMessages = selectedMessages;
}
```

When the user submits the form, selectedMessages will contain the messages that the user checked. It's very simple, then, to do something with these messages in an event handler.

---

1. This is one of several ways to use checkboxes. I explain the different ways in the sidebar on page 162.

For example, with the Delete button associated to the delete() event handler, here's how we would delete the selected messages:

email_19/src/stripesbook/action/MessageListActionBean.java

```java
public Resolution delete() {
    for (Message message : selectedMessages) {
        folderDao.deleteMessage(message);
    }
    return new RedirectResolution(getClass());
}
private FolderDao folderDao = MockFolderDao.getInstance();
```

Making sure that at least one message is selected is easy too. When no checkbox is checked, the corresponding property on the action bean will be **null**. So, all we have to do is make selectedMessages a required field:

email_19/src/stripesbook/action/MessageListActionBean.java

```java
@Validate(required=true, on={"delete", "moveToFolder"})
private List<Message> selectedMessages;
```

Let's not forget to display the potential error message to the user! Simply adding an <s:errors> tag under the message table and an error message in the resource bundle does the trick:

email_19/web/WEB-INF/jsp/message_list.jsp

```jsp
<div><s:errors field="selectedMessages"/></div>
```

email_19/res/StripesResources.properties

```
selectedMessages.valueNotPresent=You must select at least one message.
```

Now, clicking the Delete button with no selected checkbox gives an error message, as shown here:

| □ | 2008-04-11 22:42 | Jason Wilson | freddy@stripesl |
| □ | 2008-04-02 23:52 | automailer | hockeypool-list |

⊗ **You must select at least one message.**

Delete Move to folder: Select a folder... ▾ Move

8.2 Select Boxes

To move the selected messages to a different folder, the user must first select a folder. For that, we'll add a select box to the left of the Move button:

Move to folder: Select a folder... ▾ Move

A Bit More About How Checkboxes Work

In Stripes you can use checkboxes with different types of properties in the action bean: with an individual property, a Collection, or a Map.

- With an individual property:

```
<s:checkbox name="property" value="value1"/>
```

```
T property;
```

If the checkbox is checked, property is set to value1 with the usual type conversion to the type T. If the checkbox is unchecked, property is set to its *default value*: null for Object, false for boolean, 0 for int, and so on.

- With a Collection property:

```
<s:checkbox name="property" value="value1"/>
<s:checkbox name="property" value="value2"/>
...
<s:checkbox name="property" value="valueN"/>
```

```
Collection<T> property;
```

For each checked checkbox, the corresponding value (value1, value2, ...) is added to the property collection. Again, values are converted to the type T.

If no checkbox is checked, property is set to null.

- With a Map property:

```
<s:checkbox name="property.key1" value="value1"/>
<s:checkbox name="property.key2" value="value2"/>
...
<s:checkbox name="property.keyN" value="valueN"/>
```

```
Map<K,V> property;
```

If *at least one* checkbox is checked, the property map contains *every* key: key1, key2, ..., keyN. For each key, the value is the corresponding value1, value2, and so on, if the checkbox is checked or is null if the checkbox is unchecked.

Type conversion occurs for converting both keys to K and values to V.

If no checkbox is checked, property is set to null.

No matter how you use checkboxes, the value= attribute of the *<s:checkbox>* tag is optional. If omitted, the default value is true.

The <s:select> tag creates a select box that allows a single selection by default. Stripes offers helper tags that generate the options of the select box from a Collection, an enum, or a Map. In our case, we want the options to be the list of folders. We can obtain this list from the FoldersViewHelper class that we wrote on page 146. Here's the code to create the select box:

email_19/web/WEB-INF/jsp/common/message_action.jsp

```
<jsp:useBean class="stripesbook.view.FoldersViewHelper" id="folders"/>
  Move to folder:
  <s:select name="selectedFolder">
    <s:option value="">Select a folder...</s:option>
    <s:options-collection collection="${folders.folders}"
      value="id" label="name"/>
  </s:select>
  <s:submit name="moveToFolder" value="Move"/>
  <s:errors field="selectedFolder"/>
```

By using <s:options-collection> within <s:select>, we can easily generate options from the list of folders. Each option has a value and a label obtained by calling the value= and label= properties on each object of the collection. Here, getId() and getName() are called on each Folder object. The user sees the name of the folder as each option of the select box, and the folder's ID is set on the selectedFolder property of the action bean.

Also notice the first option, labeled "Select a folder...." The <s:option> tag creates a single option that's added to the select box. But we don't want this option to be a valid selection—we're just using it so that the user sees the "Select a folder..." message in the select box. We can use value="" so that the option sends the empty string as a value. Since Stripes treats empty strings as **null**, the select box acts like a blank input field when the "Select a folder..." option is selected. By making selectedFolder a required field with @Validate(required=true, on="moveToFolder"), clicking Move without selecting a folder will show an error message:

Move to folder: Select a folder... ▾ | Move | ⊗ **Please select a folder.**

This way of distinguishing the first option as a message to the user (and *not* a valid option) is much more elegant than putting a value of -1 or some other "magic number" for that option. Our code is not polluted with checks for this special value in the action bean and the manual creation of a required-field validation error. Using an empty string and making the field required with @Validate fits in very naturally into the Stripes validation mechanism.

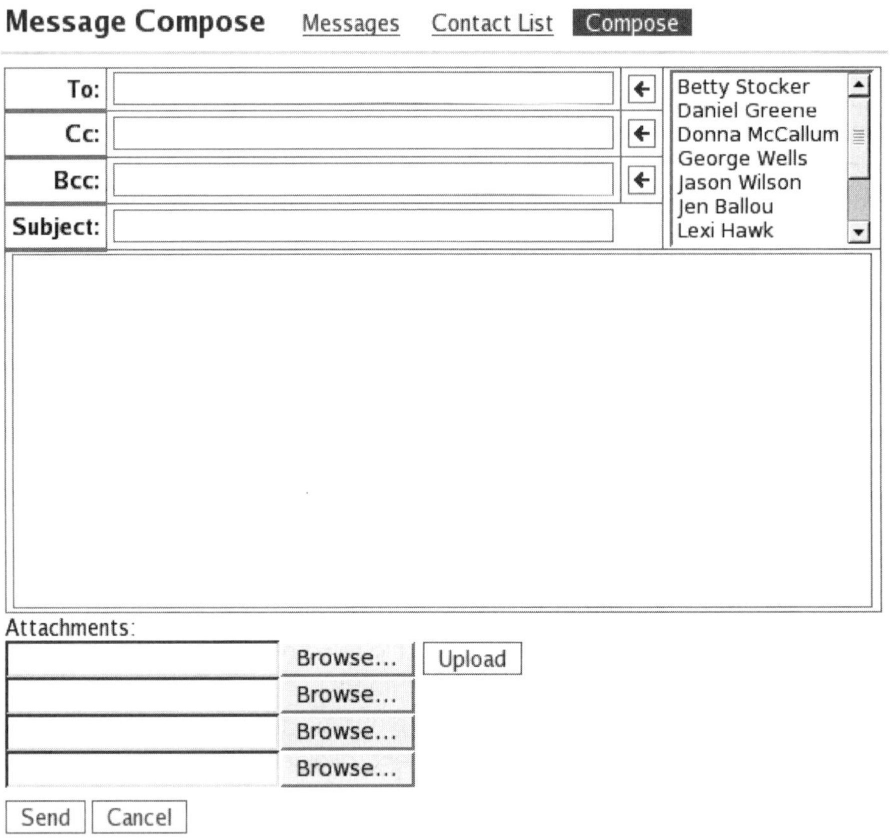

Figure 8.3: THE MESSAGE COMPOSE PAGE

Using Multiple Selection Boxes

Select boxes can also allow the user to select more than one item at a time. For example, the Message Compose page, shown in Figure 8.3, has a select box on the right side that contains the list of contacts. The user can easily add recipients by selecting the contacts and clicking one of the arrow buttons.

To allow multiple selection in the select box, add multiple="*true*" to the <*s:select*> tag and, optionally, the size= attribute to indicate how many rows to show at a time.

email_19/web/WEB-INF/jsp/message_compose.jsp

```
<jsp:useBean class="stripesbook.action.ContactListActionBean"
  id="contacts"/>
  <!-- ... -->
  <s:form beanclass="stripesbook.action.MessageComposeActionBean">
    <!-- ... -->
▶           <s:select name="contacts" multiple="true" size="7">
              <s:options-collection collection="${contacts.contacts}"
                value="id" sort="firstName"/>
            </s:select>
    <!-- ... -->
  </s:form>
</s:layout-component>
```

Inside <s:select>, the <s:options-collection> tag generates options from the list of contacts obtained from ContactListActionBean. Notice that you can use the sort= attribute to indicate the property by which to sort the objects of the collection. We're sorting the contacts by their first name.

A multiple-selection box acts much like a series of checkboxes that are bound to a Collection property. In this case, the selected contacts are bound to the contacts property of the MessageComposeActionBean class:

email_19/src/stripesbook/action/MessageComposeActionBean.java

```
private List<Contact> contacts;
public List<Contact> getContacts() {
    return contacts;
}
public void setContacts(List<Contact> contacts) {
    this.contacts = contacts;
}
```

Stripes automatically puts the selected contacts in the list so that we can add them to the To, Cc, or Bcc field.

8.3 Image Buttons and Text Areas

Continuing with the Message Compose page, let's add the image buttons with arrows that are next to the contact list select box and add the text area where the user can compose the text of the message.

Using Image Buttons

The <s:image> tag creates an image button that invokes the action bean event handler indicated in the name= attribute.

More Select Box Features

Besides the *<s:options-collection>* tag, you can also use *<s:options-map>* and *<s:options-enumeration>* to generate options in a select box from a Map and an enum, respectively. With *<s:options-map>*, the collection of values is the map's set of Map.Entry objects, as obtained from entrySet( ). For *<s:options-enumeration>*, specify the enumeration in the enum= attribute to generate options based on the values defined by the enumeration.

With all three *<s:options-xx>* tags, you can also use the group= attribute to generate *<optgroup/>* tags within a select box. This groups options together with a different label for each group. For example, say the Folder class had a type property. With two folders named Inbox and Reference having the *Received* type and with two folders named Outbox and Archive having the *Sent* type, you could use group="type" to group folders by their type:

```
<s:select name="selectedFolder">
  <s:options-collection collection="${actionBean.folders}"
    value="id" label="name" group="type"/>
</s:select>
```

This would generate a select box, as shown here:

Here's one more tip. If you have a collection of objects from which you want to generate options in a select box but want to display labels in different formats without polluting your model class with formatting code, you can always implement a Formatter with the different format types and patterns you need. Then, you can generate the options with the plain *<s:option>* tag and use *<s:format>* to format the label in different ways. For example:

```
<s:select name="...">
 <c:forEach items="${someCollection}" var="item">
  <s:option value="${item.id}">
   <s:format value="${item}" formatType="..." formatPattern="..."/>
  </s:option>
 </c:forEach>
</s:select>
```

The src= attribute contains the path to the image:

```
email_19/web/WEB-INF/jsp/message_compose.jsp
```

```
<c:set var="arrow" value="/images/arrow.png"/>
<tr>
  <th>To:</th>
  <td><s:text name="message.to" size="60"/></td>
▶ <td><s:image name="addTo" src="${arrow}"/></td>
</tr>
<tr>
  <th>Cc:</th>
  <td><s:text name="message.cc" size="60"/></td>
▶ <td><s:image name="addCc" src="${arrow}"/></td>
</tr>
<tr>
  <th>Bcc:</th>
  <td><s:text name="message.bcc" size="60"/></td>
▶ <td><s:image name="addBcc" src="${arrow}"/></td>
</tr>
```

This generates <input type="image" ...> tags. So, what does the <*s:image*>
tag do for us? It adds the application context path in front of the image
path and gives us the ability to look up images and alternate text in
localized resource bundles, as we'll see in Section 11.2, *Localizing Image
Buttons*, on page 225.

When the user clicks an arrow button, the selected contacts are added
to the addresses that are in the field next to the button. But the user
may have also entered other addresses directly in the text field. Combining the input of the text field with the input from the select box is
somewhat tricky; we'll discuss this in the next chapter. Let's continue
working with form input controls.

Adding the text area for the message text is a one-liner with the tag
<*s:textarea*>:

```
email_19/web/WEB-INF/jsp/message_compose.jsp
```

```
<s:textarea name="message.text" cols="87" rows="12"/>
```

Again, using the Stripes equivalent instead of the plain HTML tag has
the benefit of automatically repopulating the value—we don't want the
user to lose the text if the form is submitted and a validation error
occurs.

Tim Says...

Input Tags Mimic the HTML Tags As Closely As Possible

Stripes input tags try very hard to mimic their HTML counterparts as closely as possible. This means that, in general, if you already know how to use HTML input, select, textarea, form tags, and so on, then you should feel right at home with the Stripes tags. Even the class attribute for specifying CSS classes is the same.

There are, of course, some deviations. First is one you may have already noticed—where in HTML you would write <input type="X">, in Stripes you write <s:X>. For example, you would write <s:radio> instead of <input type="radio">. The main reason for doing this is to make your life easier—each of the different input types has different required and permitted attributes. Making them separate tags allows the set of fields to be validated at compile time and checked by most popular IDEs. Keeping them as one tag would lead to unhelpful code completion and more runtime errors.

In addition, several Stripes tags add attributes to the list supported by their HTML equivalents. This is done to allow you to activate additional functionality offered by Stripes. For example, the beanclass attribute on the Stripes form tag allows you to specify the action bean class to target instead of having to specify the URL, and the format* attributes on the input tags allow you to specify how values should be formatted when written to the page.

Lastly, as Freddy discusses, there are several "helper" tags that have no equivalent in HTML that help produce things such as lists of options from collections and enumerations.

Figure 8.4: THE MESSAGE DETAILS PAGE

8.4 Using Cross-page Controls

The Message Details page (shown in Figure 8.4) appears when the user clicks a message subject on the Message List page. There's nothing spectacular about the Message Details page, but what's interesting is that the controls at the bottom are the same as in the Message List page; the only difference is that deleting or moving to a folder applies to the currently displayed message rather than a series of messages checked off in the Message List page. Let's see how we can define the controls in *one* place and reuse them in these two different contexts.

We'll start by putting the controls in a separate JSP (message_action.jsp) under the common directory since it's being used in more than one place:

```
email_19/web/WEB-INF/jsp/common/message_action.jsp
<jsp:useBean class="stripesbook.view.FoldersViewHelper" id="folders"/>
<div id="action">
  <s:submit name="delete" value="Delete"/>
  Move to folder:
  <s:select name="selectedFolder">
    <s:option value="">Select a folder...</s:option>
    <s:options-collection collection="${folders.folders}"
      value="id" label="name"/>
  </s:select>
  <s:submit name="moveToFolder" value="Move"/>
  <s:errors field="selectedFolder"/>
</div>
```

This code will be *included* in message_list.jsp and message_details.jsp with the <%@include%> directive. Unlike <jsp:include/>, <%@include%>

does not execute a request to the target; rather, it pulls the source code into the JSP at the location of the directive:

email_19/web/WEB-INF/jsp/message_list.jsp

```
<s:form beanclass="stripesbook.action.MessageListActionBean">
  <d:table ...>
    <!-- ... -->
    <d:column>
      <s:checkbox name="selectedMessages" value="${message.id}"/>
    </d:column>
    <!-- ... -->
  </d:table>
  <c:if test="${not empty folder.messages}">
    <div><s:errors field="selectedMessages"/></div>
    <%@include file="/WEB-INF/jsp/common/message_action.jsp"%>
  </c:if>
</s:form>
```

email_19/web/WEB-INF/jsp/message_details.jsp

```
<s:form beanclass="stripesbook.action.MessageListActionBean">
  <%@include file="/WEB-INF/jsp/common/message_action.jsp"%>
  <div>
    <s:hidden name="selectedMessages"
      value="${actionBean.message.id}"/>
  </div>
</s:form>
```

Notice that in both cases the included code becomes nested within an <*s:form*> tag. Indeed, the code from message_action.jsp is not valid on its own, because it contains form input controls with no parent <*s:form*> tag.

For the Message List page, the controls are included only if the folder is not empty; it doesn't make sense to have controls for deleting or moving messages when no messages are being displayed in the page!

For the Message Details page, the user does not have to select messages because the controls apply to the currently displayed message. But we *do* need a parameter to indicate this message; the <*s:hidden*> tag takes care of that.

The great thing about doing this, besides reusing the message_action.jsp code in two different contexts, is that we don't even need to change anything in MessageListActionBean. Both forms submit the selectedMessages parameter to a property of type List<Message>. The Message Details page happens to submit only one value. The event handlers for deleting and moving messages work the same either way: they iterate over the list of selected messages, as we can see in the complete source for MessageListActionBean:

email_19/src/stripesbook/action/MessageListActionBean.java

```
package stripesbook.action;
public class MessageListActionBean extends BaseActionBean {
    private static final String LIST="/WEB-INF/jsp/message_list.jsp";

    @DefaultHandler
    public Resolution list() {
        return new ForwardResolution(LIST);
    }
    public Resolution delete() {
        for (Message message : selectedMessages) {
            folderDao.deleteMessage(message);
        }
        return new RedirectResolution(getClass());
    }
    public Resolution moveToFolder() {
        for (Message message : selectedMessages) {
            folderDao.addMessage(message, selectedFolder);
        }
        return new RedirectResolution(getClass());
    }
    @Validate(required=true, on={"delete", "moveToFolder"})
    private List<Message> selectedMessages;
    public List<Message> getSelectedMessages() {
        return selectedMessages;
    }
    public void setSelectedMessages(List<Message> selectedMessages) {
        this.selectedMessages = selectedMessages;
    }
    @Validate(required=true, on="moveToFolder")
    private Folder selectedFolder;
    public Folder getSelectedFolder() {
        return selectedFolder;
    }
    public void setSelectedFolder(Folder selectedFolder) {
        this.selectedFolder = selectedFolder;
    }
    private FolderDao folderDao = MockFolderDao.getInstance();
}
```

8.5 Radio Buttons

To wrap up our discussion of form input controls, let's use radio buttons to add a feature to the Contact Form page: entering the contact's gender, as shown in Figure 8.5, on the next page.

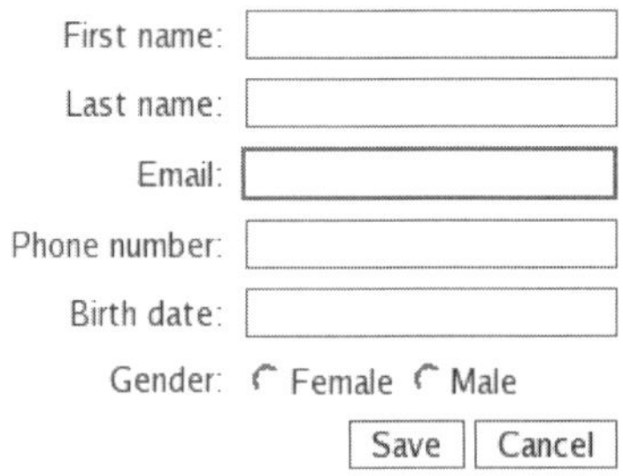

Figure 8.5: USING RADIO BUTTONS FOR THE CONTACT'S GENDER

We'll need a Gender property in the Contact class:

email_19/src/stripesbook/model/Gender.java

```java
package stripesbook.model;
public enum Gender {
    Female,
    Male
}
```

email_19/src/stripesbook/model/Contact.java

```java
package stripesbook.model;
public class Contact extends ModelBase {
    /* ... */
    private Gender gender;
    /* ... */
    public Gender getGender() {
        return gender;
    }
    public void setGender(Gender gender) {
        this.gender = gender;
    }
}
```

The value the user enters for the gender must be either Female or Male, case sensitive. It's much easier and less error-prone for the user to choose a radio button than having to type those values in a text field. Also, radio buttons allow only one selection, making them appropriate for the gender property.

The <s:radio> tag creates a radio button. Its name= attribute serves an additional purpose besides containing the name of the action bean property: it also *groups* buttons that have the same name. Only one radio button from a group can be selected at a time.

Since we added the gender property to the Contact class, the name= of each radio button will be contact.gender. We just need ContactFormActionBean to supply the possible values for the gender:

email_19/src/stripesbook/action/ContactFormActionBean.java

```
public Gender[] getGenders() {
    return Gender.values();
}
```

This makes it easy to create the radio buttons for the gender in contact_form.jsp:

email_19/web/WEB-INF/jsp/contact_form.jsp

```
<c:forEach var="gender" items="${actionBean.genders}">
  <s:radio name="contact.gender" value="${gender}"/>${gender}
</c:forEach>
```

In the value= attribute is the actual value to submit as input to the action bean property if the radio button is selected. This is the same as if the user had typed that value in a text field. The value can be different from the label that is shown next to the radio button; in fact, notice that the label is not part of the <s:radio> tag at all. You can display the label wherever you want.

The radio buttons for the gender now appear in the contact form, as shown here:

Gender: ⊙ Female ⊙ Male

What's Next?

We learned about the different types of form input controls and how they work with Stripes tags and action bean properties. Along the way, we got quite a lot done in the webmail application. In the next chapter, we'll finish implementing the features of the Message List, Message Details, and Message Compose pages.

Nothing in life is to be feared; it is only to be understood.
Now is the time to understand more, so that we may fear
less.
▶ Marie Curie

Chapter 9

Advanced Features Made Easy

The webmail application is moving along nicely. Let's finishing implementing the three message pages.

9.1 Managing Session Data

In the list of folders that appears on the left of the Message List and Message Details pages, the currently selected folder is indicated with an arrow next to the name of the folder, as we can see in Figure 9.1.

We need a place to store the currently selected Folder object. As the user navigates in different pages of the application, it'd be nice to remember the last selected folder so that we show its contents when the user returns to the Message List page.

Such per-user state information is usually stored in the session. If you've worked with the Servlet API's HttpSession interface before, you know that things can get messy when you litter your code with calls to setAttribute() and getAttribute(). Both these methods require us to use

Name	Messages	21 items found, displaying 1 to 10.[First/Prev] 1, 2,	
		Date	From
Inbox ←	21	☐ 2008-04-19 14:42	Habibi
Sent	2	☐ 2008-04-15 18:09	Jen Ballou
Reference	4	☐ 2008-04-13 16:34	autocalendar
Trash	0	☐ 2008-04-11 22:44	Lou Thompson
		☐ 2008-04-11 22:42	Jason Wilson

Figure 9.1: SHOWING THE CURRENTLY SELECTED FOLDER

an arbitrary key, so we'll have to declare constants somewhere in our code. The session returns the data as an Object, so we have to cast that back to our original data type. For example:

```
// Current folder
Folder folder = ...;

// Key used to store the folder
String FOLDER = "folder";

// Store the folder in the session
HttpSession session = request.getSession();
session.setAttribute(FOLDER, folder);

// Retrieve the folder from the session
// Needs a cast because getAttribute() returns Object
folder = (Folder) session.getAttribute(FOLDER);
```

Ugh. That's not pretty. It's nevertheless necessary if we're going to use the session. But we can hide this code in the back of the closet and rarely have to look at it again. Stripes provides a clean solution for session-related code with the ActionBeanContext class. As you know, this object is always available in action beans via the getContext() method. Also, ActionBeanContext provides getRequest() to obtain the current request and, from there, the session. All this makes ActionBeanContext the perfect place to encapsulate the code that deals with HttpSession and to shield the rest of the application from constants, casts, and ugly goblins.

By creating a class that extends ActionBeanContext, we can add methods that manage objects in the session. A custom ActionBeanContext subclass is considered an extension, so Stripes loads it automatically if we put the class in a package that we configured with the Extension.Packages parameter in web.xml.[1]

The following MyActionBeanContext class stores and retrieves the current Folder object using the session, taking care of setting a default when no previous selection exists.

---

1. See the sidebar on page 104 if you need a refresher on Stripes extensions.

email_19/src/stripesbook/ext/MyActionBeanContext.java

```java
package stripesbook.ext;
public class MyActionBeanContext extends ActionBeanContext {
    private static final String FOLDER = "folder";
    public void setCurrentFolder(Folder folder) {
        setCurrent(FOLDER, folder);
    }
    public Folder getCurrentFolder() {
        Folder folder = MockFolderDao.getInstance().read().get(0);
        return getCurrent(FOLDER, folder);
    }
    protected void setCurrent(String key, Object value) {
        getRequest().getSession().setAttribute(key, value);
    }
    @SuppressWarnings("unchecked")
    protected <T> T getCurrent(String key, T defaultValue) {
        T value = (T) getRequest().getSession().getAttribute(key);
        if (value == null) {
            value = defaultValue;
            setCurrent(key, value);
        }
        return value;
    }
}
```

All we need to do now is adjust the getter and setter methods in BaseAc-tionBean so that they use MyActionBeanContext. That way, the cast of ActionBeanContext to MyActionBeanContext is done in only one place:

email_19/src/stripesbook/action/BaseActionBean.java

```java
package stripesbook.action;
public abstract class BaseActionBean implements ActionBean {
    private MyActionBeanContext context;

    public MyActionBeanContext getContext() {
        return context;
    }
    public void setContext(ActionBeanContext context) {
        this.context = (MyActionBeanContext) context;
    }
}
```

Notice that we're using a feature introduced in the JDK 1.5, which is to allow overriding a method (getContext()) and returning an object whose type (MyActionBeanContext) is a subclass of the type returned by the superclass (ActionBeanContext). This removes the need for casting to MyActionBeanContext elsewhere in the code—the only cast is in the setContext() method.

It's now very clean and simple to retrieve the currently selected folder. Action beans can call getContext().getCurrentFolder(), and JSPs can use ${actionBean.context.currentFolder}. Neither has to bother with the session-tinkering details.

The layout_folders.jsp file can now display the list of folders, using the currently selected folder to determine where to place the arrow:

email_19/web/WEB-INF/jsp/common/layout_folders.jsp

```
<jsp:useBean class="stripesbook.view.FoldersViewHelper" id="folders"/>
<!-- ... -->
<s:layout-definition>
  <!-- ... -->
      <div id="folders">
        <d:table name="${folders.folders}" id="folder">
          <d:column title="Name">
            <s:link
              beanclass="stripesbook.action.MessageListActionBean">
              <s:param name="folder" value="${folder.id}"/>
              ${folder.name}
            </s:link>
            <c:if test="${actionBean.context.currentFolder eq folder}">
              <img src="${contextPath}/images/arrow.png"
                style="border: none; vertical-align: bottom"/>
            </c:if>
          </d:column>
          <d:column title="Messages" style="text-align: right">
            ${fn:length(folder.messages)}
          </d:column>
        </d:table>
      </div>
      <!-- ... -->
</s:layout-definition>
```

We've also created links on the names of the folders. Clicking a folder name changes the selected folder and displays the messages it contains. This has to work across all pages that use layout_folders.jsp, so we add the setter method that changes the currently selected folder in BaseActionBean:

email_19/src/stripesbook/action/BaseActionBean.java

```
public void setFolder(Folder folder) {
    getContext().setCurrentFolder(folder);
}
```

Now the currently selected folder will be changed with the <s:param> tag that we used, with the folder= parameter name and the folder Id as a value. With a type converter, the Id is automatically converted to a Folder object.

> ### ∖∣∕ Joe Asks...
> ### ✵ᷓ   Why Not Just Use a context.currentFolder Parameter to Change the Currently Selected Folder?
>
> We added a setter method on BaseActionBean to set the currently selected folder on the MyActionBeanContext object:
>
> ```
> public void setFolder(Folder folder) {
>     getContext().setCurrentFolder(folder);
> }
> ```
>
> The folder is retrieved in the JSP with ${action-Bean.context.currentFolder}, so why not use the same parameter to change the value, like this?
>
> ```
> <s:link ...>
>   <s:param name="context.currentFolder" value="${folder.id}"/>
>   ...
> </s:link>
> ```
>
> This won't work because setting a value on an ActionBean-Context object from a request parameter is blocked by Stripes for security purposes. Indeed, ActionBeanContext contains all the information concerning the current request and response, so it would be unsafe to allow users to bind into this object with context.*xx* parameters. Imagine what would happen if any user could gain administrator access just by adding context.user.admin=true to the end of a URL! Binding indirectly, as we did for the currently selected folder, ensures that nothing funny is going on behind your back.

The message_list.jsp file renders the layout_folder.jsp layout to include the list of folders and uses ${actionBean.context.currentFolder} to obtain the current folder and display the messages that it contains:

`email_19/web/WEB-INF/jsp/message_list.jsp`

```
► <c:set var="folder" value="${actionBean.context.currentFolder}"/>
  <s:layout-render name="/WEB-INF/jsp/common/layout_folders.jsp"
    title="Message List" currentSection="MessageList">
    <s:layout-component name="body">
►     <d:table name="${folder.messages}" requestURI="" id="message"
        pagesize="10" defaultsort="2" defaultorder="descending">
        <d:column title="Date" sortable="true">
          <s:format value="${message.date}"
            formatPattern="yyyy-MM-dd HH:mm"/>
        </d:column>
```

```
        <d:column property="from" sortable="true"/>
        <d:column property="to" sortable="true"/>
        <d:column title="Subject" sortable="true">
          <s:link
            beanclass="stripesbook.action.MessageDetailsActionBean">
            <s:param name="message" value="${message.id}"/>
            ${message.subject}
          </s:link>
        </d:column>
      </d:table>
    </s:layout-component>
  </s:layout-render>
```

The folder list is now fully functional, and we're just getting warmed up.

9.2   Altering Form Values in the Action Bean

Remember that in the Message Compose page we had a list of contacts in a select box and arrow buttons to add the selected contacts to the list of recipients:

Each arrow button invokes an event handler that builds a string from the text field and the selected contacts. It's tempting to just change the value of the message's to, from, or bcc property in the action bean and expect the new value to show up in the corresponding text field:

email_19/src/stripesbook/action/MessageComposeActionBean.java

```java
public Resolution addTo() {
    getMessage().setTo(getRecipientString(getMessage().getTo()));
    return new ForwardResolution(COMPOSE);
}
public Resolution addCc() {
    getMessage().setCc(getRecipientString(getMessage().getCc()));
    return new ForwardResolution(COMPOSE);
}
public Resolution addBcc() {
    getMessage().setBcc(getRecipientString(getMessage().getBcc()));
    return new ForwardResolution(COMPOSE);
}
private String getRecipientString(String previous) {
    if (contacts != null) {
```

```
        StringBuilder result = new StringBuilder();

        for (Contact contact : contacts) {
            result.append(contact).append(',');
        }
        result.setLength(result.length() - 1);
        String recpt = (previous == null) ? "" : previous + ",";
        return recpt + result.toString();
    }
    return previous;
}
```

This code looks fine, but it won't work! Well, not yet, anyway, and I'll tell you why. To decide how to populate a form input field, Stripes uses a *population strategy*, which is an extension represented by the PopulationStrategy interface. Out of the box, Stripes uses the DefaultPopulationStrategy, which prefers values from request parameters to values from action bean properties when populating a form input field. Consider this scenario, in which the user does the following:

- Types Fred in the To field
- Selects Daniel Greene from the contact box
- Clicks the arrow button next to the To field

The request parameters will be as follows:

```
message.to=Fred
contacts=(ID of Daniel Greene)
```

In the addTo() event handler, our clever code combines the two parameters to set the message.to action bean property to Fred, Daniel Greene. But the message.to= request parameter is still "Fred," and that's the value used by Stripes to populate the To text field.

So, what's a developer to do? Stripes provides an alternate population strategy, BeanFirstPopulationStrategy, which looks at the action bean property *before* the request parameter. That's what we want. Since it is a Stripes extension, we just have to create a class that extends BeanFirstPopulationStrategy and add it to our extension package, stripesbook.ext:

email_19/src/stripesbook/ext/MyPopulationStrategy.java

```
package stripesbook.ext;
public class MyPopulationStrategy extends BeanFirstPopulationStrategy{
}
```

Tim Says...
ActionBeanContext Isn't Limited to HttpSession

Freddy covered an example of using the action bean context to insulate the rest of your code from accessing things that are stored in HttpSession. In my opinion, an even greater benefit is that because your code is insulated from the implementation details, you can actually change how you store and access items without any impact.

Let's say, for example, that your HttpSession object is getting too big—you're storing too much in it. In such a situation you might choose another strategy: store some identifier in a cookie and then look up the actual object when needed. The following is an example of how you might do that, and no caller will ever know the difference:

```java
package stripesbook.ext;
public class MyActionBeanContext extends ActionBeanContext {
  private static final String FOLDER = "folder";
  private Folder currentFolder = null;

  public void setCurrentFolder(Folder folder) {
    Cookie c = new Cookie(FOLDER, String.valueOf(folder.getId()))
    getResponse().addCookie(c);
  }
  public Folder getCurrentFolder() {
    if (this.currentFolder == null) {
      Cookie c = findCookie(FOLDER);
      int id = (c != null) Integer.parseInt(c.getValue()) : 0;
      this.currentFolder = MockFolderDao.getInstance().read(id);
    }
    return this.currentFolder;
  }
  private Cookie findCookie(String name) {
    for (Cookie c : getRequest().getCookies()) {
      if (c.getName().equals(name)) {
        return c;
      }
    }
    return null;
  }
}
```

> ## ϟϟ Joe Asks...
>
> ### Why Isn't BeanFirstPopulationStrategy Used by Default?
>
> Why indeed? After all, it combines the best of both worlds: it uses values you've set on action bean properties, and it falls back to request parameters. It's certainly a good choice for new Stripes applications. However, because BeanFirstPopulation-Strategy wasn't introduced until Stripes 1.4, making it the default would risk breaking backward compatibility in ways that would be very difficult to track down. Perhaps a future version of Stripes will make BeanFirstPopulationStrategy the default—with a big loud warning about backward incompatibility—but as of Stripes 1.5, you have to tell Stripes to use it.

MyPopulationStrategy is just an empty class, but since it extends BeanFirst-PopulationStrategy, the effect is indeed to load this population strategy.[2] Just like that, Stripes uses the value that we set in the action bean property to populate the text field. Our code combines recipients from the text field, and the select box now works.

9.3 Using Indexed Properties

The Message Compose page includes fields for uploading files as attachments, as shown in Figure 9.2, on the following page.

The user can upload up to four files at a time. After clicking the `Upload` button, the files are attached, and the user can upload more files.

Before we get to uploading files, we need to discuss how Stripes makes it easy to manage a series of fields like we have for the attachments. Notice that we're (arbitrarily) using four fields at a time—but we certainly don't need four properties in the action bean.

Whenever we're dealing with a series of rows of input fields that we want to bind to the same property of an action bean, we'll want to use what Stripes calls *indexed properties*.

---

2. You can also use a configuration parameter instead of an empty class; see the sidebar on the following page.

Using an Empty Class or a Configuration Parameter to Load a Stripes Extension

We added an empty class that extends BeanFirstPopulationStrat-egy as a way of loading a Stripes extension. I like using this trick because no additional configuration is involved, all extensions are together in an extension package, and I'll have a class ready if I need to customize the population strategy. If you don't like this empty class idea, you can use a configuration param-eter in web.xml instead:

```
<filter>
  <filter-name>StripesFilter</filter-name>
  <filter-class>
    net.sourceforge.stripes.controller.StripesFilter
  </filter-class>
  <!-- ... -->
  <!-- Configure the population strategy -->
  <init-param>
    <param-name>PopulationStrategy.Class</param-name>
    <param-value>
      net.sourceforge.stripes.tag.BeanFirstPopulationStrategy
    </param-value>
  </init-param>
</filter>
```

In fact, you always have the choice of getting Stripes to load an extension either by adding it to an extension package or by configuring it explicitly with a web.xml parameter. For a com-plete list of configuration parameters, check out Appendix A, on page 365.

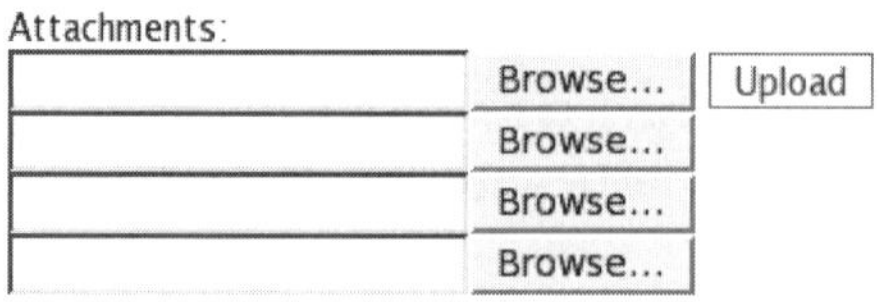

Attachments:
```
[                    ] Browse... | Upload |
[                    ] Browse...
[                    ] Browse...
[                    ] Browse...
```

Figure 9.2: FIELDS FOR UPLOADING ATTACHMENTS

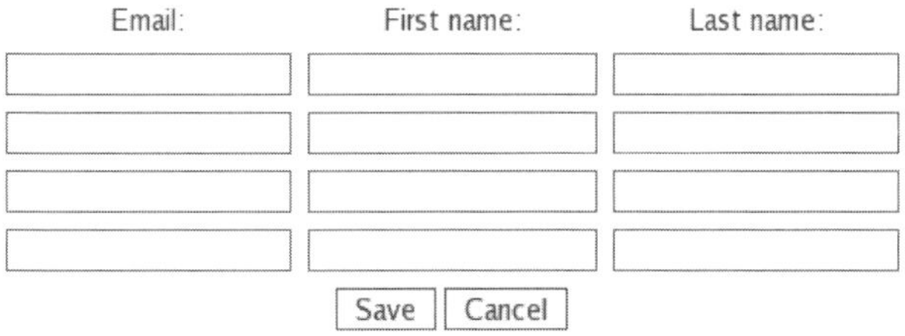

Figure 9.3: USING ROWS OF INPUT FIELDS

Here's how it works: we use square brackets and indices in the name= of the field:

`email_19/web/WEB-INF/jsp/message_compose.jsp`

```
<c:forEach var="index" begin="0" end="3">
  <div><s:file name="attachments[${index}]"/></div>
</c:forEach>
```

The previous code generates fields with the following names:

```
attachments[0]
attachments[1]
attachments[2]
attachments[3]
```

The fields are bound to a single attachments property of type List on the action bean. Stripes will populate the list with the items entered by the user, stopping at the last field that contains a value. For example, if the user enters "picture.jpg" in the second field, attachments will contain [null, "attachments"]. This keeps the items in order while omitting needless trailing null values.

Indexed properties work well with nested properties, too. If we have a form with rows of fields to create Contact objects as illustrated in Figure 9.3, we could use a loop and generate the following field names:

```
contacts[0].email       contacts[2].email
contacts[0].firstName   contacts[2].firstName
contacts[0].lastName    contacts[2].lastName
contacts[1].email       contacts[3].email
contacts[1].firstName   contacts[3].firstName
contacts[1].lastName    contacts[3].lastName
```

We could then bind these fields to a single contacts property of type List<Contact>. Without indexed properties, we'd need as many properties on the action bean as we have in the form (contact1, contact2, contact3, and contact4), and we'd have to assemble the list of contacts ourselves. Indexed properties make it all much easier.

What's even cooler about indexed properties is that Stripes is smart enough to ignore rows that are left completely empty. In the example from Figure 9.3, on the preceding page, say we made email a required field. In a row where the user enters a first name but no email, Stripes would trigger a validation error. But in other rows where the user left all the fields blank, Stripes would just ignore the row altogether. This way, we can make the email a required field without forcing the user to fill in *every* row of fields.

We can also use a Map to work with indexed properties. In that case, the value between the square brackets, [ ], is the key in the map. Since order does not matter in a map, only the fields filled in by the user will generate key-value pairs in the map. Even if the user enters a value in the second field and leaves the first field blank, the map will not contain any null entries.

Finally, we can use more than one level of indexed properties. For example, with an action bean property named contacts of type Map<String,List <Contact>>, we could use these indexed properties:

```
contacts['to'][0].email
contacts['to'][1].email
contacts['to'][2].email
contacts['cc'][0].email
contacts['cc'][1].email
contacts['cc'][2].email
```

If the user enters values in the fields such that the parameters have these values:

```
contacts['to'][0].email=fred@stripesbook.org
contacts['to'][1].email=nadia@stripesbook.org
contacts['cc'][0].email=lily@stripesbook.org
```

then the contacts property in the action bean would be populated as follows:

```
contacts = {
  "to" = [
          Contact(email=fred@stripesbook.org),
          Contact(email=nadia@stripesbook.org)
        ],
  "cc" = [
          Contact(email=lily@stripesbook.org)
        ]
}
```

9.4 Working with Files

Whew! Now that we've covered all that theory about indexed properties, let's get back to uploading files. We'll also discuss streaming them back to the user when viewing an email that contains attachments.

Uploading Files

Uploading files is somewhat problematic in any web application due to a few quirks in the HTTP specification. The multipart/form-data MIME type allows submitting a request that includes one or more files, but the parts can arrive in any order. For example, a file may be sent before the request parameters. This means the file must be received completely before getting the rest of the request data and having all the information needed to process the request.[3]

Because of this limitation, all the request data must be processed before being able to set properties and call an event handler on an action bean. To be able to give the action bean access to the uploaded files, these are saved in a temporary directory on the server's disk. After the request data processing is complete, the event handler is called and is given access to the files that were saved on disk.

Fortunately, Stripes shields us from most of these nasty details. We can add the controls for uploading a file with the <s:file> tag in a JSP and retrieve the file in an action bean with a property of type FileBean. We can read the file and process it, or we can just save it to a directory and filename of your choice.

Let's see how this works by adding support for uploading attachments on the Message Compose page. First, we add the controls in the JSP with the <s:file> tag:

email_19/web/WEB-INF/jsp/message_compose.jsp

```
<div>Attachments:</div>
<div><s:errors field="attachments"/></div>
<div class="left">
  <c:forEach var="index" begin="0" end="3">
    <div><s:file name="attachments[${index}]"/></div>
  </c:forEach>
</div>
<div class="left">
  <s:submit name="upload" value="Upload"/>
</div>
```

---

3. See http://tools.ietf.org/html/rfc2388 for more information on the multipart/form-data MIME type.

This creates the controls that we saw in Figure 9.2, on page 184. We're using indexed properties, so we'll use the List<FileBean> type for the attachments property in the action bean:

```
email_19/src/stripesbook/action/MessageComposeActionBean.java
private List<FileBean> attachments;
public List<FileBean> getAttachments() {
    return attachments;
}
public void setAttachments(List<FileBean> attachments) {
    this.attachments = attachments;
}
```

The FileBean class gives us access to the file that was saved in a temporary directory when an uploaded file was received. To use a FileBean object, we can either:

• Read the file as an input stream by calling getInputStream(), or as a reader with getReader(), and then delete the temporary file by calling delete().

• Save the file in a location of your choice by calling save(File). In this case, the temporary file is *moved* (not *copied*) to the directory and filename that you specify, so there's no need to call delete(). If you mistakenly call delete() anyway, don't worry—Stripes will realize that the temporary file is already gone and will just ignore the method call.

In our case, we just want to save the file in a directory designated to contain attachments. Here, then, is the upload() event handler that is invoked when the user clicks the Upload button:

```
email_19/src/stripesbook/action/MessageComposeActionBean.java
public Resolution upload() throws Exception {
❶   if (attachments != null) {
        for (FileBean attachment : attachments) {
❷           if (attachment != null) {
❸               if (attachment.getSize() > 0) {
                    addAttachment(attachment);
                }
                else {
                    ValidationError error = new SimpleError(
                        attachment.getFileName()
                        + " is not a valid file.");
                    getContext().getValidationErrors().add(
                        "attachments", error);
                }
            }
        }
    }
```

```
        return new ForwardResolution(COMPOSE);
    }
    private void addAttachment(FileBean fileBean) throws Exception {
        Attachment attachment = new Attachment();

        attachment.setFileName(fileBean.getFileName());
        attachment.setContentType(fileBean.getContentType());
        attachment.setSize(fileBean.getSize());

        attachmentDao.save(attachment);
❹       fileBean.save(new File(attachmentDao.getFilePath(attachment)));
        getMessage().addAttachment(attachment);
    }
```

We have to guard against a few nulls and zeroes. First, we must check that the attachments property is not null (❶), because the user may have clicked the Upload button without filling in any of the attachments fields. Since attachments are not required fields, we just do nothing in this case.

Next, when looping through the items in the list, we have to make sure the FileBean object is not null (❷). The user may have entered a filename in the second attachment field but left the first one blank. As we saw earlier regarding the use of indexed properties with lists, the first item would be null in this case.

Finally, if the user enters an invalid file path in the attachment field, a FileBean object of size 0 appears in the list. So, we check for that (❸) and produce a validation error if we encounter a zero-sized FileBean.

When all is well and good, the uploaded file is added to the email as an Attachment object, which is a simple representation of an attachment:

email_19/src/stripesbook/model/Attachment.java

```
package stripesbook.model;
public class Attachment extends ModelBase {
    private String fileName;
    private long size;
    private String contentType;
    /* getters and setters... */
}
```

At ❹, the actual file is saved in a directory on the server. The attachment DAO takes care of the details of managing the directories and filenames used for attachments.

Meanwhile back on the Message Compose page, the user has uploaded attachments. They are shown with an icon, which, when clicked, will

Figure 9.4: SHOWING ATTACHMENTS WITH DELETE BUTTONS

delete the attachment from the message, as illustrated in Figure 9.4. Here is the code that displays the attachments in the page:

```
email_19/web/WEB-INF/jsp/message_compose.jsp
<s:hidden id="deleteIndex" name="deleteIndex"/>
<c:forEach items="${actionBean.message.attachments}"
  var="attach" varStatus="loop">
  <s:image name="deleteAttachment" src="/images/delete.gif"
    onclick="getElementById('deleteIndex').value=${loop.index}"
    style="border: none; vertical-align: bottom"/>
  ${attach.fileName} (${attach.size} bytes)
  <br/>
</c:forEach>
```

Notice that we have a variable number of attachments, but every delete image button is bound to the same deleteAttachment() event handler. We need a parameter to indicate *which* attachment to delete, so we've added a deleteIndex hidden input. This parameter is set to the attachment index in the onclick= attribute. The code in the action bean deletes the attachment from the email, and the DAO takes care of deleting the file from the disk.[4]

```
email_19/src/stripesbook/action/MessageComposeActionBean.java
public Resolution deleteAttachment() throws Exception {
    Attachment attachment =
        getMessage().getAttachments().remove(deleteIndex);

    attachmentDao.delete(attachment.getId());

    return new ForwardResolution(COMPOSE);
}
```

---

4. Deleting items by index is fine here because we don't have more than one user composing the same email message. However, if you're modifying data that can be accessed simultaneously by multiple users, it's dangerous to use list indices because deleting an item changes the indices of all subsequence items. Use map keys instead, because deleting an entry does not affect the other keys.

```
private int deleteIndex;
public int getDeleteIndex() {
    return deleteIndex;
}
public void setDeleteIndex(int deleteIndex) {
    this.deleteIndex = deleteIndex;
}
```

The Message Compose page now supports uploading attachments. Before we move on to streaming the files back to the user when viewing an email that has attachments, we need to talk about one more thing regarding file uploads.

To avoid malicious users from causing harm to your web application by uploading extremely large files, Stripes imposes a default maximum size of 10MB. This is the *total* size of the request data, including all uploaded files, request parameters, request headers—everything.[5] You can change the maximum allowed size by adding a parameter to the Stripes filter in web.xml:

```
<init-param>
  <param-name>FileUpload.MaximumPostSize</param-name>
  <param-value>5M</param-value>
</init-param>
```

This would set the limit to 5MB. You can use K, M, or G (uppercase or lowercase) as a suffix to indicate kilobytes, megabytes, or gigabytes. Without a suffix, the value is assumed to be in bytes. If you use a suffix, make sure not to put any spaces between the value and the suffix. Also note that any extra characters after the suffix are ignored. This means that you could, as a matter of preference, use 5MB instead of 5M.

Streaming Files

Now that the webmail supports uploading files as attachments, we should also allow users to download attachments when they view a message.

We'll start by displaying the attachments on the Message Details page. This is fairly straightforward—we just need to loop through the attachments and display each one with a link to an event handler on the action bean.

---

5. This is another limitation of the HTTP specification. Before processing a request, the only information that's available is the total size of the request data.

Parsing multipart/form-data

Correctly parsing data that arrives in the multipart/form-data MIME type is surprisingly difficult. Instead of reinventing the wheel, Stripes delegates this unpleasant piece of work to third-party libraries that have already solved the problem. The Stripes distribution includes two such libraries: Apache Commons File-Upload* and COS.[†]

Stripes automatically uses the implementation that it finds in the class path. To use Commons File Upload, copy commons-fileupload.jar and commons-io.jar to the WEB-INF/lib directory. For COS, use cos.jar. If Stripes finds *both* libraries, Commons FileUpload is chosen.

So, how do you decide between Commons FileUpload and COS? Basically, the advantage of COS is that it's only one JAR file instead of two. However, the license for Commons FileUpload is more permissive; it caches small files in memory instead of writing them to disk, improving performance; and, unlike COS, Commons FileUpload is still being maintained.

Of course, if you know of another implementation, you can plug it in. The strategy for handling multipart form data is represented in Stripes by the MultipartWrapper interface. This is an extension, so placing your implementation in an extension package would have Stripes use it automatically.

---

*. http://jakarta.apache.org/commons/fileupload/
†. http://servlets.com/cos/

email_19/web/WEB-INF/jsp/message_details.jsp

```
<c:if test="${not empty actionBean.message.attachments}">
  <div>Attachments:</div>
  <div>
    <c:forEach var="attachment"
      items="${actionBean.message.attachments}">
    <s:link event="downloadAttachment"
      beanclass="stripesbook.action.MessageDetailsActionBean">
      <s:param name="attachmentId" value="${attachment.id}"/>
      ${attachment.fileName}
    </s:link>
    (${attachment.size} bytes)
    <br/>
    </c:forEach>
  </div>
</c:if>
```

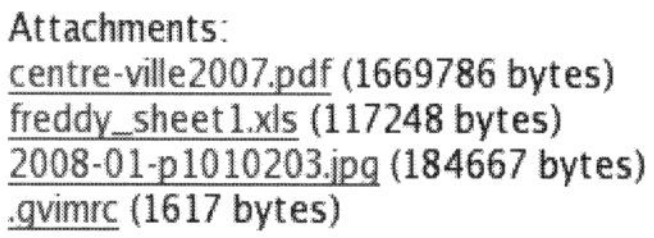

Attachments:
centre-ville2007.pdf (1669786 bytes)
freddy_sheet1.xls (117248 bytes)
2008-01-p1010203.jpg (184667 bytes)
.gvimrc (1617 bytes)

Figure 9.5: DISPLAYING ATTACHMENTS WITH LINKS TO DOWNLOAD THE FILES

This displays the attachments, as shown in Figure 9.5. When the user clicks a filename, Stripes sets the attachmentId parameter and calls the downloadAttachment() event handler of MessageDetailsActionBean.

We now need to stream the file to the user. We can send binary data as a response to the browser by returning a StreamingResolution from an event handler. StreamingResolution requires a content type and the data to be sent. We can also set the filename that will be suggested to the user when prompted to save the file. In our case, everything is provided by the attachment:

`email_19/src/stripesbook/action/MessageDetailsActionBean.java`

```java
public Integer attachmentId;

public Resolution downloadAttachment() throws Exception {
    Attachment attachment = attachmentDao.read(attachmentId);
    String fileName = attachment.getFileName();
    String filePath = attachmentDao.getFilePath(attachment);
    return new StreamingResolution(attachment.getContentType(),
        new FileInputStream(filePath)).setFilename(fileName);
}
private AttachmentDao attachmentDao =
    MockAttachmentDao.getInstance();
```

The constructors of the StreamingResolution class accept the data in the form of an InputStream, a Reader, or a String. You can also build the data yourself by subclassing StreamingResolution and overriding the stream(HttpServletResponse) method. For example:

```java
return new StreamingResolution(contentType) {
  protected void stream(HttpServletResponse resp) throws Exception {
    OutputStream output = resp.getOutputStream();
    output.write(data);
  }
}.setFilename("some_file.ext");
```

Wrapping Up

Wow. We used many new Stripes features to finish the Message List, Message Details, and Message Compose pages of the webmail application. I think it's time for a break, don't you? An ice cream cone or a hot chocolate would hit the spot, depending on the season. . . . When you're ready, we'll implement the two remaining pages: the Registration and Login pages.

Everything you can imagine is real.
► Pablo Picasso

Chapter 10

Registering and Logging In

We now have a fairly complete webmail application, but we don't have anything that creates user accounts and asks the user to log in. Let's add those features with the Registration and Login pages. We'll learn a few more Stripes techniques along the way.

10.1 The Registration Page

The first thing a user will have to do to use the webmail application is to create an account using the Registration page, shown in Figure 10.1.

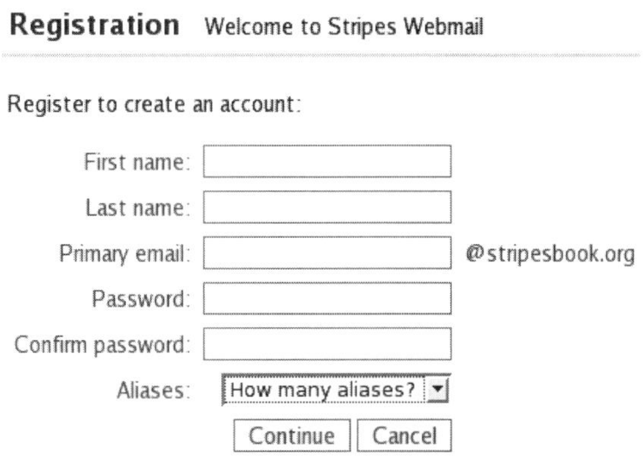

Figure 10.1: THE REGISTRATION PAGE

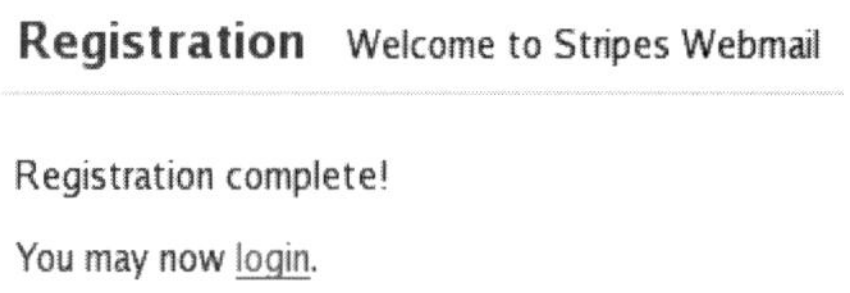

Registration Welcome to Stripes Webmail

Registration complete!

You may now login.

Figure 10.2: REGISTRATION CONFIRMATION PAGE

To represent a user in the application, we'll use a simple User model class:

```
email_19/src/stripesbook/model/User.java
package stripesbook.model;
public class User extends ModelBase {
    private String firstName;
    private String lastName;
    private String username;
    private String password;
    private List<String> aliases;

    /* getters and setters... */
}
```

With this class, we can identify users when they log in with their username and password. The application uses the primary email as the username and allows the user to create up to five *aliases*, which are different email addresses that point to the same account. That way, a user can tell his buddies that his email address is dannyboy@stripesbook.org but give potential business clients daniel.greene@stripesbook.org instead.

Once the user fills in all the fields and clicks the [Continue] button, the application validates that the primary email isn't already taken by another user. Of course, the password and confirm password must match. If all is well, the next page of the registration process appears.

That next page depends on how many aliases the user has chosen. If the user decided on *zero* aliases, the registration is complete, and we show the confirmation page (Figure 10.2). With one or more aliases, the next page allows the user to enter those aliases, as shown in Figure 10.3, on the facing page, and then we show the confirmation page.

We have several interesting features to implement for the registration process, so let's get to work.

Registration Welcome to Stripes Webmail

Enter your email aliases:

Alias 1: [   ] @stripesbook.org
Alias 2: [   ] @stripesbook.org
Alias 3: [   ] @stripesbook.org
Alias 4: [   ] @stripesbook.org

[Continue] [Cancel]

Figure 10.3: REGISTRATION PAGE TO ENTER EMAIL ALIASES

10.2 Adding Password and Confirm Password Boxes

The registration page includes a text box to enter the password. To make sure no one who is spying over the user's shoulder can see the password, the field shows all characters as asterisks (*):

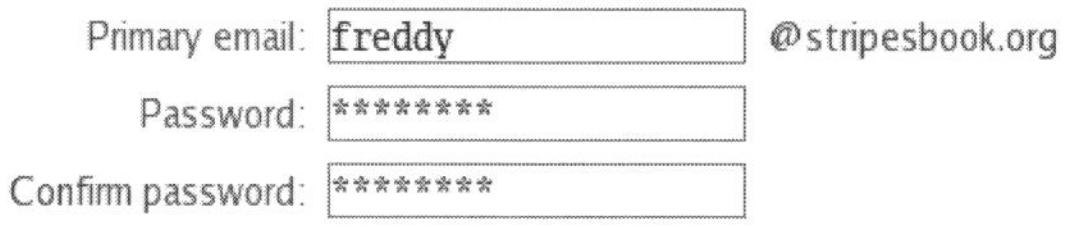

Primary email: [freddy   ] @stripesbook.org
Password: [********]
Confirm password: [********]

To create such a text box with Stripes, just use *<s:password>* instead of *<s:text>*. Here's a first look at the registration JSP:

`email_19/web/WEB-INF/jsp/register.jsp`

```
<s:layout-render name="/WEB-INF/jsp/common/layout_main.jsp"
  title="Registration">
  <s:layout-component name="body">
    <p>Register to create an account:</p>
    <s:form beanclass="stripesbook.action.RegisterActionBean">
      <table class="form">
        <!-- s:text fields for first, last and user name... -->
        <tr>
          <td><s:label for="user.password"/>:</td>
          <td><s:password name="user.password"/></td>
        </tr>
        <tr>
          <td><s:label for="confirmPassword"/>:</td>
          <td><s:password name="confirmPassword"/></td>
        </tr>
        <!-- rest of the form... -->
      </table>
    </s:form>
  </s:layout-component>
</s:layout-render>
```

Since the user is choosing a password and does not see the text in the password box, we ask the user to retype the password in the "Confirm password" box as a double-check. Confirming the password is done only at registration time. Therefore, we should define the confirmPassword property in the action bean, not in the User class. Here, then, is a starting point for RegisterActionBean:

email_19/src/stripesbook/action/RegisterActionBean.java

```java
package stripesbook.action;
public class RegisterActionBean extends BaseActionBean {
    private static final String VIEW = "/WEB-INF/jsp/register.jsp";
    @DefaultHandler
    @DontValidate
    public Resolution view() {
        return new ForwardResolution(VIEW);
    }
    @ValidateNestedProperties({
        @Validate(field="firstName", required=true),
        @Validate(field="lastName",  required=true),
        @Validate(field="username",  required=true),
        @Validate(field="password",  required=true)
    })
    private User user;
    public User getUser() {
        return user;
    }
    public void setUser(User user) {
        this.user = user;
    }
    @Validate(required=true)
    private String confirmPassword;
    public String getConfirmPassword() {
        return confirmPassword;
    }
    public void setConfirmPassword(String confirmPassword) {
        this.confirmPassword = confirmPassword;
    }
    @Validate(required=true, minvalue=0, maxvalue=5)
    private Integer numberOfAliases;
    public Integer getNumberOfAliases() {
        return numberOfAliases;
    }
    public void setNumberOfAliases(Integer numberOfAliases) {
        this.numberOfAliases = numberOfAliases;
    }
    @ValidationMethod
    public void validateUsernameAndPasswords(ValidationErrors errors){
        String username = user.getUsername();
        if (userDao.findByUsername(username) != null) {
```

```
            errors.addGlobalError(
                new SimpleError(username + " is already taken."));
        }
        if (!user.getPassword().equals(confirmPassword)) {
            errors.addGlobalError(
                new SimpleError("The passwords do not match."));
        }
    }
}
    private UserDao userDao = MockUserDao.getInstance();
}
```

In the validation method, we make sure the username is not already taken by someone else and that the password and confirm password fields match.

As we can see, all fields are required. That will work fine as is, but with six fields in total, a blank form will bombard the user with error messages. We can do something about that by hooking into the validation process.

10.3 Dealing with a Bunch of Required Fields

Right now, there'll be as many error messages in the registration form as there are missing fields. That can add up to a lot of error messages. Instead, we can put *one* general error message at the top of the form and just highlight the missing fields, as illustrated in Figure 10.4, on the next page.

Doing this is surprisingly easy. First, the action bean implements ValidationErrorHandler so that its handleValidationErrors() method is called at the end of the validation process. Next, that method checks for the presence of any field errors, which can be only required-field errors in this case. If there's at least one field error, the method adds a global error:

email_19/src/stripesbook/action/RegisterActionBean.java

```
public class RegisterActionBean extends BaseActionBean
▶    implements ValidationErrorHandler
{
    public Resolution handleValidationErrors(ValidationErrors errors){
        if (errors.hasFieldErrors()) {
            errors.addGlobalError(
                new SimpleError("All fields are required."));
        }
        return null;
    }
}
```

Registration Welcome to Stripes Webmail

Register to create an account:

- All fields are required.

First name: [   ]
Last name: [Daoud   ]
Primary email: [freddy   ] @stripesbook.org
Password: [   ]
Confirm password: [   ]
Aliases: [2   ▾]
[Continue]

Figure 10.4: HIGHLIGHTING REQUIRED FIELDS WITH JUST ONE MESSAGE AT THE TOP

Finally, we display the global error message above the form:

`email_19/web/WEB-INF/jsp/register.jsp`

```
<p>Register to create an account:</p>
<s:errors globalErrorsOnly="true"/>
<s:form beanclass="stripesbook.action.RegisterActionBean">
```

Without any other <s:errors> tag in the page, individual required-field error messages are not shown—just the global message. The field errors still cause Stripes to add class="error" to the corresponding input fields. By having a style for this class in the CSS file, the missing fields are automatically highlighted. That's it. We don't have to change anything else in the JSP. Beautiful.

10.4 Using Validation Metadata

At the bottom of the registration page, the user chooses how many email aliases they want to create. This must be a number between 0 and 5. That's easy enough to validate in the action bean:

`email_19/src/stripesbook/action/RegisterActionBean.java`

```
@Validate(required=true, minvalue=0, maxvalue=5)
private Integer numberOfAliases;
```

We could let users enter the number of aliases in a text box, but they would get a validation error if they entered an invalid number or a value outside the allowed range. A select box makes the valid choices more obvious and reduces the chance of error:

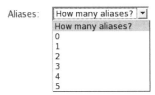

We'll generate a select box by looping from 0 to 5 in a *<c:forEach>* tag and generating an option for each value of the loop. We could use begin=0 and end=5 in the *<c:forEach>* tag, but that doesn't feel right. We'd be duplicating the minimum and maximum values specified in the validation. If we change minvalue= or maxvalue= in @Validate, we'd have to remember to go in the JSP and change the values in begin= and end= as well.

There's a better way. Stripes provides information about validations at runtime with the ValidationMetadata interface. By retrieving this information for the numberOfAliases field, we can make the minimum and maximum values dynamically available for the JSP to retrieve:

email_19/src/stripesbook/action/RegisterActionBean.java

```java
public int getMinAliases() {
    return getAliasValidation().minvalue().intValue();
}
public int getMaxAliases() {
    return getAliasValidation().maxvalue().intValue();
}
private ValidationMetadata getAliasValidation() {
    return StripesFilter.getConfiguration()
      .getValidationMetadataProvider()
      .getValidationMetadata(getClass())
      .get("numberOfAliases");
}
```

We're now ready to create the select box with the *<s:select>* tag and nested *<s:option>* tags:

email_19/web/WEB-INF/jsp/register.jsp

```jsp
<s:select name="numberOfAliases">
  <s:option value="" label="How many aliases?"/>
  <c:forEach  begin="${actionBean.minAliases}"
    var="index" end="${actionBean.maxAliases}">
    <s:option value="${index}" label="${index}"/>
  </c:forEach>
</s:select>
```

By using the validation information instead of hard-coded values in the JSP, we can change the minimum and maximum allowed number of aliases in the action bean's validation and sleep well at night. The JSP automatically uses the new values when generating the options in the select box.

10.5 Creating a Wizard

After the user has filled in all fields and chosen to have one or more aliases, the second page of registration appears. In Figure 10.3, on page 197, we can see this page after the user selected four aliases. After filling out the aliases, the user sees a page confirming that registration is complete. If the user chooses zero aliases, the registration process goes straight to the confirmation page.

We want the registration form to alter its flow according to the user input, and in the case of entering aliases, we want to create a form where the number of text fields depends on what the user chose in the previous page.

A form broken up into two or more pages is called a *wizard*. Wizards are useful for forms that involve multiple steps, such as our registration process, and can also be used just to break up a form that includes a large number of fields. In the latter situation, you avoid intimidating the user with a big daunting form that endlessly scrolls down the screen. Splitting a form across a few pages makes it easier to digest.

In Figure 10.5, on the next page, we can see the flow for our registration wizard. Notice that with a wizard, the same action bean handles all the pages of a wizard. Here, RegisterActionBean handles requests from both register.jsp and aliases.jsp, as well as the initial request from elsewhere in the application to arrive at the registration process (labeled *Start* in the diagram) and the redirect requests from the register() and save() event handlers.

Let's take it one step at a time. First, linking to RegisterActionBean calls its default event handler, which forwards to register.jsp:

email_19/src/stripesbook/action/RegisterActionBean.java

```
private static final String VIEW = "/WEB-INF/jsp/register.jsp";
@DefaultHandler
@DontValidate
public Resolution view() {
    return new ForwardResolution(VIEW);
}
```

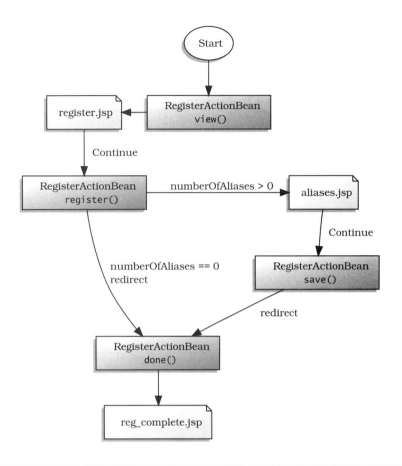

Figure 10.5: REGISTRATION WIZARD FLOW

The form in register.jsp contains the input fields for the first page of the wizard:

email_19/web/WEB-INF/jsp/register.jsp

```
<s:form beanclass="stripesbook.action.RegisterActionBean">
  <table class="form">
    <!-- input fields... -->
    <tr>
      <td></td>
      <td>
        <s:submit name="register" value="Continue"/>
        <s:submit name="cancel" value="Cancel"/>
      </td>
    </tr>
  </table>
</s:form>
```

Once the user has filled in the fields and clicked the ⌞Continue⌟ button, the register() event handler decides on the next page:

email_19/src/stripesbook/action/RegisterActionBean.java

```java
private static final String ALIASES = "/WEB-INF/jsp/aliases.jsp";
private static final String DONE = "/WEB-INF/jsp/reg_complete.jsp";
public Resolution register() {
    if (numberOfAliases > 0) {
        return new ForwardResolution(ALIASES);
    }
    return save();
}
public Resolution save() {
    userDao.save(user);
    return new RedirectResolution(getClass(), "done");
}
@DontValidate
public Resolution done() {
    return new ForwardResolution(DONE);
}
@DontValidate
public Resolution cancel() {
    return new RedirectResolution(LoginActionBean.class);
}
```

If the user has chosen to have one or more aliases, the action bean forwards to aliases.jsp, which displays the form for the user to fill out the aliases:

email_19/web/WEB-INF/jsp/aliases.jsp

```html
<p>Enter your email aliases:</p>
<s:form beanclass="stripesbook.action.RegisterActionBean">
  <s:errors/>
  <table class="form">
    <c:forEach begin="0" end="${actionBean.numberOfAliases - 1}"
      var="index">
      <tr>
        <td>
          <s:label for="user.aliases[${index}]"/> ${index + 1}:
        </td>
        <td><s:text name="user.aliases[${index}]"/></td>
        <td>@stripesbook.org</td>
      </tr>
    </c:forEach>
    <tr>
      <td></td>
      <td>
        <s:submit name="save" value="Continue"/>
        <s:submit name="cancel" value="Cancel"/>
      </td>
```

```
    </tr>
  </table>
</s:form>
```

RegisterActionBean includes a validation method to validate the aliases:

email_19/src/stripesbook/action/RegisterActionBean.java

```
    @ValidationMethod(on="save")
    public void validateAliases(ValidationErrors errors) {
        if (sizeOf(user.getAliases()) != numberOfAliases) {
            errors.addGlobalError(
                new SimpleError("Please enter all aliases."));
        }
        else {
            for (String alias : user.getAliases()) {
                if (alias == null) {
                    errors.addGlobalError(
                        new SimpleError("Please enter all aliases."));
                    break;
                }
                if (userDao.findByUsername(alias) != null) {
                    errors.addGlobalError(
                        new SimpleError(alias + " is already taken."));
                }
            }
        }
    }
    public Resolution handleValidationErrors(ValidationErrors errors){
        if (errors.hasFieldErrors()) {
            errors.addGlobalError(
                new SimpleError("All fields are required."));
        }
        return null;
    }
    private int sizeOf(List<?> list) {
        return (list == null ? 0 : list.size());
    }
    /* ... */
    private UserDao userDao = MockUserDao.getInstance();
}
```

Once the registration process is complete, either because the user has filled out the aliases or chosen to have no aliases, the action bean redirects to its done() event handler, which forwards to reg_complete.jsp:

email_19/web/WEB-INF/jsp/reg_complete.jsp

```
<p>Registration complete!</p>
You may now
<s:link beanclass="stripesbook.action.LoginActionBean">
  login
</s:link>.
```

Everything is fairly straightforward about the registration process, except for two issues that are raised by wizard forms:

1. With required fields on the different pages of a wizard, how do we prevent the required fields that are in page 2 from causing validation errors when the user submits the form that's on page 1?

2. When the user has submitted the form on page 1 and moves on to page 2, how do we "remember" the values that were submitted on page 1? Where do we store the accumulated values so that we can retrieve them and save everything at the end of the wizard?

Fortunately, Stripes has built-in support for wizards and deals with these issues for us. The first thing you have to do is add the @Wizard annotation to the action bean class:

```
@Wizard
public class RegisterActionBean ...
```

As illustrated in Figure 10.6, on the facing page, we have forms in register.jsp and aliases.jsp that are associated to RegisterActionBean. When Stripes sees an <s:form> tag for which the action bean is annotated with @Wizard, it generates some special values in the form to keep track of what's going on between each page of the wizard. When a form is submitted, Stripes detects which input fields were in the form and does not generate required-field validation errors for fields that are *not* in the form. That takes care of issue #1. For issue #2, Stripes generates hidden inputs that contain all the values that have been submitted in the previous pages of the wizard so that they are "carried over" as the user goes through the pages of the wizard. When the user submits the the last page, it's as if the user had submitted one big form with all the input fields filled in. You can save the data in the action bean just like you would for a regular single-page form.

That's a lot going on behind the scenes, but from our point of view, all we had to do was add one annotation, and the wizard is almost ready. Looking again at Figure 10.6, on the next page, notice that the view() and done() events are *not* called from a form. Indeed, view() is called from a plain link to RegisterActionBean (to start the process), and done() is called from a redirect after saving the registration data.

When an event handler of a @Wizard action bean is called, Stripes looks for the special values that it generated within the <s:form> tag. To prevent malicious users from bypassing the wizard process, Stripes throws an exception if those special values are missing. But we can still tell

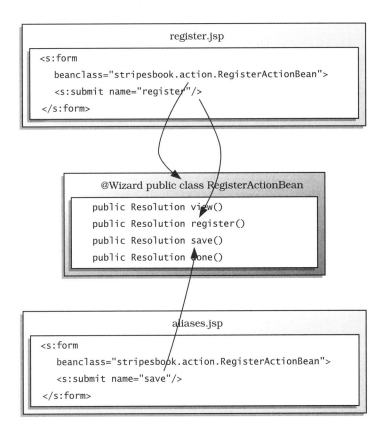

Figure 10.6: REGISTER() AND SAVE() ARE ASSOCIATED TO A FORM; VIEW() AND
DONE() ARE NOT.

Stripes that some event handlers are allowed to be called from outside
a wizard form. These special events are called *start events*, and you
indicate their names in the @Wizard annotation:

`email_19/src/stripesbook/action/RegisterActionBean.java`

```
@Wizard(startEvents={"view","done"})
public class RegisterActionBean extends BaseActionBean
    implements ValidationErrorHandler
{
    /* ... */
}
```

Now, view() and done() will not cause Stripes to throw an exception.
Our registration wizard is complete!

> ⑂ **Joe Asks...**
>
> ___**What About Going Back to the Previous Page?**___
>
> If we want to allow the user to go back to the previous page in a wizard, we have to take into account that the default behavior is to perform validation on the data that the user entered in the current page before invoking the event handler that sends the user to the previous page. If the user entered invalid data or did not fill in required fields, validation errors will occur.
>
> To let the user go back without forcing them to enter valid data in the current page, we have to "manually" adjust the validations with the on= attribute of @Validate or with @DontValidate on the event handler.
>
> Of course, if the user goes back to the previous page using the browser's ⌞Back⌝ button, any values that they entered on the current page will be lost. Hitting ⌞Back⌝ does not send any data to the server, so there's not much we can do about that!

10.6 The Login Page

After registering, the user is ready to log in at the page shown in Figure 10.7, on the facing page.

After tackling that registration wizard, this page seems so simple that you could implement it with your eyes closed. In fact, the only part that's worth a look is the validation of the username and password:

`email_19/src/stripesbook/action/LoginActionBean.java`

```java
@ValidationMethod
public void validateUser(ValidationErrors errors) {
    User user = userDao.findByUsername(username);
    if (user == null) {
        errors.add("username",
            new SimpleError("The primary email was not found."));
    }
    else if (!user.getPassword().equals(password)) {
        errors.add("password",
            new SimpleError("The password is incorrect."));
    }
}
private UserDao userDao = MockUserDao.getInstance();
```

Login   Welcome to Stripes Webmail

Please login:

Primary email: [＿＿＿＿＿＿＿＿] @stripesbook.org

Password: [＿＿＿＿＿＿＿＿]

[Login]

Register to create an account.

Figure 10.7: THE LOGIN PAGE

Besides being required fields, the username must exist, and the password must match. This logic is in a validation method because it involves querying the user DAO. Notice that the code checks for the existence of the username first and then verifies the password. This way, we can tell the user specifically which of the username or password is incorrect after a failed login.

At this point, we have a fairly complete webmail application. We still need to address security issues and could add some polish by gracefully handling any exceptions that might occur. We've been using mock DAOs—we should eventually move on to using a real database. We'll cover all those topics—and more—in Part III. Before getting to that, let's see how we can make the application available in multiple languages.

Chapter 11

Parlez-Vous Français?
Making It Multilingual

The webmail application is shaping up nicely. With its crisp design, amazing set of features, and outstanding user friendliness, the calls have been pouring in asking for its release to the public. Users from all over the world will be using the application! With such global exposure, it'd be nice to offer the interface in different languages. In this chapter, we'll discuss everything related to making an application available in more than one language, and we'll be translating the webmail application to French as an example.

11.1 Offering an Application in Multiple Languages

Several tools are at your disposal for making the translation of an application into other languages as painless as possible. At the heart of the process are Java's Locale and ResourceBundle classes. A *locale* represents a language, a country, a region, a culture. . . everything you would consider when you want to present information to a user in the manner that's most natural for them. A *resource bundle* contains all the locale-specific information and isolates it from the rest of the code. This makes it easier not only to support multiple languages but also to add more languages later.

Locales and Resource Bundles

A locale is represented by several parameters, but let's keep things simple and just use the language. Languages are represented by two-letter codes, such as en for English and fr for French.[1] Using new Locale("fr") would create a locale for French.

A resource bundle has a unique *base name* and multiple files, one for each locale. When the resource bundle named MyBundle is used and the language is French, Java automatically looks for MyBundle_fr in the class path. If it doesn't find it, it uses MyBundle as a default.

The file can be implemented in different ways but always contains a set of key-value pairs. The implementation that we'll use is the .properties file; in fact, you've already seen the Stripes default resource bundle, StripesResources.properties. In a multilingual application, you would have resource bundle files such as the following:

```
StripesResources_fr.properties // French
StripesResources_es.properties // Spanish
StripesResources_it.properties // Italian
StripesResources.properties    // default (English, in our case)
```

Each file would contain the same keys but with values translated in the specific language. For example, StripesResources.properties might contain this:

```
greeting=Hello
```

and StripesResources_fr.properties would have this:

```
greeting=Bonjour
```

That's pretty simple. Now that we have the basics of locales and resource bundles down, let's see what we have to do in Stripes to make the application available in French with a StripesResources_fr.properties file. First, we need to let Stripes know about our localization plans.

Configuring the List of Supported Locales

When a request arrives at Stripes, the headers contain the list of the user's preferred locales, as configured in their browser. Stripes compares this to the list of locales supported by the application and chooses the best match. By default, a Stripes application supports one locale: the system's default, which is English in our case. So, the first thing we have to do is set the list of supported locales to English and French using the language codes.

---

1. See Javadocs for the java.util.Locale class for more details on language codes and the other parameters you can use for a locale.

Locales and Character Encodings

We can be more specific when configuring locales with the LocalePicker.Locales parameter by appending a country to the language. For example, fr_FR and fr_CA both designate French while distinguishing between France and Canada. We can also append a variant: es_ES_Traditional indicates traditional Spanish from Spain. Again, refer to the java.util.Locale Javadocs for complete information on these parameters.

At the end of a locale, we can also append a colon (:) and indicate a character encoding. For example, de:UTF-8 specifies the German locale with UTF-8 character encoding.

In JSPs, we can specify the character encoding with the pageEncoding= attribute of the page directive:

```
<%@page pageEncoding="UTF-8" %>
```

A top-level <s:layout-definition> JSP is a good place for setting the character encoding for all JSPs.

This is configured with the Stripes filter's LocalePicker.Locales parameter in web.xml:

`email_20/web/WEB-INF/web.xml`

```
<filter>
  <filter-name>StripesFilter</filter-name>
  <filter-class>
    net.sourceforge.stripes.controller.StripesFilter
  </filter-class>
  <!-- other init params... -->
  <init-param>
    <param-name>LocalePicker.Locales</param-name>
    <param-value>en,fr</param-value>
  </init-param>
</filter>
```

Now, if a user accesses the application with French as their preferred language, Stripes will use the French locale and therefore the Stripes-Resources_fr.properties file. Right now it won't find it and fall back on StripesResources.properties, still showing the application in English! So, the next step is to create the StripesResources_fr.properties file and learn what keys Stripes uses when searching for localized values.

Let's use the Login page as an example. After submitting the page with an existing primary email but with an incorrect password, you get the screen shown in Figure 11.1, on the next page.

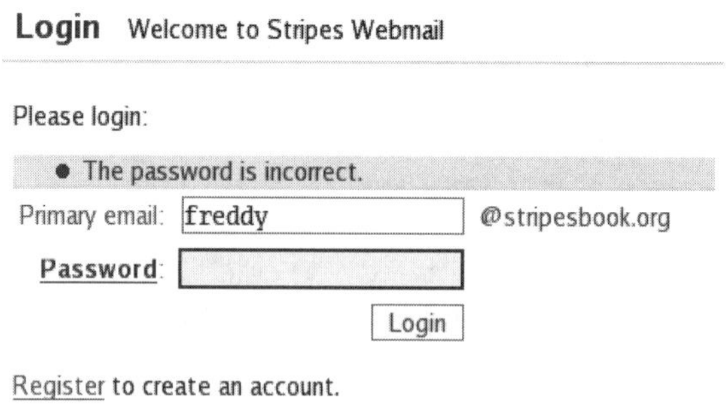

Login   Welcome to Stripes Webmail

Please login:

● The password is incorrect.

Primary email: `freddy`   @stripesbook.org

Password: [   ]

[Login]

Register to create an account.

Figure 11.1: THE LOGIN PAGE IN ENGLISH

The text we see on this page comes from three sources:

- *Form field labels*: This includes the "Primary email" and "Password" labels as well as the Login button.
- *Error and information messages*: In this case, this is "The password is incorrect."
- *Free-form text*: Basically, that's all the other text we see in the page.

11.2   Translating the Text of an Application

Let us now see how Stripes looks up resource bundle keys for the three sources of text.

Translating Form Field Labels

Stripes looks up form field labels in the *Form field bundle*, which is in StripesResources by default.

We've seen how the <*s:label*> tag can be used to look up the text for a field label in the resource bundle. For example, if the contact.firstName field is in the stripesbook.action.ContactFormActionBean and we use <s:label for="contact.firstName"> in the JSP, Stripes looks for a label in this order of priority:

1. In the resource bundle, using the key:
   stripesbook.action.ContactFormActionBean.contact.firstName
2. In the resource bundle, using the key:
   contact.firstName

3. In the Java code:

@Validate(label="whatever is here")

4. In the JSP:

<s:label for="contact.firstName">whatever is here</s:label>

Options 1 and 2 are the most interesting to us, because we can just use the key in the resource bundle file for each language. Option 3 is a hard-coded string and cannot be made available in more than one language. We can use option 4 with the *<fmt:message>* tag within the body of the *<s:label>* tag if we can't use either of the keys from options 1 and 2.

We already had *<s:label>* tags in login.jsp to use the resource bundle for the field labels:

email_20/web/WEB-INF/jsp/login.jsp

```
<s:form beanclass="stripesbook.action.LoginActionBean">
  <s:errors/>
  <table class="form">
    <tr>
►     <td><s:label for="username"/>:</td>
      <td><s:text name="username"/></td>
      <td>@stripesbook.org</td>
    </tr>
    <tr>
►     <td><s:label for="password"/>:</td>
      <td><s:password name="password"/></td>
    </tr>
    <tr>
      <td></td>
►     <td><s:submit name="login"/></td>
    </tr>
  </table>
</s:form>
```

To use the resource bundle keys for the Login button, we didn't add any code—in fact, we removed code! How's that for getting more for less? We previously had the value= attribute for the label of the button. Omitting this attribute causes Stripes to use the value in name= to look up the button label in the resource bundle in the same way as field labels. Now, adding the following entries in the resource bundles will make the field and button labels available in English and French:

email_20/res/StripesResources.properties

```
stripesbook.action.LoginActionBean.username=Primary email
stripesbook.action.LoginActionBean.password=Password
stripesbook.action.LoginActionBean.login=Login
```

```
email_20/res/StripesResources_fr.properties
```
```
stripesbook.action.LoginActionBean.username=Courriel principal
stripesbook.action.LoginActionBean.password=Mot de passe
stripesbook.action.LoginActionBean.login=Envoyer
```

The nice thing about the resource bundle keys that Stripes uses is that we can keep your keys organized with the action bean class name prefix and use keys without the prefix for text that is the same across more than one action bean. For example, the following resource bundle entry:

```
cancel=Cancel
```

would label all <s:submit name="cancel"/> buttons with "Cancel." If all these buttons will be labeled "Cancel," why repeat the same text as many times as there are action beans? Furthermore, we can still override this and use a different label in a specific page. If we wanted to use "Abort" instead of "Cancel" on the Register page, we would add this:

```
stripesbook.action.RegisterActionBean.cancel=Abort
```

since this key has priority over the previous, nonprefixed key.

Translating Error and Information Messages

For error and information messages, Stripes looks in the *error message bundle* for the text to be displayed, which is also in StripesResources by default. The classes involved in creating localized messages are LocalizableMessage, LocalizableError, and ScopedLocalizableError, as shown in Figure 11.2, on the facing page, with their relationship to the other Stripes message classes.

We've seen how LocalizableError and ScopedLocalizableError work in Section 6.3, *Changing the Error Message Text*, on page 124. Both classes look for messages in the resource bundle with a series of keys based on the action bean and the nature of the error. We already have key-value pairs for these messages in StripesResources.properties, so we just have to use the same keys and translate the text in StripesResources_fr.properties. Here are some examples:

```
email_20/res/StripesResources.properties
```
```
validation.required.valueNotPresent={0} is a required field
contact.lastName.valueTooShort=\
  The last name must be at least {2} characters.
contact.birthDate.invalidDate=The birth date is not valid.
contact.birthDate.valueFailedExpression=\
  The birth date is in the future.
```

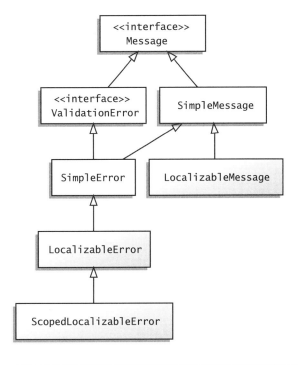

Figure 11.2: The Stripes message classes

```
validation.required.valueNotPresent={0} est un champ requis
contact.lastName.valueTooShort=\
    Le nom de famille doit avoir au moins {2} caract\u00e8res.
contact.birthDate.invalidDate=La date de naissance n''est pas valide.
contact.birthDate.valueFailedExpression=\
    La date de naissance est dans le futur.
```

That funny \u00e8 sequence in the French text is a Unicode escape. Java .properties files allow only the ISO8859-1 character encoding, but you can get Unicode characters using \unnnn, where nnnn is the hexadecimal value of the character. For example, \u00e8 represents the è character. You'll find a chart of Unicode characters at http://mindprod. com/jgloss/ascii.html.

That's great for all the error messages that are generated automatically, but what about the ones that we created ourselves?

Remember that we used the SimpleError class, such as these messages in the LoginActionBean:

```
email_19/src/stripesbook/action/LoginActionBean.java
@ValidationMethod
public void validateUser(ValidationErrors errors) {
    User user = userDao.findByUsername(username);
    if (user == null) {
        errors.add("username",
            new SimpleError("The primary email was not found."));
    }
    else if (!user.getPassword().equals(password)) {
        errors.add("password",
            new SimpleError("The password is incorrect."));
    }
}
```

The text is hard-coded in the Java code. To make the text translatable, we use LocalizableError, and pass in the resource bundle key:

```
email_20/src/stripesbook/action/LoginActionBean.java
@ValidationMethod
public void validateUser(ValidationErrors errors) {
    User user = userDao.findByUsername(username);
    if (user == null) {
        errors.add("username",
            new LocalizableError("primaryEmailNotFound"));
    }
    else if (!user.getPassword().equals(password)) {
        errors.add("password",
            new LocalizableError("passwordIncorrect"));
    }
}
```

This allows us to take the text out of the Java code and move it to resource bundles, making it ready to be translated. Stripes automatically tries keys with the action bean class name prefix before trying prefixless keys, so we can use the same patterns as with form field labels. Deciding to use the prefixes, we now have the messages in English and French in StripesResources.properties and StripesResources_fr.properties as follows:

```
email_20/res/StripesResources.properties
stripesbook.action.LoginActionBean.primaryEmailNotFound=\
  The primary email was not found.
stripesbook.action.LoginActionBean.passwordIncorrect=\
  The password is incorrect.
```

email_20/res/StripesResources_fr.properties

```
stripesbook.action.LoginActionBean.primaryEmailNotFound=\
  Le courriel principal n''existe pas.
stripesbook.action.LoginActionBean.passwordIncorrect=\
  Le mot de passe est incorrect.
```

The constructor for LocalizableError also accepts an optional list of parameters that replaces tokens starting at {2}.[2] For example, the error message on the Register page for a username that is already taken uses the LocalizableError class as follows:

email_20/src/stripesbook/action/RegisterActionBean.java

```
if (userDao.findByUsername(username) != null) {
    errors.addGlobalError(
      new LocalizableError("usernameAlreadyTaken", username));
}
```

The messages are now translated in the resource bundles:

email_20/res/StripesResources.properties

```
stripesbook.action.RegisterActionBean.usernameAlreadyTaken=\
  {2} is already taken.
```

email_20/res/StripesResources_fr.properties

```
stripesbook.action.RegisterActionBean.usernameAlreadyTaken=\
  {2} est d\u00e9j\u00e0 pris.
```

Making information messages translatable works in a similar way. Instead of using the SimpleMessage class and hard-coded text, use LocalizableMessage and resource bundle keys:

email_20/src/stripesbook/action/ContactFormActionBean.java

```
public Resolution save() {
    Contact contact = getContact();
    getContactDao().save(contact);
    getContext().getMessages().add(
      new LocalizableMessage(getClass().getName()+".contactSaved",
        contact)
    );
    return new RedirectResolution(ContactListActionBean.class);
}
@DontValidate
public Resolution cancel() {
    getContext().getMessages().add(
      new LocalizableMessage(getClass().getName()+".actionCancelled")
    );
    return new RedirectResolution(ContactListActionBean.class);
}
```

_____

2. Remember that {0} and {1} are reserved for the field name and the value entered by the user.

email_20/res/StripesResources.properties

```
stripesbook.action.ContactFormActionBean.contactSaved=\
  {0} has been saved.
stripesbook.action.ContactFormActionBean.actionCancelled=\
  Action cancelled.
```

email_20/res/StripesResources_fr.properties

```
stripesbook.action.ContactFormActionBean.contactSaved=\
  {0} a \u00e9t\u00e9 enregistr\u00e9(e).
stripesbook.action.ContactFormActionBean.actionCancelled=\
  Action annul\u00e9e.
```

Notice the two ways in which information messages differ from error messages:

- Since there is no field name and value entered by the user, tokens for replacing parameters in the text start at {0}.

- Stripes doesn't add the action bean class name prefix, so the resource bundle key is just used as is. We're adding the class name prefix ourselves so that the keys consistently use the same pattern as for error messages. Doing this is, of course, completely optional.

Translating Free-Form Text

What's left to translate is the free-form text. Stripes stays out of this one because the JSTL already provides the <fmt:message> tag for retrieving text from a resource bundle. For example, <fmt:message key="hello"/> displays the text for the hello key. You can also store the text in a variable with the var= attribute, as in <fmt:message key="hello" var="greeting"/>, and display it later in the JSP with ${greeting}.

The JSTL, however, doesn't know that we're using StripesResources. Add the following context parameter at the top of web.xml to tell the JSTL to use StripesResources as the default resource bundle:

email_20/web/WEB-INF/web.xml

```
<context-param>
  <param-name>
    javax.servlet.jsp.jstl.fmt.localizationContext
  </param-name>
  <param-value>StripesResources</param-value>
</context-param>
```

You can now use the *<fmt:message>* tag with corresponding key-value pairs in the StripesResources resource bundle. As with the LocalizableMessage class, you choose arbitrary keys, and they are used as is, without a prefix. Let's say that we still want to prefix the keys with the action bean class name. Adding ${actionBean.class.name} in front of the key will do it:[3]

email_20/web/WEB-INF/jsp/common/taglibs.jsp

```
<c:set var="contextPath" value="${pageContext.request.contextPath}"/>
▶ <c:set var="prefix" value="${actionBean.class.name}"/>
```

email_20/web/WEB-INF/jsp/login.jsp

```
▶ <fmt:message var="title" key="${prefix}.title"/>
  <s:layout-render name="/WEB-INF/jsp/common/layout_main.jsp"
    title="${title}">
    <s:layout-component name="body">
▶     <p><fmt:message key="${prefix}.pleaseLogin"/>:</p>
      <s:form beanclass="stripesbook.action.LoginActionBean">
      <!-- same as before... -->
      </s:form>
      <s:link beanclass="stripesbook.action.RegisterActionBean">
▶       <fmt:message key="${prefix}.register"/>
      </s:link>
▶     <fmt:message key="${prefix}.toCreateAnAccount"/>.
    </s:layout-component>
  </s:layout-render>
```

The translated text is in the resource bundles:

email_20/res/StripesResources.properties

```
stripesbook.action.LoginActionBean.title=Login
stripesbook.action.LoginActionBean.pleaseLogin=Please login
stripesbook.action.LoginActionBean.toCreateAnAccount=\
  to create an account
stripesbook.action.LoginActionBean.register=Register
```

email_20/res/StripesResources_fr.properties

```
stripesbook.action.LoginActionBean.title=Identification
stripesbook.action.LoginActionBean.pleaseLogin=Veuillez vous identifier
stripesbook.action.LoginActionBean.toCreateAnAccount=\
  pour cr\u00e9er un compte
stripesbook.action.LoginActionBean.register=Enregistrez-vous
```

All the text for the Login page is now translated in StripesResources_fr. properties, and the page is available in French, as shown in Figure 11.3, on the following page.

---

3. Using the action bean prefix is, of course, totally optional. You can also use plain keys.

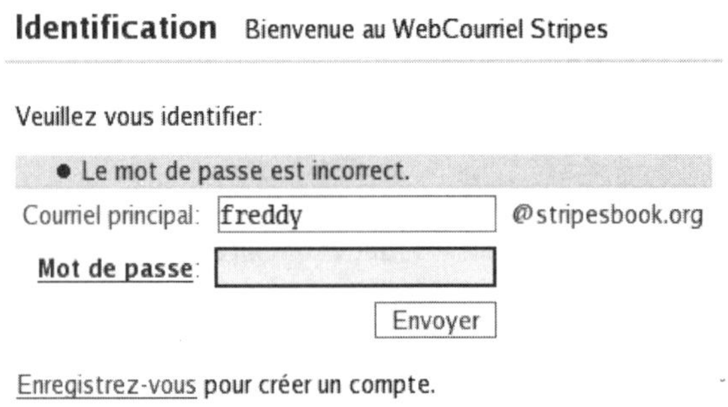

Identification Bienvenue au WebCourriel Stripes

Veuillez vous identifier:

● Le mot de passe est incorrect.

Courriel principal: freddy @stripesbook.org

Mot de passe: [   ]

[Envoyer]

Enregistrez-vous pour créer un compte.

Figure 11.3: THE LOGIN PAGE IN FRENCH

Translating the Other Parts of the Application

Back on page 148, we created a view helper that manages the menu displayed at the top:

Message List [Messages] Contact List Compose

The label for each menu item was hard-coded in the Section enumeration; we now need to make it translatable. We can do that by removing the text and replacing it with a resource bundle text key. We'll build the key using a section. prefix followed by the name of the enumeration constant:

```
email_20/src/stripesbook/action/MenuViewHelper.java
public enum Section {
    MessageList(MessageListActionBean.class),
    ContactList(ContactListActionBean.class),
    Compose(MessageComposeActionBean.class);

    private String textKey, beanclass;
    Section(Class<? extends ActionBean> beanclass) {
        this.textKey = "section." + name();
        this.beanclass = beanclass.getName();
    }
    public String getTextKey() { return textKey; }
    public String getBeanclass() { return beanclass; }
}
```

The JSP that displays the menu is easily adapted by retrieving the text from the resource bundle using the text key provided by each section.

Joe Asks...

Do I Use One or Two Single Quotes in the .properties Files?

For form field labels and free-form text, use a single quote as follows:

```
message=That's a great idea!
```

However, for error and information messages, you need to use two single quotes:

```
message=That''s a great idea!
```

As you can see in Figure 11.2, on page 217, all message classes inherit from SimpleMessage, which uses Java's MessageFormat class to produce the message. MessageFormat requires a single quote to be escaped with another single quote, because a single quote on its own has a special meaning. Refer to the MessageFormat Javadocs for more details.

email_20/web/WEB-INF/jsp/common/menu.jsp

```
<c:forEach var="section" items="${actionBean.sections}">
►    <fmt:message var="text" key="${section.textKey}"/>
     <c:choose>
       <c:when test="${section eq actionBean.currentSection}">
►        <span class="currentSection">${text}</span>
       </c:when>
       <c:otherwise>
         <s:link beanclass="${section.beanclass}" class="sectionLink">
►          ${text}
         </s:link>
       </c:otherwise>
     </c:choose>
</c:forEach>
```

We can now place the translated text in the resource bundles:

email_20/res/StripesResources.properties

```
section.MessageList=Messages
section.ContactList=Contact List
section.Compose=Compose
```

email_20/res/StripesResources_fr.properties

```
section.MessageList=Messages
section.ContactList=Liste des contacts
section.Compose=Composition
```

We've seen how to translate the three types of text (form field labels, error/information messages, and free-form text). Lather, rinse, and repeat for each page, and you have a fully translated French webmail application! Well, almost. The only thing we haven't seen so far is how to localize certain types of input controls, so let's discuss them briefly.

Localizing Radio Buttons

In the previous chapter, we added radio buttons for the gender in the contact form:

Gender: ⊙ Female ⊙ Male

Stripes doesn't generate labels for radio buttons; they are just text after the *<s:radio>* tag. You can use the *<fmt:message>* tag and use the value of the gender object with ${gender} to build the key:

email_20/web/WEB-INF/jsp/contact_form.jsp

```
<c:forEach var="gender" items="${actionBean.genders}">
  <s:radio name="contact.gender" value="${gender}"/>
  <fmt:message key="${prefix}.${gender}"/>
</c:forEach>
```

Now you can put the text in the resource bundles as follows:

email_20/res/StripesResources.properties

```
stripesbook.action.ContactFormActionBean.Female=Female
stripesbook.action.ContactFormActionBean.Male=Male
```

email_20/res/StripesResources_fr.properties

```
stripesbook.action.ContactFormActionBean.Female=F\u00e9minin
stripesbook.action.ContactFormActionBean.Male=Masculin
```

The radio buttons are now translated:

Sexe: ⊙ Féminin ⊙ Masculin

Localizing Select Boxes

For select boxes with options generated by Stripes with *<s:options-enumeration>*, *<s:options-collection>*, or *<s:options-map>*, you can add entries in the resource bundle with the keys that Stripes uses to look up localized labels. For example, we used *<s:options-collection>* to render a select box with the list of Folder objects.

email_20/web/WEB-INF/jsp/common/message_action.jsp

```
<s:select name="selectedFolder">
  <s:option value="">
    <fmt:message key="messageList.selectAFolder"/>...
  </s:option>
▶ <s:options-collection collection="${folders.folders}"
▶   value="id" label="name"/>
</s:select>
```

For each Folder, Stripes calls getId() for the value and getName() for the label. To look up localized labels, Stripes looks for a key that starts with the class name (Folder), optionally prefixed by the package (stripesbook. action), and followed either by the string returned by getName() or by getId(). Using the class name without the package, followed by the name of the folder, we get the following entries in the resource bundles:

email_20/res/StripesResources.properties

```
Folder.Inbox=Inbox
Folder.Sent=Sent
Folder.Reference=Reference
Folder.Trash=Trash
```

email_20/res/StripesResources_fr.properties

```
Folder.Inbox=R\u00e9ception
Folder.Sent=Envoi
Folder.Reference=R\u00e9f\u00e9rence
Folder.Trash=Poubelle
```

That's all we need to translate the options in the select box. Options rendered by <s:options-enumeration> and <s:options-map> work essentially in the same way: the class name with or without the package prefix, followed by the label or the value. If we had used a select box for the gender and <s:options-enumeration> to generate options from the Gender enumeration, we could have added these entries in the French resource bundle:

```
stripesbook.model.Gender.Female=F\u00e9minin
stripesbook.model.Gender.Male=Masculin
```

Localizing Image Buttons

One last type of input control that it is worth mentioning while talking about localization is the image button. If we're using localized images, you can use the resource bundle to get the <s:image> tag to use the image associated to the current locale. As with other input controls, the key is the same as the name= attribute of the tag, optionally prefixed with the action bean class name. To indicate the path to the image, append the .src suffix to the key; for the alternate text, use the .alt suffix. For example:

```
stripesbook.action.MessageComposeActionBean.addTo.src=images/fr/arrow.png
stripesbook.action.MessageComposeActionBean.addTo.alt=Ajouter
```

11.3 Switching Between Languages

Although the application now automatically appears in French if that's the user's preferred language, we might also want to let the user choose the language directly in the application. This could be a link at the bottom of the page, as illustrated in Figure 11.4, on page 228.[4] This saves the user from having to change the browser's settings and caters to those bilingual users who might feel like switching languages according to their mood.

One way to implement this feature is to use a request parameter that tells the application what locale to use, such as locale=fr. This value is stored in the session and used until the user switches the language again.

To make this possible, we'll need an extension to the Stripes module called the *locale picker*. On each request, Stripes uses an implementation of the LocalePicker interface to determine the locale and character encoding:

```
public interface LocalePicker extends ConfigurableComponent {
    public Locale pickLocale(HttpServletRequest request);

    public String pickCharacterEncoding(HttpServletRequest request,
        Locale locale);
}
```

The default implementation looks in the request for a list of preferred locales and compares it to the list of locales supported by the application, as we discussed earlier. We can extend the default class and add the behavior of first looking for the locale= parameter in the request and in the session before falling back to the behavior of the parent class.

---

4. Of course, if the application became available in more than two languages, we'd use something else: several links, a select box, or what have you. Right now we'll stick to a single link that switches between English and French.

email_20/src/stripesbook/ext/MyLocalePicker.java

```java
package stripesbook.ext;
public class MyLocalePicker extends DefaultLocalePicker {
    public static final String LOCALE = "locale";

    @Override
    public Locale pickLocale(HttpServletRequest request) {
        HttpSession session = request.getSession();

        // Look in the request.
        String locale = request.getParameter(LOCALE);
        if (locale != null) {
            session.setAttribute(LOCALE, locale);
        }
        // Not found in the request? Look in the session.
        else {
            locale = (String) session.getAttribute(LOCALE);
        }
        // Use the locale if found.
        if (locale != null) {
            return new Locale(locale);
        }
        // Otherwise, use the default.
        return super.pickLocale(request);
    }
}
```

In the pickLocale() method, the locale= request parameter has priority
for choosing the locale. Next comes the last selected locale, which is
stored in the session. Finally, when the user first accesses the application, the method falls back to the default behavior of using the value
supplied by the browser until the user clicks the link to change the
language.

Again, we can just add MyLocalePicker to the stripesbook.ext package, and
it will automatically be loaded by Stripes because we designated this
package in web.xml as the package for Stripes extensions. Gotta love
that!

Now we can add a link to switch from one language to the other at the
bottom of each page by adding this code to layout_main.jsp:

email_20/web/WEB-INF/jsp/common/layout_main.jsp

```jsp
<fmt:message var="otherLocale" key="layout.otherLocale"/>
<s:link href="${actionBean.lastUrl}">
  <s:param name="locale" value="${otherLocale}"/>
  <fmt:message key="layout.otherLanguage"/>
</s:link>
```

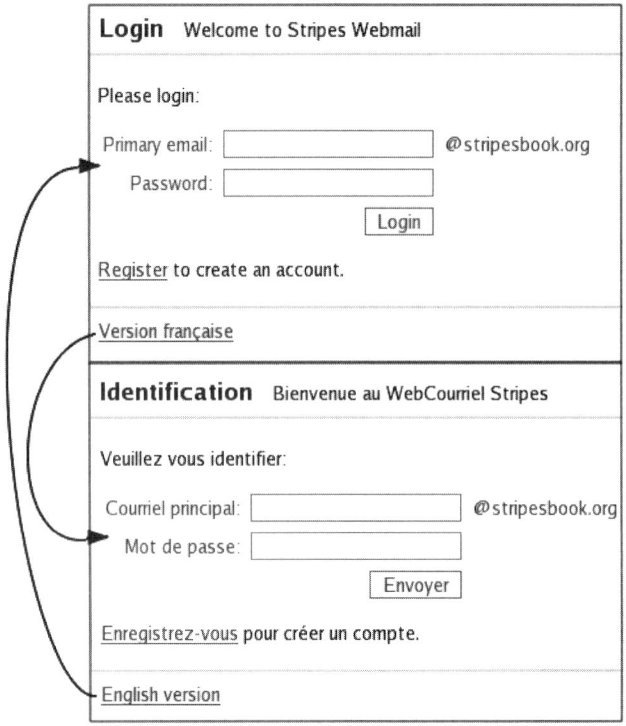

Figure 11.4: The Login page with a link to switch languages

Since this link is displayed in every page of the application, it just resubmits the previous request with the locale= parameter tacked on at the end. By adding a getLastUrl() to BaseActionBean, we can obtain the URL with ${actionBean.lastUrl}. Indeed, different action beans are used in different pages, but they all extend BaseActionBean, making it the appropriate place to add the helper method.

All that's left is to add the entries in the resource bundles. We just have to be careful not to get mixed up: the values in the English resource bundle refer to French, and vice versa:

`email_20/res/StripesResources.properties`

```
layout.otherLanguage=Version fran\u00e7aise
layout.otherLocale=fr
```

`email_20/res/StripesResources_fr.properties`

```
layout.otherLanguage=English version
layout.otherLocale=en
```

We now have a link, as shown in Figure 11.4, on the facing page, which appears on every page and automatically switches whatever page the user is on to the other language. We needed only a custom locale picker, a link in the layout JSP, the text in the resource bundles, and a helper method to the base action bean. This is all thanks to the "pluggability" of Stripes, its layout mechanism, dynamic ${actionBean} attribute, and easy-to-use localization!

11.4 Using Different Resource Bundles

So far, we've used the default StripesResources bundle for all localized text. Although using action bean class name prefixes helps in keeping the keys organized, you might prefer to have separate bundles for form field names, messages, and free-form text. Or you might want to continue using just one bundle but use a different name. Whatever the reason, let's look at how you can change the name of the resource bundle used for each type of text. As a bonus, we'll also look at how we can gain full control over the localization strategy, implementing a one-resource-bundle-per-action-bean convention as an example.

Changing the Names of the Resource Bundles

Remember that localized text comes from three sources. You can change the resource bundle name for all three sources independently— it's up to you to decide whether you want the same or different bundles for each source. Let's look at an example of the latter. Instead of Stripes-Resources, we'll use the following:

- fieldLabels for the form field labels
- errors for the error and information messages
- text for the free-form text

Let's also put the resource bundles under the translations directory instead of in the root as with StripesResources.

We already know how to specify the resource bundle for free-form text with the JSTL context parameter. To change the Stripes resource bundles, use initialization parameters to the Stripes filter, as shown here:

email_21/web/WEB-INF/web.xml

```
<context-param>
  <param-name>
    javax.servlet.jsp.jstl.fmt.localizationContext
  </param-name>
```

```
▶         <param-value>translations/text</param-value>
        </context-param>
        <filter>
          <filter-name>StripesFilter</filter-name>
          <filter-class>
            net.sourceforge.stripes.controller.StripesFilter
          </filter-class>
          <!-- other init params...-->
          <init-param>
            <param-name>
▶             LocalizationBundleFactory.FieldNameBundle
            </param-name>
▶           <param-value>translations/fieldLabels</param-value>
          </init-param>
          <init-param>
            <param-name>
▶             LocalizationBundleFactory.ErrorMessageBundle
            </param-name>
▶           <param-value>translations/errors</param-value>
          </init-param>
        </filter>
```

The resource bundle files must now be under translations within the class path. For example:

```
/WEB-INF/classes/translations/errors.properties
/WEB-INF/classes/translations/errors_fr.properties
/WEB-INF/classes/translations/fieldNames.properties
/WEB-INF/classes/translations/fieldNames_fr.properties
/WEB-INF/classes/translations/text.properties
/WEB-INF/classes/translations/text_fr.properties
```

This gives us the possibility of using separate resource bundles for each type of text and putting the files in the directories of our choice. Of course, we can also use these configuration parameters to change the name of the resource bundle from StripesResources to something else, but we can use the same name for all three and use just one resource bundle for all localized text.

Implementing a One-Resource-Bundle-per-Action-Bean Convention

By implementing our own subclass of ResourceBundle, we can implement just about any localization strategy you want. Let's look at how that would work if we decided to organize resource bundles by using one bundle for each action bean. The convention might be that the base name of the resource bundle is the same as the package and class

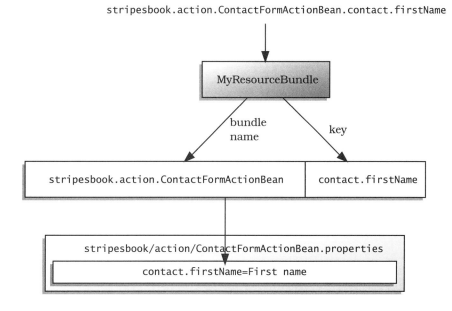

Figure 11.5: USING A CUSTOM RESOURCE BUNDLE

name of the action bean. For example, the resource bundle files for the following:

```
stripesbook.action.ContactFormActionBean
```

would look like this:

```
stripesbook/action/ContactFormActionBean.properties
stripesbook/action/ContactFormActionBean_fr.properties
```

As usual, the files would have to be found in the classpath, such as under the WEB-INF/classes directory.

The trick here is that the name of the resource bundle has to be determined "on the fly" according to the class name at the beginning of the key. We need a custom ResourceBundle (MyResourceBundle, say) that looks at the key, extracts the class name and uses it as a resource bundle name, and looks up the value using the rest of the key, as illustrated in Figure 11.5.

The two methods you have to override when subclassing ResourceBundle are getKeys() and handleGetObject(). Here, then, is the code for MyResourceBundle:

email_22/src/stripesbook/ext/MyResourceBundle.java

```java
package stripesbook.ext;
public class MyResourceBundle extends ResourceBundle {
    private Locale locale;
    public MyResourceBundle(Locale locale) {
        this.locale = locale;
    }
    @Override
    public Enumeration<String> getKeys() {
        return null;
    }
    @Override
    protected Object handleGetObject(String fullKey) {
        Object result = null;

        // Look for a class name in the full key
        for (int i = fullKey.length() - 1; i > 0; i--) {
            if (fullKey.charAt(i) == '.') {
                String className = fullKey.substring(0, i);
                try {
                    Class.forName(className);
                    // Found a class name, use the rest as a key
                    String key = fullKey.substring(i + 1);
                    result = getResult(locale, className, key);
                }
                catch (ClassNotFoundException exc) {
                }
            }
        }
        if (result == null) {
            // Found nothing, try the application's default bundle
            String name=DefaultLocalizationBundleFactory.BUNDLE_NAME;
            result = getResult(locale, name, fullKey);
        }
        return result;
    }
    // Just returns null if the bundle or the key is not found,
    // instead of throwing an exception.
    private String getResult(Locale loc, String name, String key) {
        String result = null;
        ResourceBundle bundle = ResourceBundle.getBundle(name, loc);
        if (bundle != null) {
            try { result = bundle.getString(key); }
            catch (MissingResourceException exc) { }
        }
        return result;
    }
}
```

This is actually a fake resource bundle (or, to put it more elegantly, a *decorator*), because it intercepts the call to handleGetObject() and dynamically delegates to the "real" resource bundle using the class name contained in the key. That's why getKeys() returns **null**: MyResourceBundle doesn't have any keys of its own.

If nothing is found when looking for a class name or for a key in the class name bundle, MyResourceBundle looks in the default Stripes resource bundle. This way, you can use StripesResources for text that is not associated with any specific action bean. You can also put keys without a class name and use them as a default for the whole application, overriding them in action bean bundles if necessary. Using our earlier example, where you had buttons labeled "Cancel" throughout the application, but wanted to use "Abort" on the Register page, you would have cancel=Cancel in StripesResources and cancel=Abort in the stripesbook/action/RegisterActionBean bundle.

We've already done most of the work to support our "modular" resource bundles. We now have to tell Stripes to use MyResourceBundle. Although packaged in stripesbook.ext, MyResourceBundle is not a Stripes extension, just a custom ResourceBundle. The Stripes extension for changing the ResourceBundle implementation is the LocalizationBundleFactory interface, which has a method for the form field bundle and one for the error message bundle. We'll return MyResourceBundle for both:

`email_22/src/stripesbook/ext/MyLocalizationBundleFactory.java`

```java
package stripesbook.ext;
public class MyLocalizationBundleFactory
    implements LocalizationBundleFactory
{
    public ResourceBundle getFormFieldBundle(Locale locale) {
        return new MyResourceBundle(locale);
    }
    public ResourceBundle getErrorMessageBundle(Locale locale) {
        return new MyResourceBundle(locale);
    }
    public void init(Configuration configuration) { }
}
```

What about the free-form text, which is handled by the JSTL? How do we tell the JSTL to use MyResourceBundle? We could do that (with <fmt:setBundle>), but then we'd have to make sure to prefix every key with the action bean class name, since the JSTL does not do that automatically. That's too much work, isn't it? There's an easier way. We can set the JSTL bundle to the class name of the current action bean with a one-liner added to the end of taglibs.jsp.

email_22/web/WEB-INF/jsp/common/taglibs.jsp

```
<fmt:setBundle basename="${actionBean.class.name}"/>
```

Every page already uses taglibs.jsp, so just like that, we've set the bundle globally. Now the JSTL will dynamically use the action bean class as a base name for its resource bundle. That's it—we don't even need the javax.servlet.jsp.jstl.fmt.localizationContext context parameter in web.xml in this case.

With this nifty maneuver, the *<fmt:message>* keys in the JSPs don't need a prefix. For example, in the Login page, we now have this:

email_22/web/WEB-INF/jsp/login.jsp

```
▶ <fmt:message var="title" key="title"/>
  <s:layout-render name="/WEB-INF/jsp/common/layout_main.jsp"
    title="${title}">
    <s:layout-component name="body">
▶     <p><fmt:message key="pleaseLogin"/>:</p>
      <!-- ... -->
      <s:link beanclass="stripesbook.action.RegisterActionBean">
▶       <fmt:message key="register"/>
▶     </s:link> <fmt:message key="toCreateAnAccount"/>.
    </s:layout-component>
  </s:layout-render>
```

Since the page is associated to stripesbook.action.LoginActionBean, that becomes the resource bundle for the localized text:

email_22/res/stripesbook/action/LoginActionBean.properties

```
title=Login
pleaseLogin=Please login
register=Register
toCreateAnAccount=to create an account
```

email_22/res/stripesbook/action/LoginActionBean_fr.properties

```
title=Identification
pleaseLogin=Veuillez vous identifier
register=Enregistrez-vous
toCreateAnAccount=pour cr\u00e9er un compte
```

Very clean. The keys are concise, and the resources are grouped together with the action bean class in matching .properties files.

The only exception to this resource bundle pattern is using StripesResources for free-form text not associated with a specific action bean, such as in the layout JSPs. In those cases, add <fmt:setBundle base-

name="StripesResources"/> in the layout JSP after the **taglib** import, and
the text will come from StripesResources. For example:

email_22/web/WEB-INF/jsp/common/layout_main.jsp

```
<%@include file="/WEB-INF/jsp/common/taglibs.jsp"%>
▶ <fmt:setBundle basename="StripesResources"/>
<s:layout-definition>
  <!DOCTYPE HTML PUBLIC "-//W3C//DTD HTML 4.01//EN"
    "http://www.w3.org/TR/html4/strict.dtd">
  <html>
    <!-- ... -->
          <s:layout-component name="menu">
▶           <fmt:message key="layout.welcome"/>
          </s:layout-component>
          <!-- ... -->
  </html>
</s:layout-definition>
```

Those keys will now be found in the StripesResources bundle:

email_22/res/StripesResources.properties

```
layout.welcome=Welcome to Stripes Webmail
```

email_22/res/StripesResources_fr.properties

```
layout.welcome=Bienvenue au WebCourriel Stripes
```

You can also use the StripesResources bundle in this manner for a JSP
that's being used by more than one action bean. By doing this, you
avoid having to duplicate the keys used by that JSP in each action
bean's corresponding .properties file.

Très Bien!

Supporting multiple languages in an application doesn't have to be a
complicated task. Using the Stripes key lookup patterns and resource
bundles (either the defaults or your own), you can make your applications available in multiple languages without a Herculean effort. As
your application grows, you can keep your translated text organized,
whether it's in one or more resource bundles. You can also implement
your own resource bundle strategy—the choice is yours.

Regardless of how we organize your resource bundles, all localized text
is isolated from the rest of the code. We still have one JSP per page,
no matter in how many languages we translate the application. Adding
another language at a later stage is not a problem either—we need only
to add the locale code to the list of supported languages and translate
the resource bundles.

Tim Says...

Localized Text Storage—Isn't That a Pain?

Stripes makes it relatively easy (or at least, I hope less painful) to localize an application and support more than one language. But one area we know is a little weak is supporting different structures for storing all your localized text. Freddy showed an inventive solution—breaking up the resource bundle using a decorator—but it did feel a bit like a hack.

Wouldn't it be nice to be able to store your localized text in a database or in a set of files structured how you choose? Although Stripes 1.5 relies on two ResourceBundles for the entire application, we are looking to change things around for the next version. At that time we hope to "hide" the entire process of finding localized text behind a pluggable component so that other strategies can be plugged in with minimal effort—just like in other parts of Stripes. Most likely such a component will be given access to the action bean, the current locale, and one or more keys in order to provide the localized text.

Until that time, if you want to store localized text in a different way than Stripes wants it, you have two options. The first is to do something like Freddy did and implement your own ResourceBundle to look for text in different places. The second option is to store the text however you like and use your build system to pull it all together into the two resource bundles that Stripes wants.

Part III

In High Gear

Friendships make prosperity more shining and lessens adversity by dividing and sharing it.
▶ Cicero

Chapter 12

Completing the Stack

Stripes is a very "friendly" framework in the sense that it makes the integration of third-party libraries quite simple. In this chapter, we'll look at inviting a few friends to the party: Java Persistence API (JPA), Hibernate, Spring, and JUnit. We'll store the model data of our webmail application in a real database, make it easier to swap DAO implementations by using dependency injection, and write some automated unit tests.

12.1 Persistence with Stripersist, JPA, and Hibernate

So far, we've been using mock DAOs to store the webmail data. This was on purpose so that you could focus on learning core aspects of Stripes without getting distracted by database issues. Now that you've acquired a considerable amount of Stripes knowledge, it's time to complete the stack from the model to the database.

You can make the link between Java model objects and a database in many ways: using plain JDBC, using a library that facilitates the interaction with JDBC but places the responsibility of writing SQL on you, using an Object-Relational Mapping (ORM) framework, and so on. Each solution has its advantages and disadvantages. I can't possibly demonstrate every possibility, and I won't debate the pros and cons of each. Rather, I'll show you an ORM example with JPA and Hibernate.[1] I chose this combination because JPA is Sun's standard persistence specification and because there's a library specifically designed to integrate

---

1. These live at http://java.sun.com/javaee/technologies/persistence.jsp and http://www.hibernate.org.

JPA with Stripes. Now, since JPA is only a specification, you also need an implementation; I chose Hibernate because it's widely used. I don't use anything Hibernate-specific in the sample code, so things should work the same if you decided to replace Hibernate with any other JPA implementation, such as OpenJPA (http://openjpa.apache.org) or JPOX (http://www.jpox.org).

Aaron Porter, Stripes committer, smart developer, and all-around nice guy, wrote a library that facilitates the integration of JPA in Stripes, named Stripersist.[2] Crack your knuckles, we're going to set up a database and use JPA, Hibernate, and Stripersist to implement the persistence of the webmail application model data.

Setting Up a Database

Of course, we'll need a database to get started. Any database that has a JDBC driver will do, such as Postgres (http://www.postgresql.com) and MySQL (http://www.mysql.com). If you're using a commercial database, chances are that they provide a JDBC driver as well.

I use HSQLDB (http://www.hsqldb.org) for the sample application because setting it up is extremely simple. I also like that it comes with a GUI so that you can browse the database and poke around. If you have Ant installed, you can just go to the directory where you unpacked the source code bundle and start the database server using this:

```
ant dbstart
```

Launching the GUI (shown in Figure 12.1, on the facing page) is also very easy:

```
ant dbgui
```

Finally, to shut down the server, use the following:

```
ant dbstop
```

When running the examples that use the database, make sure to start the database server before launching the web application.

Setting Up JPA, Hibernate, and Stripersist

Now that the database is ready, the next step is to set up JPA, Hibernate, and Stripersist. You'll find all the required JAR files in the lib/hibernate and lib/stripersist directories of the sample code bundle.

---

2. Stripersist is part of the Stripes-Stuff project at http://www.stripes-stuff.org.

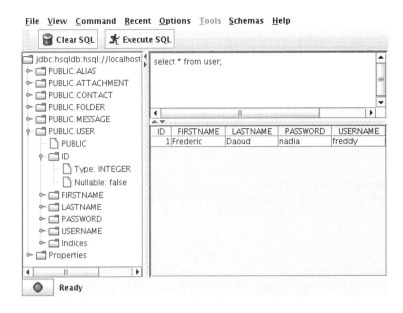

Figure 12.1: THE HSQLDB GUI CLIENT

The Ant build script automatically builds the WAR files with all the required JARs.

The JPA configuration is placed in the WEB-INF/classes/META-INF/persistence.xml file. This is where you tell JPA to use Hibernate and configure Hibernate to use the HSQLDB database:

`email_23/res/META-INF/persistence.xml`

```xml
<persistence xmlns="http://java.sun.com/xml/ns/persistence"
  xmlns:xsi="http://www.w3.org/2001/XMLSchema-instance"
  xsi:schemaLocation="http://java.sun.com/xml/ns/persistence
    http://java.sun.com/xml/ns/persistence/persistence_1_0.xsd"
  version="1.0">
  <persistence-unit name="stripes_webmail">
    <!-- Tell JPA to use Hibernate -->
    <provider>org.hibernate.ejb.HibernatePersistence</provider>

    <!-- Hibernate settings -->
    <properties>
      <!-- Autodetect entity classes -->
      <property name="hibernate.archive.autodetection" value="class"/>

      <!-- Automatically create the SQL schema -->
      <property name="hibernate.hbm2ddl.auto" value="create"/>
```

```
<!-- Tell Hibernate to use HSQLDB -->
<property name="hibernate.dialect"
  value="org.hibernate.dialect.HSQLDialect"/>

<property name="hibernate.connection.driver_class"
  value="org.hsqldb.jdbcDriver"/>

<!-- Configure the JDBC database connection -->
<property name="hibernate.connection.url"
  value="jdbc:hsqldb:hsql://localhost:9001/webmail"/>

<property name="hibernate.connection.username" value="sa"/>
<property name="hibernate.connection.password" value=""/>
<property name="jdbc.batch_size" value="0"/>

<!-- Configure the connection pool -->
<property name="hibernate.c3p0.min_size" value="5"/>
<property name="hibernate.c3p0.max_size" value="20"/>
<property name="hibernate.c3p0.timeout" value="300"/>
<property name="hibernate.c3p0.max_statements" value="50"/>
<property name="hibernate.c3p0.idle_test_period" value="3000"/>
    </properties>
  </persistence-unit>
</persistence>
```

Setting up Stripersist is a one-liner in the web.xml file. Add the Stripersist package to the list of Stripes extension packages:

email_23/web/WEB-INF/web.xml

```
<init-param>
  <param-name>Extension.Packages</param-name>
  <param-value>
    stripesbook.ext,
    org.stripesstuff.stripersist
  </param-value>
</init-param>
```

You're ready to go!

Using JPA Annotations in the Model

Now that the database, JPA, Hibernate, and Stripersist are rearing to work for us, the next step is to tell JPA about our model classes, which we've been gradually adding to the application throughout most of the book. JPA provides several annotations that we add to classes and properties so that JPA can figure out how to do the mapping between the model and database tables.

Let's have a global view of our webmail application's model. As illustrated in Figure 12.2, on the next page, there are users, aliases, contacts, folders, messages, and attachments. We have to let JPA know

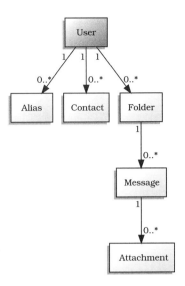

Figure 12.2: THE WEBMAIL APPLICATION MODEL CLASSES

about these model classes. which the JPA calls *entities*. Add the @Entity annotation on each model class:

email_23/src/stripesbook/model/User.java

```
@Entity
public class User extends ModelBase {
```

Entities are managed by JPA and also discovered by Stripersist. We'll see what Stripersist does for us in the next section. Let's finish annotating the model for JPA.

Each model class has a property that uniquely identifies individual objects. The @Id annotation must be added to that property for each entity. Rather than repeat this property in each model class, we can use an abstract base class:

email_23/src/stripesbook/model/ModelBase.java

```
@MappedSuperclass
public abstract class ModelBase {
    @Id
    @GeneratedValue
    private Integer id;
    public Integer getId() { return id; }
    public void setId(Integer id) { this.id = id; }
}
```

ModelBase is not itself an entity. By using @MappedSuperclass, JPA will add its properties to each @Entity subclass. The @Id and @Generated-Value annotations indicate that id is the identifier property and its values should be automatically generated by the database. This is inherited by each of our model classes because they all extend ModelBase.

Look again at Figure 12.2, on the preceding page. We've identified the entities, and now we need to establish the relationships between them. If we work our way from the top to the bottom of the diagram, all entities have zero or more of the entity below: a user has zero or more folders, a folder has zero or more messages, and so on. JPA refers to these types of relationships as *one-to-many* if you're reading the diagram from top to bottom or *many-to-one* if you're going from bottom to top.

JPA provides the @OneToMany and @ManyToOne annotations to describe these relationships. The User class has a @OneToMany relationship with the Contact class, and the Contact class has a @ManyToOne relationship with the User class. We indicate these relationships by adding the annotations to the properties:

email_23/src/stripesbook/model/User.java

```
@Entity
public class User extends ModelBase {
    @OneToMany(mappedBy="user")
    private Set<Contact> contacts;

    /* Getters and setters... */
}
```

Notice that the mappedBy= attribute of @OneToMany corresponds to the name of the property in the Contact class that refers to the User:

email_23/src/stripesbook/model/Contact.java

```
@Entity
public class Contact extends ModelBase {
    @ManyToOne
    private User user;

    /* Getters and setters... */
}
```

We've identified the other side of the relationship with @ManyToOne on the user property of the Contact class. After doing the same for the other relationships between entities, we're done with adding JPA annotations to the model.

When the application starts, Hibernate generates and executes SQL commands to create the database schema. The tables automatically contain columns that correspond to the properties of the entity classes as well as extra columns to manage the one-to-many/many-to-one relationships. The data is moved between the database and the model classes, in both directions, without requiring us to write a single line of SQL. And that's not all—Stripersist allows us to use our entity classes directly, taking care of reading objects from the database for us. Let's talk about that in more detail.

Stripersist Type Conversion and Formatting

Stripersist registers entity classes and does type conversion for them on the fly. The type converter finds the @Id property on each @Entity class (or @MappedSuperclass) and uses it to convert a String to an entity class by loading the corresponding object from the database. Stripersist also creates formatters that do the opposite, which is to produce a String from the model object's @Id.

We discussed writing type converters to load model objects from ID parameters back in Section 5.4, *Using a Type Converter and Formatter to Load Model Objects*, on page 106. With Stripersist, we don't need to do this ourselves; Stripersist's type converter does it automatically. Here's how it works. Say we have a Contact class with an @Id property of type ID. Refer to Figure 12.3, on the following page:

1. A request comes in with a someContact=5 parameter to be bound to an action bean's someContact property of type Contact. Since Contact has the @Entity annotation, Stripersist's TypeConverter<Entity> is invoked.

2. The type converter finds the @Id property on the Contact class and determines its type, ID.

3. Stripersist asks Stripes for a type converter for ID and calls its convert() method with the String parameter "5".

4. The type converter returns the converted id value of type ID. This works automatically if Stripes has a built-in type converter for the ID type; otherwise, we need to provide our own.

5. The type converter then calls the JPA EntityManager's find() method with the converted id object.

6. The EntityManager loads the Contact object from the database and returns it.

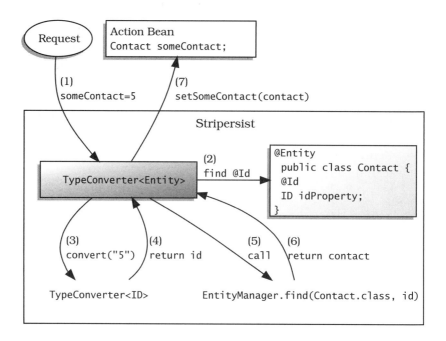

Figure 12.3: THE STRIPERSIST ENTITY TYPE CONVERTER

7. Finally, Stripersist's type converter returns the Contact object, which is set on the someContact property of the action bean.

All this work that Stripersist does means we can use entity classes directly. For example, remember how the contact form allowed the user to update an existing contact. We needed a hidden field in the form to identify the contact; now, we don't need to manually write a type converter or a formatter to support that. We can just use a Contact property on the action bean directly in the <s:hidden> tag:

email_23/web/WEB-INF/jsp/contact_form.jsp

```
<div><s:hidden name="contact"/></div>
```

This produces a parameter with the value of the @Id property of the Contact object that is being updated. When the user submits the form, that value will be converted to a Contact object. Voilà! You can now use ID parameters for all entities: User, Folder, Message, and so on.

Using Stripersist and JPA in the DAOs

We've gotten pretty far already. We now need to write the code that creates, updates, and deletes model objects, as well as reads them by something else than their @Id. The DAOs are the perfect place for this code. Remember our generic DAO interface:

```
email_23/src/stripesbook/dao/Dao.java
```

```java
package stripesbook.dao;
public interface Dao<T,ID extends Serializable> {
    public List<T> read();
    public T read(ID id);
    public void save(T t);
    public void delete(T t);
    public void commit();
}
```

The mock DAOs that we were previously using just assumed an ID property of type Integer. Now that we're using the @Id annotation to indicate the ID property, we have to be a little more flexible. That's why the Dao interface is generic not only for the model type T but also the type of the ID property, ID. JPA requires @Id property types to be Serializable, which is why the Dao imposes this restriction.

The DAO interface also includes a commit() method so that transactions can be committed. More about this very shortly. Because the methods in the Dao interface are common to all model objects, it makes sense to write an abstract base class that provides a generic implementation for any type. Each specific DAO extends this base class and needs to provide only what is specific to the corresponding model class.

Let's create the BaseDaoImpl class and use a little bit of Java generics magic to detect the model class that the DAO is dealing with:

```
email_23/src/stripesbook/dao/impl/stripersist/BaseDaoImpl.java
```

```java
package stripesbook.dao.impl.stripersist;
public abstract class BaseDaoImpl<T,ID extends Serializable>
    implements Dao<T,ID>
{
    private Class<T> entityClass;

    @SuppressWarnings("unchecked")
    public BaseDaoImpl() {
        entityClass = (Class<T>)
            ((ParameterizedType) getClass().getGenericSuperclass())
            .getActualTypeArguments()[0];
    }
    /* methods... */
}
```

When a concrete DAO subclass is instantiated, entityClass will contain the specific model class. This is very handy to write the rest of the BaseDaoImpl code in a generic fashion. For example, here's how we implement the read methods:

`email_23/src/stripesbook/dao/impl/stripersist/BaseDaoImpl.java`

```
@SuppressWarnings("unchecked")
public List<T> read() {
    return Stripersist.getEntityManager()
        .createQuery("from " + entityClass.getName())
        .getResultList();
}
public T read(ID id) {
    return Stripersist.getEntityManager().find(entityClass, id);
}
```

There are a few things going on here. First, Stripersist.getEntityManager() returns an implementation of the JPA's EntityManager interface that we can use to work with the database. JPA requires you to create an Entity-ManagerFactory (normally at application startup), use it to create an EntityManager, close() the EntityManager when you're done with it, and close() the EntityManagerFactory when the application shuts down. Stripersist takes care of all that housekeeping for you!

Next, the entity's class name is dynamically added to the query passed to createQuery() in order to retrieve the list of objects for that entity. Finally, EntityManager provides a method to retrieve an entity object by its ID, which is used in the read(ID) method.

Note that we called Stripersist.getEntityManager() with no parameters. This works because we defined only one *persistence unit* in the persistence.xml file:

```
<persistence-unit name="stripes_webmail">
  ...
</persistence-unit>
```

With more than one persistence unit, we would pass the name of the persistence unit as a parameter, as in Stripersist.getEntityManager("stripes_webmail").

At this point, we're only reading objects. We also need to create, update, and delete objects. Unlike reading, these operations involve changing the database. You are no doubt familiar with database *transactions*; in a nutshell, a transaction is a way to group one or more operations for which it is important that either *all* or *none* of the operations go through to the database. The typical example is a bank transaction that involves transferring money from one account to another. Two operations are involved: withdrawing from one account and depositing to the other account. These must both go through or both be canceled. Otherwise, what happens if the withdrawal works but the deposit fails? The account holder loses the money.

To prevent that from happening, the transaction *begins*, the withdrawal and deposit operations are carried out, and only if all goes well is the transaction *committed* to the database. If something goes wrong during the operations, the transaction is *rolled back*, and the database is left unchanged.

With JPA, you are responsible for beginning, committing, and rolling back transactions. But hold on—Stripersist already does two out three of those for you. Every time you call Stripersist.getEntityManager(), Stripersist begins the transaction (unless it's already active). At the very end of each request, Stripersist automatically rolls back the transaction if it wasn't committed. So, all you really need to do is to commit transactions after modifying the database and make sure to use a RedirectResolution, as we discussed Section 3.7, *The Redirect-After-Side-Effect Pattern*, on page 56.

We're now ready to implement the save() and delete() methods in the base DAO:

`email_23/src/stripesbook/dao/impl/stripersist/BaseDaoImpl.java`

```
@SuppressWarnings("unchecked")
public void save(T object) {
    Stripersist.getEntityManager().persist(object);
}
public void delete(T object) {
    Stripersist.getEntityManager().remove(object);
}
public void commit() {
    Stripersist.getEntityManager().getTransaction().commit();
}
```

Wow, after all that theory, there's not much to the code, is there? In both methods, Stripersist.getEntityManager() implicitly begins a transaction. We either save or delete the model object (which JPA calls persist() and remove()), and the client code is responsible for committing the transaction with a call to commit() on the Dao interface. Done and done!

Our base DAO now fully implements the generic DAO interface. Before moving on to the specific DAOs, let's add a couple of convenience methods to the base for finding objects that match a given field.

```java
@SuppressWarnings("unchecked")
public T findBy(String fieldName, Object value) {
    Query query = Stripersist.getEntityManager()
        .createQuery(getQuery(fieldName, null))
        .setParameter(fieldName, value);
    return getSingleResult(query);
}
@SuppressWarnings("unchecked")
public T findBy(String fieldName, Object value, User user) {
    Query query = Stripersist.getEntityManager()
        .createQuery(getQuery(fieldName, user))
        .setParameter(fieldName, value)
        .setParameter("user", user);
    return getSingleResult(query);
}
private String getQuery(String fieldName, User user){
    String query =
        "from " + entityClass.getName() + " t " +
        "where t." + fieldName + " = :" + fieldName;
    if (user == null) {
        return query;
    }
    return query + " and t.user = :user";
}
@SuppressWarnings("unchecked")
private T getSingleResult(Query query) {
    try {
        return (T) query.getSingleResult();
    }
    catch (NonUniqueResultException exc) {
        return (T) query.getResultList().get(0);
    }
    catch (NoResultException exc) {
        return null;
    }
}
}
```

These two findBy() methods find an object according to a specified field. Unlike the first method, the second method constrains the search to a specific user. Both methods use a query constructed with the JPA query syntax, which looks similar to SQL but supports, among other things, *named* parameters that start with a colon (:).

With this code in the base DAO, it's now very easy to implement the subclasses by extending the base and implementing the methods defined in each specific DAO interface. For example, remember that the ContactDao interface added the findByEmail() method.

> ## More About JPA
>
> Going into a more in-depth discussion about JPA annotations, the JPA query language, and other JPA classes is—wait for it—outside the scope of this book. See Part V of *The Java EE 5 Tutorial* (JBC+06) for detailed explanations about everything related to using JPA.

`email_23/src/stripesbook/dao/ContactDao.java`

```java
package stripesbook.dao;
public interface ContactDao extends Dao<Contact,Integer> {
    public Contact findByEmail(String email, User user);
}
```

The implementation is trivial:

`email_23/src/stripesbook/dao/impl/stripersist/ContactDaoImpl.java`

```java
package stripesbook.dao.impl.stripersist;
public class ContactDaoImpl extends BaseDaoImpl<Contact,Integer>
    implements ContactDao
{
    public Contact findByEmail(String email, User user) {
        return findBy("email", email, user);
    }
}
```

Our DAOs can now use Stripersist and JPA very easily, and the rest of the application can use the DAOs as before without being exposed to the details of the persistence layer.

Using the DAOs

We can now use the DAOs in the action beans. The BaseActionBean is a convenient place to create instances that all action beans can use:

`email_23/src/stripesbook/action/BaseActionBean.java`

```java
public abstract class BaseActionBean implements ActionBean {
    protected AttachmentDao attachmentDao = new AttachmentDaoImpl();
    protected ContactDao contactDao = new ContactDaoImpl();
    protected FolderDao folderDao = new FolderDaoImpl();
    protected MessageDao messageDao = new MessageDaoImpl();
    protected UserDao userDao = new UserDaoImpl();
}
```

Since everything revolves around the user, it's also convenient to have a getUser() method in BaseActionBean that returns the current user:

email_23/src/stripesbook/action/BaseActionBean.java
```java
protected User getUser() {
    return getContext().getUser();
}
```

Since the session is used to remember the current user, the method delegates to the action bean context, MyActionBeanContext, which stores the user ID in the session and retrieves the User object with help from the UserDao:

email_23/src/stripesbook/ext/MyActionBeanContext.java
```java
private UserDao userDao = new UserDaoImpl();
public void setUser(User user) {
    setCurrent(USER, user.getId());
}
public User getUser() {
    Integer userId = getCurrent(USER, null);
    return userDao.read(userId);
}
```

Action beans now have easy access to the current user as well as all the DAOs. For example, here's how the ContactFormActionBean saves a contact:

email_23/src/stripesbook/action/ContactFormActionBean.java
```java
public Resolution save() {
    Contact contact = getContact();
    contact.setUser(getUser());
    contactDao.save(contact);
    contactDao.commit();
    getContext().getMessages().add(
        getLocalizableMessage("contactSaved", contact)
    );
    return new RedirectResolution(ContactListActionBean.class);
}
```

Notice the call to commit() after saving the contact. Commits are done in action beans (or wherever the DAOs are used), not in the DAOs themselves, so that multiple objects can be created, updated, or deleted within a single transaction.

The webmail application is now using a real database. Our model has a few annotations, our DAOs are simple, and we're not tied to any specific JPA implementation. Life is good.

Stripersist and Security

Stripersist is very powerful but also very dangerous if you're not careful. Users should not be allowed to arbitrarily send values to the properties of objects that are connected to the JPA Entity-Manager, because a call to commit() saves *all* modifications to associated objects.

Fortunately, you can avoid trouble by restricting which properties are allowed to be bound, as we'll discuss in Section 14.1, *Controlling Parameter Binding*, on page 301.

The StripersistInit Interface

Stripersist provides one more feature: the StripersistInit interface, which is handy when you want to use Stripersist for code that needs to run at application startup. By implementing that interface and the init() and by placing your class in an extension package, your code will automatically be executed after Stripersist has finished loading. We'll talk about StripersistInit in more detail when we use it in Section 14.6, *Using Roles*, on page 315.

"But I *Want* to Use Native Hibernate/OpenJPA/JPOX/Etc.!"

Although working with JPA means your code is independent of the underlying implementation, you might be ready to concede that genericity in exchange for using the extras that your implementation provides beyond JPA.

For example, Hibernate has a query-by-criteria API that can sometimes be nicer to work with than constructing String queries. To use criteria, you need to obtain a Hibernate Session. The JPA's EntityManager interface provides the getDelegate() method specifically for that purpose: to obtain the underlying implementation. In theBaseDaoImpl class, you can add a method to obtain the Hibernate Session:

```
email_24/src/stripesbook/dao/impl/stripersist/BaseDaoImpl.java
protected Session getSession() {
    return (Session) Stripersist.getEntityManager().getDelegate();
}
```

From the Session, you can do whatever you want with Hibernate's native API, including queries by criteria. For example, you can simplify the findBy() methods:[3]

email_24/src/stripesbook/dao/impl/stripersist/BaseDaoImpl.java

```java
package stripesbook.dao.impl.stripersist;
import static org.hibernate.criterion.Restrictions.*;
public abstract class BaseDaoImpl<T,ID extends Serializable>
    implements Dao<T,ID>
{
    /* other methods... */

    @SuppressWarnings("unchecked")
    public T findBy(String fieldName, Object value) {
        Criteria criteria = getSession().createCriteria(entityClass)
            .add(eq(fieldName, value));
        return getSingleResult(criteria);
    }
    @SuppressWarnings("unchecked")
    public T findBy(String fieldName, Object value, User user) {
        Criteria criteria = getSession().createCriteria(entityClass)
            .add(and(
                eq(fieldName, value),
                eq("user", user)
            ));
        return getSingleResult(criteria);
    }
    @SuppressWarnings("unchecked")
    private T getSingleResult(Criteria criteria) {
        try {
            return (T) criteria.uniqueResult();
        }
        catch (HibernateException exc) {
            return (T) criteria.list().get(0);
        }
    }
}
```

It's nice to know that you can work with your JPA implementation's native classes if you're more comfortable using them. Stripersist will continue to work as before, but make sure you still use JPA annotations on your model classes so that Stripersist finds them.

---

3. Notice the static import of Restrictions.*, which makes it possible to write code such as and(eq(...), eq(...)). Of course, you could also choose not to use static imports and write Restrictions.and(Restrictions.eq(...), Restrictions.eq(...)) instead.

Other Resources

Stripersist makes it easy to use a JPA implementation. If JPA is altogether not for you, using another solution to communicate data between your Java model and a database—be it iBATIS (http://www.ibatis.org), Cayenne (http://cayenne.apache.org), or even plain JDBC—wouldn't be difficult with Stripes. Using a DAO layer is all about hiding the implementation details from the client code. You would write your DAOs to use iBATIS, and Stripes would call the DAOs without being affected by what framework is used to do the work. The only difference is that you wouldn't benefit from the transaction support, type conversion, and formatting that Stripersist provides; you'd have to implement that yourself.

12.2 Dependency Injection with Spring

When you have a class that depends on the services of another class, such as an action bean needing a DAO, you can just create an instance of the dependency with the **new** operator. This approach is simple and easy to follow; you see which class is being used to satisfy the dependency directly in the code. We've been doing this so far. For example, BaseActionBean contains the implementations of the DAOs:

```
email_23/src/stripesbook/action/BaseActionBean.java
```

```java
public abstract class BaseActionBean implements ActionBean {
    protected AttachmentDao attachmentDao = new AttachmentDaoImpl();
    protected ContactDao contactDao = new ContactDaoImpl();
    protected FolderDao folderDao = new FolderDaoImpl();
    protected MessageDao messageDao = new MessageDaoImpl();
    protected UserDao userDao = new UserDaoImpl();
}
```

Although this approach is simple and straightforward, it is also limited. We're using DAO interfaces so that we can easily swap implementations without affecting the calling code. But using a different implementation means hunting down the places where we're creating new instances, replacing them with the alternative implementation and recompiling. What we gain in simplicity, we lose in flexibility (which is how these things often go).

Dependency injection is the concept of providing, *from the outside*, implementations to classes that need them. This way, classes have references only to interfaces, and not to any specific implementation. Using this technique, BaseActionBean would have references only to

AttachmentDao, ContactDao, and so on. You would then configure which implementations you'd like to use in a dependency injection framework. The framework takes care of "wiring up" classes and their dependencies for you. It becomes much easier to use different implementations, because you need to change only the configuration. Moreover, you can use different configurations for different situations, making testing much easier, as we'll see in the next section. All of this leaves your code much more flexible because you have only references to interfaces. The trade-off is more complexity; you no longer see which implementations are being used when you're reading the code. You have to look at the configuration of the dependency injection framework to figure it out.

We'll look at the support that Stripes provides for dependency injection (DI) with Spring (http://www.springframework.org). Guice (http://code. google.com/p/google-guice) is another popular choice; since Stripes does not have built-in support for Guice, we'll take the opportunity to implement it ourselves as an exercise in Section 13.4, *Interceptor Example: Adding Support for Guice*, on page 293.

Setting Up Spring

Because Spring provides many other services besides dependency injection, the distribution comes with several JAR files so that you can use only what you need. In our case, we need spring-core.jar, spring-beans.jar, spring-context.jar, and spring-web.jar to use the DI container and the web application context loader. You can also take the easy way out and just use the spring.jar file, which includes everything.

Next, set up the Spring context loader listener in web.xml:

email_25/web/WEB-INF/web.xml

```
<listener>
  <listener-class>
    org.springframework.web.context.ContextLoaderListener
  </listener-class>
</listener>
```

Spring's ContextLoaderListener automatically loads the default Spring configuration file, WEB-INF/applicationContext.xml,[4] when the web application starts up.

---

4. You can also use different configuration files by indicating them in the contextConfigLocation context parameter.

Here's how we set up this file to get Spring to load components into its container from our stripesbook.dao.impl.stripersist package:

```
email_25/web/WEB-INF/applicationContext.xml
<?xml version="1.0" encoding="UTF-8"?>
<beans xmlns="http://www.springframework.org/schema/beans"
 xmlns:xsi="http://www.w3.org/2001/XMLSchema-instance"
 xmlns:context="http://www.springframework.org/schema/context"
 xsi:schemaLocation="http://www.springframework.org/schema/beans
 http://www.springframework.org/schema/beans/spring-beans-2.5.xsd
 http://www.springframework.org/schema/context
 http://www.springframework.org/schema/context/spring-context-2.5.xsd">

  <context:component-scan
    base-package="stripesbook.dao.impl.stripersist"/>

</beans>
```

Boy, that's a lot of cruft in the XML header, isn't it? Oh, well. Looking past that, we see a single element where we're telling Spring to scan a package and look for components. Now, we need give Spring a clue about these components, which are our DAO implementations. Spring provides four annotations to do this. @Component indicates a component in general, while @Repository, @Service, and @Controller more precisely specify a persistence-, service-, or presentation-layer component. @Repository is what we want since the DAOs are in the persistence layer, so we use that annotation in the DAO implementation classes:

```
email_25/src/stripesbook/dao/impl/stripersist/ContactDaoImpl.java
@Repository("contactDao")
public class ContactDaoImpl extends BaseDaoImpl<Contact,Integer>
    implements ContactDao
```

We're telling Spring that ContactDaoImpl is a persistence-layer component named contactDao. We'll do the same for the other DAOs:

```
email_25/src/stripesbook/dao/impl/stripersist/AttachmentDaoImpl.java
@Repository("attachmentDao")
public class AttachmentDaoImpl extends BaseDaoImpl<Attachment,Integer>
    implements AttachmentDao
```

```
email_25/src/stripesbook/dao/impl/stripersist/FolderDaoImpl.java
@Repository("folderDao")
public class FolderDaoImpl extends BaseDaoImpl<Folder,Integer>
    implements FolderDao
```

```
email_25/src/stripesbook/dao/impl/stripersist/MessageDaoImpl.java
```

```java
@Repository("messageDao")
public class MessageDaoImpl extends BaseDaoImpl<Message,Integer>
    implements MessageDao
```

```
email_25/src/stripesbook/dao/impl/stripersist/UserDaoImpl.java
```

```java
@Repository("userDao")
public class UserDaoImpl extends BaseDaoImpl<User,Integer>
    implements UserDao
{
```

Finally, we must configure Stripes to use its Spring interceptor[5] by adding net.sourceforge.stripes.integration.spring to the list of extension packages:

```
email_25/web/WEB-INF/web.xml
```

```xml
<init-param>
  <param-name>Extension.Packages</param-name>
  <param-value>
    stripesbook.ext,
    org.stripesstuff.stripersist,
    net.sourceforge.stripes.integration.spring
  </param-value>
</init-param>
```

We're now ready to use our Spring-managed DAOs.

Injecting the DAOs in the Action Beans

Remember that we previously had direct references to the implementations of the DAOs in BaseActionBean. We can now get Stripes to inject the dependencies by retrieving them from the components loaded by Spring. We need only to add the @SpringBean annotation:

```
email_25/src/stripesbook/action/BaseActionBean.java
```

```java
public abstract class BaseActionBean implements ActionBean {
    @SpringBean protected AttachmentDao attachmentDao;
    @SpringBean protected ContactDao contactDao;
    @SpringBean protected FolderDao folderDao;
    @SpringBean protected MessageDao messageDao;
    @SpringBean protected UserDao userDao;
}
```

An empty @SpringBean annotation uses a naming convention. Stripes looks for the Spring-managed component with the same name as the

---

5. Don't worry about what an *interceptor* is for now. We'll discuss that topic in Section 13.3, *Everything Is Possible: Interceptors*, on page 288.

property: attachmentDao, contactDao, folderDao, messageDao, and user-Dao. These match the names that we used in the @Repository annotations. We can also specify the name in the @SpringBean annotation:

```
@SpringBean("myContactDao")
protected ContactDao contactDao;
```

In this case, Stripes uses the name myContactDao instead of the name of the property. Again, the name must match the name that we use in the @Repository annotation of the corresponding component so that Stripes can find it, so we'd have to use myContactDao there as well.

Now, BaseActionBean is coded only against the DAO interfaces. Spring takes care of loading the implementations, and Stripes sets them on the action bean. If you want to use a different set of implementations, all you have to do is change the package in applicationContext.xml. You don't have to change BaseActionBean or recompile any code. In Section 12.3, *Testing with Spring and Injected Mock Objects*, on page 266, we'll see how we can use this flexibility to load the "real" set of DAO implementations when running the application and use a set of mocks when executing automated tests.

Injecting Dependencies in Other Stripes Objects

@SpringBean indicates where to inject a Spring-managed dependency. Stripes does this automatically for action beans, but not for other Stripes objects such as the action bean context, type converters, formatters, and so on. In the webmail application, we need DAOs in MyActionBeanContext:

email_23/src/stripesbook/ext/MyActionBeanContext.java

```
public class MyActionBeanContext extends ActionBeanContext {
    private FolderDao folderDao = new FolderDaoImpl();
    private UserDao userDao = new UserDaoImpl();
}
```

How do we inject Spring-managed dependencies in there? I could tell you that we can just refactor MyActionBeanContext so that it doesn't depend on any DAOs. That would involve moving code between MyActionBeanContext and BaseActionBean and modifying a few JSPs that currently obtain information from MyActionBeanContext. Sure, that would work, but I'd be punting on the issue, wouldn't I? No, let's face the problem and see how we can use DI on MyActionBeanContext.

We already know that a custom action bean context is a Stripes extension. The module that Stripes uses to *create* instances of the action bean context is also a Stripes extension, called the action bean context factory. We can easily extend the Stripes default implementation, obtain the action bean context object that it creates, and inject dependencies before returning it. Stripes provides a convenient SpringHelper.injectBeans() method to detect @SpringBean annotations and then inject dependencies:

email_25/src/stripesbook/ext/MyActionBeanContextFactory.java

```java
package stripesbook.ext;
public class MyActionBeanContextFactory
    extends DefaultActionBeanContextFactory
{
    @Override
    public ActionBeanContext getContextInstance(
        HttpServletRequest req, HttpServletResponse resp)
        throws ServletException
    {
        ActionBeanContext actionBeanContext
            = super.getContextInstance(req, resp);

        ServletContext servletContext =
            StripesFilter.getConfiguration().getServletContext();

        SpringHelper.injectBeans(actionBeanContext, servletContext);

        return actionBeanContext;
    }
}
```

@SpringBean now works in MyActionBeanContext:

email_25/src/stripesbook/ext/MyActionBeanContext.java

```java
public class MyActionBeanContext extends ActionBeanContext {
    @SpringBean private FolderDao folderDao;
    @SpringBean private UserDao userDao;
}
```

We can also use this technique to inject Spring dependencies into other non-action-bean Stripes objects—type converters, formatters, and so on. Subclass the Stripes default factory, call the superclass method to create the object, and use SpringHelper.injectBeans() on the object before returning it. Besides a ServletContext object, injectBeans() also accepts an ActionBeanContext or a Spring ApplicationContext to be able to load the components from Spring.

Other Resources

@SpringBean works to inject dependencies by annotating either a property or a setter method. This type of dependency injection is called *setter-based*, because the object is first created with a zero-parameter constructor, and then dependencies are injected on its properties. *Constructor-based* DI, on the other hand, injects dependencies via parameters of the class's constructor.

Stripes supports only setter-based injection because action beans are created with a zero-parameter constructor. Stripes-Spring, available at http://www.silvermindsoftware.com/stripes, is a Stripes plug-in that adds support for constructor-based dependency injection on action beans. Constructor-based DI has the following advantages:

- It makes a class's dependencies more obvious because they are all in the constructor, rather than scattered in properties or setter methods.

- Once the dependencies have been injected via the constructor, they can be made immutable by not providing a setter method.

Check out the Stripes-Spring project if you'd like to use constructor-based DI on action beans.

12.3 Automated Testing with Mock Objects

Have you ever felt uneasy at the thought of making a change to your code because you were worried about the impact on the rest of the application? Felt weary of having to retest everything? Felt unsettled because you might have missed something? Writing automated tests can help you feel more confident about changing, refactoring, and improving your code.[6]

Stripes comes with a set of mock objects that allow you to write automated tests for the action beans of your web applications. These mocks simulate most of what happens in a servlet container so that you can easily exercise the different functionalities that revolve around action beans, including the following:

- Submitting a form and verifying the results

---

6. The benefits and methodology of *test-driven development* are thoroughly discussed in Kent Beck's *Test Driven Development: By Example* [Bec02].

- Checking the presence or absence of validation errors
- Confirming that type conversion is working properly
- Verifying which URL is being returned
- Testing URL binding

We'll start with a testing framework, JUnit, available at http://www.junit. org. You can run JUnit in a variety of ways: with Ant, with your IDE, or as a stand-alone program. You'll find that the book's source code bundle is set up to run the tests with Ant. No matter how you run the tests, the code remains the same.

For example, the following is a "Hello, World!" test: annotating a method with @Test tells JUnit to run it as a test, and the Assert class contains methods to test for many different kinds of conditions.[7]

email_26/src/stripesbook/test/basic/HelloWorldTest.java

```java
package stripesbook.test.basic;
import org.junit.Test;
import static org.junit.Assert.*;
public class HelloWorldTest {
    @Test
    public void testHello() {
        String expected = "HELLO";
        String result = "hello".toUpperCase();
        assertEquals(expected, result);
    }
}
```

With that minimal introduction to JUnit, we're now ready to write some Stripes test code.

Testing with Stripes Mocks

Stripes provides a rich set of classes that mock the different parts of the Servlet API (HTTP request, response, and so on). Although we can use each part individually, most of the time it's easier to use the higher-level MockRoundtrip object and let it take care of managing the request, response, and other underlying parts. Using MockRoundtrip involves three steps:

1. Set up a MockServletContext object with parameters much like the ones in the web.xml file. We need to do this only once for all the tests that run within the same context.

---

7. I'll be using only basic JUnit code here. See Thomas and Hunt's *Pragmatic Unit Testing in Java with JUnit* [HT03] for more advanced JUnit techniques.

> ### ☺ Joe Asks...
> #### What If I Prefer TestNG?
>
> I'm using JUnit for the automated testing examples, but this is just an arbitrary choice. TestNG is also popular (in fact, it is used to test Stripes itself). If you prefer TestNG (or any other testing framework, for that matter), you can use it instead of JUnit simply by replacing the libraries and adapting the test code. The Stripes mock objects have no dependencies on any particular testing framework. In fact, they are not even tied to Stripes; you could technically use them to test independent servlet container artifacts, such as external filters and servlets.

2. If our tests require the use of a session, create a MockHttpSession object.

3. Use a MockRoundtrip object to simulate a request (link with or without parameters, form submission, . . .) to an action bean, and verify the results. If we created a MockHttpSession object, attach it to MockRoundtrip.

Let's write a couple of automated tests for the contact form as an example. We begin with a method marked as @BeforeClass so that JUnit will run it only *once*, before running all the @Test methods.

email_26/src/stripesbook/test/stripesmock/ContactFormActionBeanTest.java

```java
package stripesbook.test.stripesmock;
public class ContactFormActionBeanTest {
    private static MockServletContext mockServletContext;
    private static MockHttpSession mockSession;

    @BeforeClass
    public static void setup() throws Exception {
        mockServletContext = new MockServletContext("webmail");

        Map<String,String> params = new HashMap<String,String>();
        params.put("ActionResolver.Packages", "stripesbook.action");
        params.put("Extension.Packages", "stripesbook.ext,"
            + "org.stripesstuff.stripersist");
        mockServletContext.addFilter(StripesFilter.class,
            "StripesFilter", params);

        mockServletContext.setServlet(DispatcherServlet.class,
            "DispatcherServlet", null);

        mockSession = new MockHttpSession(mockServletContext);
    }
```

The MockServletContext accepts one or more filters, but only *one* servlet at a time. Starting at ❶, we've added the Stripes filter with its parameters and the dispatcher servlet. We do not have to set up any mappings because all requests go through all filters and the servlet of a MockServletContext.

Stripes also provides a mock object to simulate the session, MockHttpSession, but it is not used unless you create an instance. This is done at ❷.

Next, we need a user to be logged in for the tests to run properly. This involves creating a mock user, courtesy of MockDataLoaderActionBean (a convenience action bean that loads mock data for testing purposes), and logging in with LoginActionBean:

`email_26/src/stripesbook/test/stripesmock/ContactFormActionBeanTest.java`

```
// Load mock user
MockRoundtrip trip = new MockRoundtrip(mockServletContext,
    MockDataLoaderActionBean.class, mockSession);
trip.execute();

// Login mock user
trip = new MockRoundtrip(mockServletContext,
    LoginActionBean.class, mockSession);
trip.setParameter("username", "freddy");
trip.setParameter("password", "nadia");
trip.execute("login");
```

As we can see, using the MockRoundtrip class is pretty simple. Indicate the action bean to which we want to submit the request, attach a session if needed, set the parameters we want to send, and call execute().

Every test that we add will now benefit from this setup. Let's write a test and learn more about MockRoundtrip.

Let's say we want to test the submission of a blank contact form. Since the email field is required, this should result in a validation error. Here is the test method:

`email_26/src/stripesbook/test/stripesmock/ContactFormActionBeanTest.java`

```
@Test
public void testEmailRequired() throws Exception {
    MockRoundtrip trip = new MockRoundtrip(mockServletContext,
        ContactFormActionBean.class, mockSession);

    trip.execute("save");

    ContactFormActionBean bean =
        trip.getActionBean(ContactFormActionBean.class);
```

```
    assertEquals(1,
        bean.getContext().getValidationErrors().size());

    assertEquals(MockRoundtrip.DEFAULT_SOURCE_PAGE,
        trip.getDestination());
}
```

Notice that to invoke an event handler, we just need to add its name as a parameter. After calling execute() on MockRoundtrip, we can retrieve the action bean and verify whatever we need to—in this case, the number of validation errors. MockRoundtrip also returns the destination, which is the source page in this case because a validation error occurred.

Testing a valid contact form (that is, with the email field filled in) is similar. In this case, we test for the destination to be back to the contact list. While we're at it, we'll also verify that type conversion for the phone number is working properly:

email_26/src/stripesbook/test/stripesmock/ContactFormActionBeanTest.java

```
@Test
public void testSaveValid() throws Exception {
    MockRoundtrip trip = new MockRoundtrip(mockServletContext,
        ContactFormActionBean.class, mockSession);

    trip.setParameter("contact.email", "test@test.com");
    trip.setParameter("contact.phoneNumber", "654-456-4567");
    trip.execute("save");

    ContactFormActionBean bean =
        trip.getActionBean(ContactFormActionBean.class);

    assertEquals(0,
        bean.getContext().getValidationErrors().size());

    PhoneNumber pn = bean.getContact().getPhoneNumber();
    assertEquals("654", pn.getAreaCode());
    assertEquals("456", pn.getPrefix());
    assertEquals("4567", pn.getSuffix());

    assertTrue(
        trip.getDestination().startsWith("/ContactList.action"));
}
```

We're checking the destination URL; conveniently, getDestination() returns the URL regardless of it being a forward or a redirect. We can also use getForwardUrl() or getRedirectUrl() to not only test the destination but also specifically verify which type of response was returned.

Finally, we can also use URLs instead of action beans to test requests with MockRoundtrip. Simply specify the URL in the constructor, as in new MockRoundtrip(mockServletContext, "/ContactForm.action").

Testing with Spring and Injected Mock Objects

The tests that we've written so far involve the complete application, including Stripersist, JPA, Hibernate, and the HSQLDB database. It's good to be able to test everything, but it also makes our tests depend on the complete chain being up and running. It'd be nice to be able to test certain things even if, say, the database isn't available.

We were previously using a set of mock DAOs to simulate a database. We can bring those back and use them so that tests become independent of the database and the persistence layer. Doing this is easy with the Spring dependency injection version of the application that we created in Section 12.2, *Dependency Injection with Spring*, on page 255. First, we reconfigure the extension packages in the Stripes filter, removing Stripersist and adding the Stripes interceptor for Spring DI:

email_27/src/stripesbook/test/stripesmock/ContactFormActionBeanTest.java

```
params.put("Extension.Packages", "stripesbook.ext,"
    + "net.sourceforge.stripes.integration.spring");
```

Next, we create a separate Spring configuration file, applicationContext-test.xml, for which we use the mock DAO package:

email_27/web/WEB-INF/applicationContext-test.xml

```
<beans xmlns="http://www.springframework.org/schema/beans"
  ...>
  <context:component-scan base-package="stripesbook.dao.mock"/>
</beans>
```

By telling Spring to use applicationContext-test.xml instead of the default applicationContext.xml, Spring will load the mock DAOs instead of their Stripersist counterparts. Configuring a different Spring configuration file is done with the contextConfigLocation context parameter:

email_27/src/stripesbook/test/stripesmock/ContactFormActionBeanTest.java

```
mockServletContext.addInitParameter("contextConfigLocation",
    "/WEB-INF/applicationContext-test.xml");

ContextLoaderListener springContextLoader =
    new ContextLoaderListener();
springContextLoader.contextInitialized(
    new ServletContextEvent(mockServletContext));
```

Notice that after adding the context parameter, we added the Spring context loader listener as well, just like we had to do in the web.xml file.

The tests we wrote previously can be run without any change. The difference is that this version allows the tests to execute independently of the database and the persistence layer. What's more, we left the original applicationContext.xml and web.xml unchanged. We have a neat separation between the application code and the test code.

Out-of-Container Testing with Mockito

Getting our tests to be executable without depending on the database or the persistence layer is nice, as is using the Stripes mock objects because we can test action bean features. However, you might like some of your tests to be even more "stand-alone," meaning that you can test a class in isolation without having to set up the Stripes mock objects.

For example, consider testing the phone number type converter by itself. We can write tests for the convert() method without any dependencies:

email_27/src/stripesbook/test/plainmock/PhoneNumberTypeConverterTest.java

```java
package stripesbook.test.plainmock;
import static org.junit.Assert.*;

public class PhoneNumberTypeConverterTest {
    private TypeConverter<PhoneNumber> typeConverter;
    private Collection<ValidationError> errors;

    @Before
    public void setup() {
        typeConverter = new PhoneNumberTypeConverterFormatter();
        errors = new ArrayList<ValidationError>();
    }
    @Test
    public void testValidPhoneNumber() {
        PhoneNumber phoneNumber = typeConverter.convert(
            "(555) 444.6667", PhoneNumber.class, errors);

        assertEquals(0, errors.size());
        assertEquals("555", phoneNumber.getAreaCode());
        assertEquals("444", phoneNumber.getPrefix());
        assertEquals("6667", phoneNumber.getSuffix());
    }
    @Test
    public void testInvalidPhoneNumber() {
        PhoneNumber phoneNumber = typeConverter.convert(
            " 55 444.667  ", PhoneNumber.class, errors);
        assertNull(phoneNumber);
        assertEquals(1, errors.size());
    }
}
```

That worked because the phone number type converter doesn't use anything other than the String input and the list of errors that we provide, both of which are simple to create. But what about a class that depends on objects that are not so easy to create, such as the MyLocalePicker, which needs an HttpServletRequest and an HttpSession?

`email_27/src/stripesbook/ext/MyLocalePicker.java`

```java
package stripesbook.ext;
public class MyLocalePicker extends DefaultLocalePicker {
    public static final String LOCALE = "locale";

    @Override
    public Locale pickLocale(HttpServletRequest request) {
        HttpSession session = request.getSession();

        // Look in the request.
        String locale = request.getParameter(LOCALE);
        if (locale != null) {
            session.setAttribute(LOCALE, locale);
        }
        // Not found in the request? Look in the session.
        else {
            locale = (String) session.getAttribute(LOCALE);
        }
        // Use the locale if found.
        if (locale != null) {
            return new Locale(locale);
        }
        // Otherwise, use the default.
        return super.pickLocale(request);
    }
}
```

Say we wanted to test the pickLocale() method according to different scenarios of what's in the request and what's in the session. It's not so simple to create mock implementations of HttpServletRequest and HttpSession. Many libraries exist to help us avoid having to create mock objects by hand. One such library is Mockito, available at http://www.mockito.org. Mockito is very simple to use and mocks just about any interface or class. When we mock an interface or a class, for example, Mockito will create a mock on the fly that responds to methods without throwing any exceptions. Furthermore, we can instruct Mockito to return specific values from method calls so that we can set up the mock according to the test we want to execute.

Let's see how that works to test MyLocalePicker. Say we wanted to test that pickLocale() returns the French locale if the locale=fr request para-

meter is present. First, we set up the mocks in the @Before method so
that it is executed before each test method:

```
email_27/src/stripesbook/test/plainmock/MyLocalePickerTest.java
package stripesbook.test.plainmock;

import static org.junit.Assert.*;
import static org.mockito.Mockito.*;

public class MyLocalePickerTest {
    private LocalePicker localePicker;
    private HttpServletRequest req;
    private HttpSession session;

    @Before
    public void setup() {
        localePicker = new MyLocalePicker();
        req = mock(HttpServletRequest.class);
        session = mock(HttpSession.class);
        stub(req.getSession()).toReturn(session);
    }
}
```

Now, we can test different scenarios by getting Mockito to stub the
request and session methods to return specific values and testing that
MyLocalePicker returns the correct Locale. Here's how we verify the result
when the request contains "fr":

```
email_27/src/stripesbook/test/plainmock/MyLocalePickerTest.java
@Test
public void testLocaleFrInRequest() {
    stub(req.getParameter(MyLocalePicker.LOCALE)).toReturn("fr");
    Locale locale = localePicker.pickLocale(req);
    assertEquals(Locale.FRENCH, locale);
}
```

Testing the result with a value of "fr" in the session instead of the request
is done in a similar manner:

```
email_27/src/stripesbook/test/plainmock/MyLocalePickerTest.java
@Test
public void testLocaleFrInSession() {
    stub(session.getAttribute(MyLocalePicker.LOCALE)).toReturn("fr");
    Locale locale = localePicker.pickLocale(req);
    assertEquals(Locale.FRENCH, locale);
}
```

Finally, we can test that a value in the request overrides a value in the session:

email_27/src/stripesbook/test/plainmock/MyLocalePickerTest.java

```java
@Test
public void testLocaleInRequestOverridesSession() {
    stub(session.getAttribute(MyLocalePicker.LOCALE)).toReturn("fr");
    stub(req.getParameter(MyLocalePicker.LOCALE)).toReturn("en");
    Locale locale = localePicker.pickLocale(req);
    assertEquals(Locale.ENGLISH, locale);
}
```

Wrapping Up

You took the webmail application to the next level in this chapter. Now, you're using a real database, you can use dependency injection if that suits you, and you can write automated tests that involve various levels of the stack.

After you've let the ideas from this chapter simmer and perhaps have played around with the examples and tried different things, you're ready to continue learning more techniques and add some polish to the application. Onward and upward!

Chapter 13

Tapping into Stripes

Are you ready? It's time to kick it up another notch. We'll tap into the inner workings of Stripes: take control of exceptions, which occur sooner or later in any application; customize URL bindings so that you can change the format of your application's URLs; and learn about interceptors, which allow you to do just about anything during Stripes' request-response life cycle.

13.1 Houston: Exception Handling

The webmail application runs quite smoothly when all is well, but what if Something Bad happens? As a simple example, what if the user types an invalid URL, such as /Admin.action? A big exception page appears, such as the one shown in Figure 13.1, on the following page, complete with an HTTP error code and a nasty stack trace, that's what! We don't want users to see that.

The ExceptionHandler Interface

The Stripes extension that lets us decide what to do with uncaught exceptions is the ExceptionHandler interface. Its handle() method is called by Stripes with the unhandled exception, the request, and then the response.

HTTP ERROR: 500

Could not locate an ActionBean that is bound to the URL [/Admin.action]

RequestURI=/email_26/Admin.action

Caused by:

```
net.sourceforge.stripes.exception.ActionBeanNotFoundException: Could no
    at net.sourceforge.stripes.controller.AnnotatedClassActionResol
    at net.sourceforge.stripes.controller.NameBasedActionResolver.g
    at net.sourceforge.stripes.controller.AnnotatedClassActionResol
    at net.sourceforge.stripes.controller.DispatcherHelper$1.interc
    at net.sourceforge.stripes.controller.ExecutionContext.proceed(
```

Figure 13.1: A TYPICAL GENERIC EXCEPTION PAGE

Here's how we can implement a simple exception handler that logs the exception and forwards to a nicer page:

email_28/src/stripesbook/ext/MyExceptionHandler.java

```java
package stripesbook.ext;
public class MyExceptionHandler implements ExceptionHandler {
    private static final String VIEW = "/WEB-INF/jsp/exception.jsp";
    private static final Log log =
        Log.getInstance(MyExceptionHandler.class);

    public void handle(Throwable exc, HttpServletRequest req,
        HttpServletResponse resp)
        throws ServletException, IOException
    {
        log.error(exc);
        req.getRequestDispatcher(VIEW).forward(req, resp);
    }
    public void init(Configuration configuration) { }
}
```

MyExceptionHandler will be loaded by Stripes because it is in an extension package that's configured in web.xml. ExceptionHandler is one of the many extension interfaces that inherits from ConfigurableComponent, an interface that defines the init(Configuration) method. Stripes calls this method after creating an instance of the extension, allowing you to perform any necessary one-time initialization. For MyExceptionHandler, the init() method is left blank. The handle() method forwards to exception.jsp, which is a simple page with an error message and a link to start over.

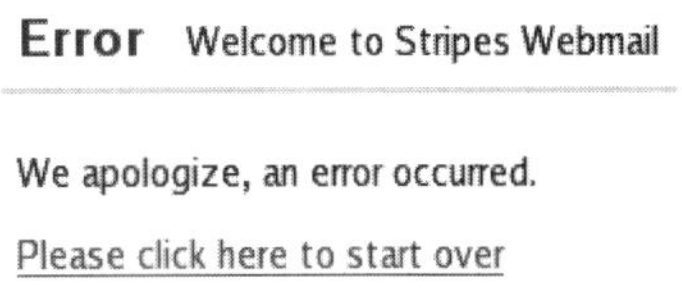

Error Welcome to Stripes Webmail

We apologize, an error occurred.

Please click here to start over

Figure 13.2: A NICER WAY OF RECOVERING FROM AN EXCEPTION

```
email_28/web/WEB-INF/jsp/exception.jsp
```

```
<fmt:message var="title" key="exception.title"/>
<s:layout-render name="/WEB-INF/jsp/common/layout_main.jsp"
  title="${title}">
  <s:layout-component name="body">
    <p>
      <fmt:message key="exception.message"/>
    </p>
    <s:link href="/">
      <fmt:message key="exception.startOver"/>
    </s:link>
  </s:layout-component>
</s:layout-render>
```

Going to /Admin.action now displays the page shown in Figure 13.2.
Ahh, much nicer!

Extending DefaultExceptionHandler

Stripes also provides the DefaultExceptionHandler class, which we can
extend and benefit from a few niceties. First, we can return a Resolution
after the exception-handling code, which makes it simpler to redirect
to another action bean, add request parameters, and so on. Second,
with DefaultExceptionHandler we can handle different types of exceptions
very easily. Just add a method that accepts exactly three parameters:
the exception type, the HttpServletRequest, and the HttpServletResponse.
When an exception occurs, Stripes automatically uses the method that
handles the specific exception type or the closest match going up the
exception's class hierarchy. This lets us have a method that generically
handles Throwable (the top of the exception hierarchy) for all exceptions
and adds methods that handle more specific exceptions in different
ways.

We can extend DefaultExceptionHandler and add a method that handles Throwable, using a ForwardResolution to display the exception page:

email_29/src/stripesbook/ext/MyExceptionHandler.java

```java
package stripesbook.ext;
public class MyExceptionHandler extends DefaultExceptionHandler {
    private static final String VIEW = "/WEB-INF/jsp/exception.jsp";
    private static final Log log =
        Log.getInstance(MyExceptionHandler.class);

    public Resolution catchAll(Throwable exc, HttpServletRequest req,
        HttpServletResponse resp)
    {
        log.error(exc);
        return new ForwardResolution(VIEW);
    }
}
```

The name of the method can be whatever we want. What's important is that the method be **public** and accept the three parameters. Returning a Resolution is optional.

Now, we can easily add handler methods for specific exceptions. For example, the exception thrown when trying the /Admin.action URL is actually an ActionBeanNotFoundException. In that case, we can use Error-Resolution to return an HTTP error code back to the client: the infamous 404. HttpServletResponse contains constants for error codes, so we'll use that:

email_29/src/stripesbook/ext/MyExceptionHandler.java

```java
public Resolution catchActionBeanNotFound(
    ActionBeanNotFoundException exc,
    HttpServletRequest req, HttpServletResponse resp)
{
    return new ErrorResolution(HttpServletResponse.SC_NOT_FOUND);
}
```

Next, we'll configure the application to use not_found.jsp for the 404 error code:

email_29/web/WEB-INF/web.xml

```xml
<error-page>
  <error-code>404</error-code>
  <location>/WEB-INF/jsp/not_found.jsp</location>
</error-page>
```

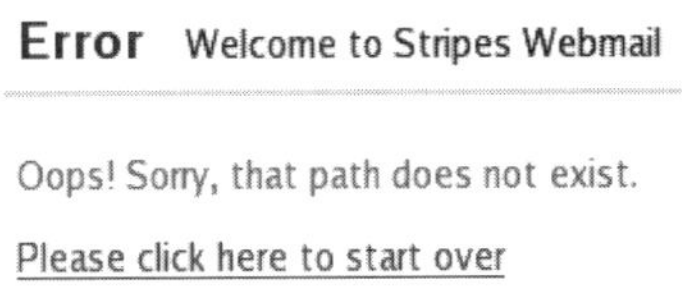

Error Welcome to Stripes Webmail

Oops! Sorry, that path does not exist.

Please click here to start over

Figure 13.3: PAGE SHOWN FOR AN INVALID PATH

---

email_29/web/WEB-INF/jsp/not_found.jsp

```
<fmt:message var="title" key="exception.title"/>
<s:layout-render name="/WEB-INF/jsp/common/layout_main.jsp"
  title="${title}">
  <s:layout-component name="body">
    <p style="color: red">
      <fmt:message key="exception.not_found.message"/>
    </p>
    <s:link href="/">
      <fmt:message key="exception.startOver"/>
    </s:link>
  </s:layout-component>
</s:layout-render>
```

Now, when the user enters /Admin.action, the page in Figure 13.3 will appear.

At this point you might be wondering, why return an ErrorResolution with the 404 code and configure web.xml to display not_found.jsp, instead of just returning a ForwardResolution to not_found.jsp? The answer is that we now handle *all* invalid URLs, not just the ones go through Stripes. No matter whether the user enters /Admin.action or /something.else, the not_found.jsp page will be displayed.

As a final example of how we can use specific exception handling to make our webmail application "smarter," let's catch the exception that is thrown when the user is composing a message and uploads an attachment that exceeds the file size limit. We saw on page 191 that the default maximum file upload size is 10MB. If the user uploads a larger total size, Stripes throws a FileUploadLimitExceededException, which includes the maximum and posted sizes. We can recover from this exception and go back to the message compose page, sending the size information as parameters.

email_29/src/stripesbook/ext/MyExceptionHandler.java

```java
public Resolution catchAttachmentsTooBig(
    FileUploadLimitExceededException exc,
    HttpServletRequest req, HttpServletResponse resp)
{
    return new RedirectResolution(MessageComposeActionBean.class,
        "recover")
        .addParameter("maximumSize", exc.getMaximum())
        .addParameter("postedSize", exc.getPosted());
}
```

This will set the maximumSize and postedSize parameters and call the recover() event handler. So, we add properties for the parameters and a recover() method in MessageComposeActionBean:

email_29/src/stripesbook/action/MessageComposeActionBean.java

```java
public Resolution recover() {
    ValidationError error = new LocalizableError(
        "maximumUpload", postedSize, maximumSize);
    getContext().getValidationErrors().add("attachments", error);
    return new ForwardResolution(COMPOSE);
}
public long maximumSize, postedSize;
```

We add the error message text in the resource bundle and the <s:errors> tag in the JSP:

email_29/res/StripesResources.properties

```
stripesbook.action.MessageComposeActionBean.maximumUpload=\
  Total attachment size ({2} bytes) exceeds the limit ({3} bytes).
```

email_29/web/WEB-INF/jsp/message_compose.jsp

```jsp
<div><fmt:message key="messageCompose.attachments"/>:</div>
<div><s:errors field="attachments"/></div>
<div class="left">
  <c:forEach var="index" begin="0" end="3">
    <div><s:file name="attachments[${index}]"/></div>
  </c:forEach>
</div>
```

The user will now see the informative message shown in Figure 13.4, on the facing page, and the user will have a chance to try again, instead of being sent to a generic error page. That plan came together rather nicely, wouldn't you say?

We now have a place where we can neatly recover from exceptions. Let's continue our quest to master the inner workings of Stripes and move on to the intricate details of URL bindings.

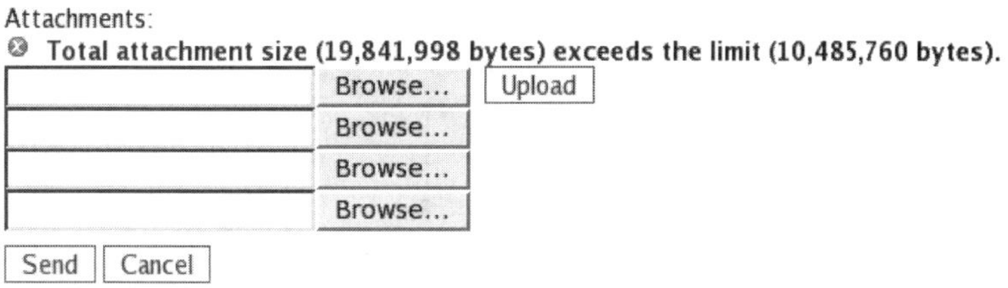

Attachments:
⊗ **Total attachment size (19,841,998 bytes) exceeds the limit (10,485,760 bytes).**

	Browse...	Upload
	Browse...	
	Browse...	
	Browse...	

Send   Cancel

Figure 13.4: ERROR MESSAGE FOR EXCEEDING THE UPLOAD SIZE LIMIT

DelegatingExceptionHandler for Multiple Exception-Handling Classes

Most of the time a single class that extends DefaultException-Handler is a good way of centralizing your exception-handling code in one place. Nevertheless, you're not out of luck if you need more than one exception-handling class. Stripes includes DelegatingExceptionHandler to do exactly that; see Section A.2, *ExceptionHandler.Class*, on page 368 for more details.

13.2 Customizing URL Bindings

So far, we've been developing the webmail application, learning Stripes, and adding features, without bothering much with URLs. That has a nice feel to it—work with action bean class names, event handler names, and parameter names, and let Stripes figure out all the URL business.

That's all well and good, but you, your boss, your customer, or an Unstoppable Force of Nature might decide that the URLs in your application must be changed. Stripes, not being a dictator, lets you change the default URL binding convention and adapt it to your requirements. You can change anything you like, from a minor tweak in the convention to completely replacing the default strategy with your own. The ActionResolver interface defines several methods that Stripes uses for URL binding. The default implementation, NameBasedActionResolver, contains protected methods that make it easy to customize different parts of the binding convention.

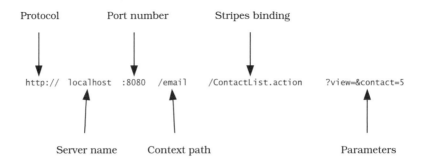

Figure 13.5: THE DIFFERENT PARTS OF A URL

Before diving in, let's make sure we're on the same page when talking about URLs. A complete URL might look like this:

```
http://localhost:8080/email/ContactList.action?view=&contact=5
```

The different parts of this URL are shown in Figure 13.5. We'll be working with the part labeled *Stripes binding*; keep in mind that URL bindings in Stripes do not include the application context path or the request parameters in the ?param1=value1&param2=value2 format (but, as we'll see, we can still embed request parameters within the Stripes binding).

Using @UrlBinding

Let's start with a simple example. We can specify the URL binding for an action bean with the @UrlBinding annotation:

```
@UrlBinding("/something/Something.action")
public class MessageListActionBean implements ActionBean
```

This binds the /something/Something.action URL to MessageListActionBean, regardless of the action bean's package and class name. When changing URL bindings this way, we still need to use the .action suffix because that's the URL mapping configured in web.xml:

email_29/web/WEB-INF/web.xml

```
<servlet-mapping>
  <servlet-name>DispatcherServlet</servlet-name>
  <url-pattern>*.action</url-pattern>
</servlet-mapping>
```

When changing URL bindings, always make sure they still correspond to the configured mapping in web.xml. If they do not, Stripes is out of the picture, and all bets are off!

Changing the .action Extension

Say we are developing the webmail application for A Beautiful Company, Inc. The owners are so proud of the company name that they want you to use the .abc extension for all URLs in the application. Our task consists of changing the default suffix that Stripes uses, .action, to .abc.

How much time do we need to do this? A couple of weeks? A couple of days? An hour?

Well, we can scratch our heads, look troubled, sigh, and tell our boss that we'll *try* to get it done within a week. The truth is that it won't take us more than a few minutes. All we need to do is change the mapping of the dispatcher servlet in the web.xml file:

`email_30/web/WEB-INF/web.xml`

```
<servlet-mapping>
  <servlet-name>DispatcherServlet</servlet-name>
  <url-pattern>*.abc</url-pattern>
</servlet-mapping>
```

and override the getBindingSuffix() method of NameBasedActionResolver:

`email_30/src/stripesbook/ext/MyActionResolver.java`

```
package stripesbook.ext;
public class MyActionResolver extends NameBasedActionResolver {
    @Override
    protected String getBindingSuffix() {
        return ".abc";
    }
}
```

That's it, we've completed the task. The whole application now proudly uses the .abc suffix in its URLs. Let's go ahead and get the bonus points from our boss for finishing way before the deadline.

Changing the Package Prefixes and Action Bean Suffixes

NameBasedActionResolver has two other protected methods that we can override to further customize URL binding. Remember that when binding an action bean to a URL, the package name up to and including any of action, stripes, web, or www is truncated. You can override getBasePackages() and return a different set of names.

The DefaultViewActionBean for Going Straight to JSPs

If you've been using the "preaction" pattern that we discussed way back on page 27, you always make sure that requests first go through an action bean before being forwarded to a JSP.

For a "stand-alone" JSP that doesn't need an action bean, you don't have to create an action bean just to forward to the JSP. Stripes has an internal DefaultViewActionBean that tries to find a JSP, according to a default set of patterns, if the URL did not match any existing action beans.

For the /path/SomeView.action URL, Stripes looks for the following JSPs, in order, and uses the first one that it finds:

- /path/SomeView.jsp
- /path/someView.jsp
- /path/some_view.jsp

If none of the paths matches an existing JSP, then you get the usual ActionBeanNotFoundException.

We've been putting our JSPs under /WEB-INF/jsp. Prepending this to each path that Stripes attempts is a simple matter of overriding a method in NameBasedActionResolver:

defaultview/src/stripesbook/ext/MyActionResolver.java

```java
package stripesbook.ext;
public class MyActionResolver extends NameBasedActionResolver {
    @Override
    protected List<String> getFindViewAttempts(String url) {
        List<String> defaultViews =
            super.getFindViewAttempts(url);

        List<String> customViews =
            new ArrayList<String>(defaultViews.size());

        for (String view : defaultViews) {
            customViews.add("/WEB-INF/jsp" + view);
        }
        return customViews;
    }
}
```

You can further customize what happens when an action bean is not found by overriding the findView() and handleActionBean-NotFound() methods of NameBasedActionResolver.

Stripes also truncates a list of suffixes from the action bean class name. Order is important here, because if a suffix is found at the end of the name, it is removed, and the truncated name is used when checking for the next suffix in the list. To understand this better, let's look at the default list of suffixes:

1. "Bean"
2. "Action"

Stripes first removes "Bean" from the end of the class name or leaves the name unchanged if it does not end in "Bean". Next, it removes "Action" from the end of the *resulting* name from the previous step. Again, the name is left unchanged if it doesn't end in "Action". So, for example:

- "LoginActionBean" → "Login".

  "LoginActionBean" becomes "LoginAction" (remove "Bean") and then becomes "Login" (remove "Action").

- "LoginBean" → "Login".

  "LoginBean" becomes "Login" (remove "Bean") and then remains "Login" (unchanged since it doesn't end in "Action").

- "LoginBeanAction" → "LoginBean".

  "LoginBeanAction" remains "LoginBeanAction" (unchanged since it doesn't end in "Bean"), then becomes "LoginBean" (remove "Action").

- "LoginActionBeanTest" → "LoginActionBeanTest".

  "LoginActionBeanTest" remains "LoginActionBeanTest" (unchanged since it doesn't end in "Bean") and again remains "LoginActionBean-Test" (unchanged since it doesn't end in "Action").

- "LoginController" → "LoginController" remains unchanged as in the previous example.

So, you see how having "Bean" and "Action", in that order, works to remove just "Bean", just "Action", or "ActionBean" from the end of the action bean class name. To change the list of suffixes, override the getActionBeanSuffixes() method of NameBasedActionResolver.

Clean URLs with a Prefix

"Clean" URLs have become popular, because they are more meaningful to the user, hide some of your implementation details, are more search-engine friendly, and are just plain better lookin'.

For example, instead of this:

`/ContactList.action?view=&contact=7`

we might have this:

`/action/contact_list/view/7`

Notice the "cleanliness" of the second URL compared to the first: no extension, no question mark, no ampersand, no equal sign. The first thing we need to do to use these clean URLs is change the mapping of the Stripes dispatcher servlet in the web.xml file from a suffix, such as .action, to a prefix, such as /action:

email_31/web/WEB-INF/web.xml

```
<servlet-mapping>
  <servlet-name>DispatcherServlet</servlet-name>
  <url-pattern>/action/*</url-pattern>
</servlet-mapping>
```

With this mapping, Stripes handles all URLs with the /action prefix. Next, we'll make the corresponding changes in NameBasedActionResolver by overriding getBindingSuffix() and getUrlBinding(). At a minimum, get-BindingSuffix() must return an empty string, and getUrlBinding() must call super.getUrlBinding() and add the "/action" prefix to the result. Just for fun, we'll also convert the URL binding to all lowercase with underscores:

email_31/src/stripesbook/ext/MyActionResolver.java

```
package stripesbook.ext;
public class MyActionResolver extends NameBasedActionResolver {
    @Override
    protected String getBindingSuffix() {
        return "";
    }
    @Override
    protected String getUrlBinding(String actionBeanName) {
        String result = super.getUrlBinding(actionBeanName);
        result = convertToLowerCaseWithUnderscores(result);
        return "/action" + result;
    }
    private String convertToLowerCaseWithUnderscores(String string) {
        StringBuilder builder = new StringBuilder();
        for (int i = 0, t = string.length(); i < t; i++) {
            char ch = string.charAt(i);
            if (Character.isUpperCase(ch)) {
                ch = Character.toLowerCase(ch);
                if (i > 1) {
                    builder.append('_');
                }
            }
            builder.append(ch);
        }
```

```
        return builder.toString();
    }
}
```

With that in place, MessageListActionBean is bound to the following:

```
/action/message_list
```

We now have cleaner default URL bindings. It's a good start, but parameters still show up at the end, like this:

```
/action/message_list?folder=1
```

To continue the cleanup, we need to use @UrlBinding and embed parameters within the URL. To embed a parameter, put its name between { } within the binding:

```
email_31/src/stripesbook/action/MessageListActionBean.java
```

```
@UrlBinding("/action/message_list/{folder}")
public class MessageListActionBean extends BaseActionBean {
```

The folder parameter now appears as this:

```
/action/message_list/1
```

Hello, clean URLs!

But wait, there's more. When we embed a parameter in a URL, we can optionally specify a default value for the parameter. That value will be used if the parameter is omitted from the request URL. For example, the following binding will use a folder parameter with a value of 1 if the request URL is /action/message_list:

```
@UrlBinding("/action/message_list/{folder=1}")
public class MessageListActionBean extends BaseActionBean {
```

Besides parameters, event names can also be embedded in the URL. For example, ContactListActionBean has the list event to see the contact list, and it has the view event to view the details of a specific contact. The special {$event} parameter embeds the event name in the URL binding:

```
email_31/src/stripesbook/action/ContactListActionBean.java
```

```
@UrlBinding("/action/contact_list/{$event}/{contact}")
public class ContactListActionBean extends ContactBaseActionBean {
```

These clean URLs now work with ContactListActionBean:

```
/action/contact_list/list    (contact parameter is not used)
/action/contact_list/view/1 (view the details of contact 1)
```

Clean URLs Without a Prefix

Normally, we need to map a prefix (or a suffix) in web.xml to determine which URLs will be handled by Stripes. It's not a Stripes-specific thing; it's a basic Servlet specification requirement. Mapping *all* URLs to Stripes with /* is usually a bad idea, because some URLs target non-Stripes resources, such as images, CSS files, JavaScript files, static .html files, and so on.

In the previous example, we used the /action prefix to differentiate requests that should go to Stripes from all other requests. So, we had URL bindings such as this:

```
/action/contact_list/...
/action/message_list/...
/action/register/...
```

That's pretty clean, but that Unstoppable Force of Nature might return and demand the removal of that /action prefix so that URLs are even simpler:

```
/contact_list/...
/message_list/...
/register/...
```

So, now what? Without a common prefix, how do we map URLs to Stripes in web.xml? We could map each prefix, such as /contact_list/*, /message_list/*, and so on. But that's way too painful, and it could come back and bite us later if we happen to have an image file under /contact_list/icon.gif, for example.

Have no fear. We can get prefixless clean URLs, without tedious configuration and without having to worry about static files conflicting with Stripes bindings. Ben Gunter, the Stripes committer who implemented clean URL support, had one more trick up his sleeve to address this requirement.

Ben came up with the clever DynamicMappingFilter to which we can map all URLs with /*. The filter takes into account that some requests target non-Stripes resources. Using DynamicMappingFilter, instead of this:

```
/action/contact_list/view/5
```

we can use this:

```
/contact_list/view/5
```

It doesn't get much cleaner than that. Here's a summary of what Dynamic-icMappingFilter does to achieve the magic:

- If the request does not produce an error, then the URL matches an existing static file. Let the request go through untouched in this case.

- If the request results in a 404 error (not found), send the request to the action bean that is bound to the URL. This becomes a regular Stripes-handled request. If no action bean is found, send along the 404 error.

- If the request produces any other error, send the error through.

Want to take the DynamicMappingFilter out for a spin? We just need to make a few changes to web.xml:

- Remove the DispatcherServlet definition.

- Remove the StripesFilter and DispatcherServlet URL mappings.

- Add the DynamicMappingFilter, and map it to /*.

With these changes, the core of the web.xml file becomes the following:

email_32/web/WEB-INF/web.xml

```
<filter>
  <filter-name>StripesFilter</filter-name>
  <filter-class>
    net.sourceforge.stripes.controller.StripesFilter
  </filter-class>
  <!-- same init-params as before... -->
</filter>

<filter>
  <filter-name>DynamicMappingFilter</filter-name>
  <filter-class>
    net.sourceforge.stripes.controller.DynamicMappingFilter
  </filter-class>
</filter>

<filter-mapping>
  <filter-name>DynamicMappingFilter</filter-name>
  <url-pattern>/*</url-pattern>
  <dispatcher>REQUEST</dispatcher>
  <dispatcher>FORWARD</dispatcher>
  <dispatcher>INCLUDE</dispatcher>
</filter-mapping>
```

To continue using the clean URL convention of converting the path to lowercase with underscores, use the same MyActionResolver extension as on page 282, but return the URL without the "/action" prefix.[1]

The URL bindings are now the same as before but without the /action prefix. For example, here is the URL binding for the contact list:

```
email_32/src/stripesbook/action/ContactListActionBean.java
```

```
@UrlBinding("/contact_list/{$event}/{contact}")
public class ContactListActionBean extends ContactBaseActionBean {
```

As we can see, we can customize URL bindings in just about any way we want and keep our boss, our customers, and those Unstoppable Forces of Nature happy.

Specifying the Event Name

Let's look at one last thing concerning URLs: the different ways that an event name can be mapped from a URL to an event handler method. By convention, the name of an event handler corresponds to the name of the method, as follows:

```
public Resolution view()
```

The name of this event handler is view. If we need to use an event handler name that does not correspond to the method name, we can set a different name with the @HandlesEvent annotation:

```
@HandlesEvent("visualize")
public Resolution view()
```

This would cause the visualize event to be handled by the view() method.

As for specifying event names in URLs, we have several options. Knowing how this works is useful when we're testing and want to manually type a URL and is particularly important when working with Ajax, as we'll see in Chapter 15, *Using JavaScript and Ajax*. So, here are the different ways of indicating an event name:

- Include a request parameter with the same name as the event name. This is what Stripes does by default, as follows:

  /ContactList.action?view=&contact=5

---

1.   Again, the lowercase-with-underscores convention is optional. To use clean URLs, the bare minimum is either to override getBindingSuffix() and return an empty string so that ".action" is not used or to annotate *every* action bean with @UrlBinding.

Tim Says...

<u>**Don't Violate Conventions with @UrlBinding**</u>

By default, Stripes will create URLs for all action beans such that they all follow a consistent convention. Freddy has shown you how to modify that convention to suit your own needs and how to use @UrlBinding to both implement clean URLs and override conventions with specific URLs. In my opinion, even when using @UrlBinding to implement clean URLs, you should try your hardest to stick to your URL naming convention!

When developing, it's helpful to be able to see a class name and immediately know what its URL will look like. For example, you see a class called awesome.SuperDuperActionBean, and you know it'll map to /awesome/super_duper, not to some other URL like /worlds_best_bean. But this isn't such a big deal—if you know the class name, you can always check the class to get its URL, right?

The better reason is this: when testing your application and something goes wrong, it's very handy to be able to look at the URL and be able to guess the action bean that's being called. In this case, if the URL doesn't follow your convention, then you have to search your entire project to figure out which action bean you want. Speaking from experience, this can be time-consuming and frustrating!

This calls the view event handler. Do not include more than one parameter that matches an event name; otherwise, Stripes will complain!

Notice that the *value* of the parameter is ignored, so it can be anything or nothing at all.

- Embed the event name in the URL by using {$event} in @UrlBinding, and construct the URL accordingly.

- Append a slash (/) and the event name after the part of the URL that binds to the action bean. For example, if the action bean is bound to /action/contact_list, /action/contact_list/view targets the view event handler. This is equivalent to the following:

```
@UrlBinding("/action/contact_list/${event}")
```

except that we don't need to add the annotation.

- Include a request parameter with the same name as the event name and ".x" added at the end, as in "view.x". This is supported because HTML image maps generate parameters in this format.

- Include a request parameter with the special name _eventName (defined by StripesConstants.URL_KEY_EVENT_NAME) and the event name as the value. For example:

/ContactList.action?_eventName=view&contact=5

The _eventName parameter overrides all of these event name-resolving criteria. This becomes important when we want to submit Ajax requests, as we'll see on page 340.

URL bindings now hold no secrets. When you're ready for some more tinkering under the Stripes hood, roll up your sleeves because we're going to discuss how to use interceptors to tap into every stage of the Stripes life cycle.

13.3 Everything Is Possible: Interceptors

Stripes goes through several *life-cycle stages* when handling a request. Each stage is clearly defined and does specific tasks. When all is said and done, a resolution is executed or an exception is thrown.

Not every request goes through *every* life-cycle stage; the sequence may be interrupted by things like validation errors, exceptions, or (drum roll, please) *interceptors*.

Interceptors are blocks of code that are executed *before* or *after* a life-cycle stage (or both). After they are done with their poking around, they can let the life-cycle sequence continue, or they can interrupt the flow.

Interceptors are a very clean and powerful way to implement features that apply to every request of an application or even just the requests targeted at a specific action bean. Before learning how to implement an interceptor, it's worth knowing the Stripes life-cycle stages.

The Stripes Life-Cycle Stages

The LifecycleStage enumeration defines the eight Stripes life-cycle stages. Here they are along with a summary of what happens at each stage:

1. RequestInit: The request is about to be handled.

2. ActionBeanResolution: The action bean that is targeted by the request is determined from the URL.

3. HandlerResolution: The name of the event and the event handler method are resolved from the URL and request parameters.

4. BindingAndValidation: The request parameters are bound to the corresponding properties of the action bean, with validation and type conversion.

5. CustomValidation: The custom validation methods are executed. Also, the handleValidationErrors() is called if the action bean implements ValidationErrorHandler.

6. EventHandling: The event handler method is executed.

7. ResolutionExecution: The resolution that was returned from any of the preceding stages is executed, producing a response to the client.

8. RequestComplete: This final stage is executed in a **finally** block to make sure that it always runs, even if an exception is thrown.

For stages 4–6, the usual rules of validation apply: a validation error normally means event handling won't be executed, and custom validation depends on previous validations as explained in Section 4.3, *Continue or Stop Validation When There Are Previous Errors?*, on page 78.

Besides exceptions and validation errors, the other way that life-cycle stages can be interrupted is by an interceptor. If, at any stage, a resolution is returned, the life cycle immediately skips to ResolutionExecution. This is how the flow can be altered.

Let's learn a bit more about interceptors and how we can tinker with The Flow of Things.

Implementing Before/After Methods

To execute code *before* or *after* one or more life-cycle stages, we must first decide whether we want the code to apply to just one action bean or to the whole application. Let's start with the former case. By adding a method to an action bean and annotating the method with @Before or @After, it will be executed before or after the life-cycle stages we specify:

```
@Before(stages=LifecycleStage.BindingAndValidation)
public void interceptor1() {
  // do something before binding and validation
}
```

```java
@After(stages={LifecycleStage.EventHandling,LifecycleStage.RequestComplete})
private void interceptor2() {
  // do something after event handling and also after request complete
}

@Before
protected Resolution interceptor3() {
  // do something before the default stage: event handling
  if (someCondition) {
    // interrupt the flow by returning a resolution
    // event handling will not execute in this case
    return new RedirectResolution(...);
  }
  // do not interrupt the flow
  return null;
}

@Before
@After
public int interceptor4() {
  // Do something before and after event handling
  // Any returned values that are not resolutions are ignored
  return 42;
}

@Before(on="save")
public int interceptor5() {
  // Do something before event handling, but only for the "save" event
}
```

Notice the following aspects illustrated in the previous examples:

- Interceptor methods can be named anything, have any access modifier (**private**, **public**, and so on), return anything (more on this in the next point), but *cannot* accept any parameters.
- The method can be **void** or return any type. If the method returns a resolution, the life-cycle sequence is interrupted, and that resolution is executed. Any other returned value is ignored.
- You specify which life-cycle stages to intercept in the stages= attribute of @Before and @After. The default stage is EventHandling. @Before cannot be run before RequestInit or ActionBeanResolution, and @After cannot be run after RequestInit, all for the same reason: the action bean does not yet exist at those points in time!
- A method can be annotated with both @Before and @After.
- We can restrict an interceptor method to specific events by indicating the event names in the on= attribute, either positively as in on={"save", "update"} or negatively as in on="!delete".

That's a neat way to intercept execution for a specific action bean. We can also write an interceptor that runs for the whole application.

Implementing Interceptors

For a global interceptor, implement the Interceptor interface, and either place the class in an extension package or configure it in the web.xml file.

The Interceptor interface is simple:

```
public interface Interceptor {
  Resolution intercept(ExecutionContext context) throws Exception;
}
```

To indicate the life-cycle stages that we want to intercept, we annotate our class with @Intercepts. For example:

```
@Intercepts(LifecycleStage.ActionBeanResolution)
public class MyInterceptor implements Interceptor {
  public Resolution intercept(ExecutionContext context) {
    // ...
  }
}
```

Instead of using @Before or @After to indicate whether our interceptor code should run before or after the life-cycle stages, we call proceed() on the ExecutionContext object that's passed to the intercept() method. That executes the life-cycle stage. So, the code we put around the call to proceed() is executed before or after, accordingly:

```
@Intercepts(LifecycleStage.ActionBeanResolution)
public class MyInterceptor implements Interceptor {
  public Resolution intercept(ExecutionContext context)
  // proceed() can throw an Exception so we have to declare it
    throws Exception
  {
    // do something before

    Resolution resolution = context.proceed();

    // do something after

    return resolution;
  }
}
```

Notice how proceed() returns a resolution; returning that value from intercept() effectively lets the life-cycle sequence continue normally. If, on the other hand, we want to interrupt the flow, we would return a different resolution from intercept().

As we are writing code in the intercept() method, the ExecutionContext object gives us information we can use as we want, including the following:

- The current life-cycle stage, which is useful when we're intercepting more than one stage
- The action bean context, which is available at every stage
- The action bean, which becomes available after the ActionBeanResolution stage
- The event handler Method object, available after the HandlerResolution stage; at this point, we can also retrieve the event handler name by calling getEventName() on the action bean context
- The ValidationErrors from the action bean context, after the BindingAndValidation stage
- The current Resolution, which is normally **null** until either a validation error occurs or the EventHandling stage has completed

If we also need configuration information, we can have our interceptor class implement the ConfigurableComponent interface. Stripes will automatically call the init(Configuration) after creating an instance of our interceptor.

In What Order Are Interceptors Executed?

If we have more than one interceptor that runs on the same life-cycle stage, the order in which they are executed may or may not be important to us. If the order matters, we must know that interceptors loaded by the Stripes extension packages mechanism are executed in no guaranteed order. We're not out of luck, though. To control the order, we move our interceptors to a nonextension package (or annotate them with @DontAutoLoad) and configure them in web.xml file, in the desired order:

```
<filter>
  <filter-name>StripesFilter</filter-name>
  <filter-class>
    net.sourceforge.stripes.controller.StripesFilter
  </filter-class>
  <!-- other init params... -->
  <init-param>
    <param-name>Interceptor.Classes</param-name>
    <param-value>
```

```
      stripesbook.nonext.Interceptor1,
      stripesbook.nonext.Interceptor2,
      stripesbook.nonext.Interceptor3
    </param-value>
  </init-param>
</filter>
```

Let's say that those three interceptors all run both before and after the same life-cycle stage. Suppose further we also have a @Before and an @After method in the action bean for the same life-cycle stage. If there are no interruptions, things happen in the following order:

1. @Before
2. Interceptor1, before
3. Interceptor2, before
4. Interceptor3, before
5. Interceptor3, after
6. Interceptor2, after
7. Interceptor1, after
8. @After

13.4 Interceptor Example: Adding Support for Guice

In Section 12.2, *Dependency Injection with Spring*, on page 255, we looked at using Spring for dependency injection. Guice (http://code. google.com/p/google-guice) is another DI container, for which Stripes does not have built-in support (at least not in the latest version of Stripes as of this writing). We'll add support for Guice DI using an interceptor. Tapping into Stripes and "guicing" up action beans is surprisingly easy!

The life-cycle stage that interests us is the ActionBeanResolution stage. Stripes creates an instance of the action bean during this stage, and the action bean context has already been manufactured. We can intercept both objects and inject Guice-annotated dependencies into them before they are returned:

email_33/src/stripesbook/ext/guice/interceptor/GuiceInterceptor.java

```
package stripesbook.ext.guice.interceptor;
@Intercepts(LifecycleStage.ActionBeanResolution)
public class GuiceInterceptor
    implements Interceptor, ConfigurableComponent
{
    /* ... */
```

```
public Resolution intercept(ExecutionContext context)
    throws Exception
{
    injector.injectMembers(context.getActionBeanContext());
    Resolution resolution = context.proceed();
    injector.injectMembers(context.getActionBean());
    return resolution;
}
}
```

That's all there is to it! Well, almost. The injector we see there is a Guice Injector object, which is configured with one or more Guice Modules. In a nutshell, a Module is a Java class that tells Guice which implementations to use for which interfaces. Then, dependencies are injected by annotating properties with Guice's @Inject annotation.

Here's how we create a Module that wires up our DAOs:

email_33/src/stripesbook/ext/guice/config/GuiceConfigModule.java

```
package stripesbook.ext.guice.config;
public class GuiceConfigModule extends AbstractModule {
    @Override
    protected void configure() {
        bind(AttachmentDao.class).to(AttachmentDaoImpl.class);
        bind(ContactDao.class).to(ContactDaoImpl.class);
        bind(FolderDao.class).to(FolderDaoImpl.class);
        bind(MessageDao.class).to(MessageDaoImpl.class);
        bind(UserDao.class).to(UserDaoImpl.class);
    }
}
```

That's pretty straightforward. Next, we have to get our interceptor to load up this Module and use it to create an Injector. A simple solution is to piggyback onto the Stripes extensions mechanism: drop our Module into an extension package, and have our interceptor automatically find it. Using the Configuration that Stripes passes to the init() method, we can call getBootstrapPropertyResolver() and from there use one of several utility methods that returns the classes that are compatible with the class or interface that we specify:

email_33/src/stripesbook/ext/guice/interceptor/GuiceInterceptor.java

```
package stripesbook.ext.guice.interceptor;
@Intercepts(LifecycleStage.ActionBeanResolution)
public class GuiceInterceptor
    implements Interceptor, ConfigurableComponent
{
    public static final String MODULES = "Guice.Modules";
```

```
    private static Injector injector;
    private static final Log log =
        Log.getInstance(GuiceInterceptor.class);

    public void init(Configuration config) throws Exception {
        List<Class<? extends Module>> moduleClasses =
            config.getBootstrapPropertyResolver()
                .getClassPropertyList(MODULES, Module.class);

        int size = moduleClasses.size();
        if (size > 0) {
            List<Module> modules = new ArrayList<Module>(size);
            for (Class<? extends Module> cls : moduleClasses) {
                modules.add(cls.newInstance());
            }
            injector = Guice.createInjector(modules);
            log.info("Created Guice injector with modules: ",
                moduleClasses);
        }
        else {
            injector = Guice.createInjector();
        }
    }
    public static Injector getInjector() {
        return injector;
    }
}
```

What this does is look for a list of Module classes configured in web.xml as an init parameter to the Stripes filter with the name Guice.Modules. If there is no such parameter, then Stripes looks for classes that implement Module in the extension packages. That way, we have the option of using an extension package or a parameter in web.xml, just like all the other Stripes extensions.

Once we have the list of Module classes, it's simple to create instances and use them to configure the Guice injector. We then use the injector in the intercept() method that we wrote earlier to inject dependencies in the action bean context and in the action bean. The injector is in a static member to give easy access to it via GuiceInterceptor.getInjector(), but otherwise it wouldn't need to be since Stripes creates only one instance of each interceptor.

Now that we have defined the Guice configuration and implemented the Guice interceptor, we can use dependency injection on action beans and the action bean context by tagging properties with Guice's @Inject annotation.

email_33/src/stripesbook/action/BaseActionBean.java

```java
public abstract class BaseActionBean implements ActionBean {
    @Inject protected AttachmentDao attachmentDao;
    @Inject protected ContactDao contactDao;
    @Inject protected FolderDao folderDao;
    @Inject protected MessageDao messageDao;
    @Inject protected UserDao userDao;
}
```

email_33/src/stripesbook/ext/MyActionBeanContext.java

```java
public class MyActionBeanContext extends ActionBeanContext {
    @Inject protected FolderDao folderDao;
    @Inject protected UserDao userDao;
}
```

That's all there is to it. To inject dependencies on other Stripes objects, we'd use the same technique as we did for Spring on page 259: subclass the default factory, retrieve the object, and inject the dependencies. Instead of this:

```java
SpringHelper.injectBeans(object, context);
```

we'd use the following:

```java
GuiceInterceptor.getInjector().injectMembers(object);
```

13.5 Another Interceptor Example: Ensuring Login

The Guice interceptor example was pretty cool in terms of implementing Guice support, but it was rather light on the actual interceptor code:

email_33/src/stripesbook/ext/guice/interceptor/GuiceInterceptor.java

```java
package stripesbook.ext.guice.interceptor;
@Intercepts(LifecycleStage.ActionBeanResolution)
public class GuiceInterceptor
    implements Interceptor, ConfigurableComponent
{
    /* ... */

    public Resolution intercept(ExecutionContext context)
        throws Exception
    {
        injector.injectMembers(context.getActionBeanContext());
        Resolution resolution = context.proceed();
        injector.injectMembers(context.getActionBean());
        return resolution;
    }
}
```

Let's look at a meatier example with a sneak preview of the next chapter about adding security. One of the many things we'll do to secure the webmail application is to ensure that the user is logged in. An interceptor is the perfect place for doing that:

`email_34/src/stripesbook/ext/LoginInterceptor.java`

```
package stripesbook.ext;
@Intercepts(LifecycleStage.ActionBeanResolution)
public class LoginInterceptor implements Interceptor {
    @SuppressWarnings("unchecked")
    private static final List<Class<? extends BaseActionBean>> ALLOW =
        Arrays.asList(
            LoginActionBean.class,
            RegisterActionBean.class
        );
    public Resolution intercept(ExecutionContext execContext)
        throws Exception
    {
        Resolution resolution = execContext.proceed();

        MyActionBeanContext ctx =
            (MyActionBeanContext) execContext.getActionBeanContext();

        BaseActionBean actionBean = (BaseActionBean)
            execContext.getActionBean();

        Class<? extends ActionBean> cls = actionBean.getClass();

        if (ctx.getUser() == null && !ALLOW.contains(cls)) {
            resolution = new RedirectResolution(LoginActionBean.class);
        }
        return resolution;
    }
}
```

Ah, now we're doing something a little more sophisticated. The interceptor runs after the ActionBeanResolution stage so that we can retrieve the current action bean. We also retrieve the action bean context and check whether it contains a user—that's how we know whether the user has logged in.

By comparing the action bean class to a list of "allowed" action beans for which the user doesn't have to be logged in, we can determine whether we need to bounce the user. If that's the case, we interrupt the life-cycle sequence by returning a RedirectResolution to the Login page instead of the resolution that was returned by the proceed() method.

13.6 The Stripes Life Cycle in More Detail

This section contains more nitty-gritty details about what happens during the Stripes life-cycle stages. These details are good to know when you're tapping deep into Stripes, but feel free to move on and come back later if you find that all this information is a little too much to absorb in one sitting.

So, here's the skinny. When a request arrives, the first thing Stripes does is create the action bean context from the factory by calling getContextInstance() on the implementation of ActionBeanContextFactory (the default is DefaultActionBeanContextFactory). The servlet context is set on the action bean context, which is in turn set on the execution context.

Next, Stripes goes through each life-cycle stage.

RequestInit

Nothing happens here. This stage exists solely to make it easy for interceptors to do something before the request-handling starts.

ActionBeanResolution

From the request URL, Stripes determines the corresponding action bean. The work is done by the getActionBean() method of the ActionResolver implementation (the default is NameBasedActionResolver). Bindings defined with @UrlBinding and @HandlesEvent have priority over naming conventions. Once the action bean has been resolved, it is set as a request attribute with the name actionBean, a constant defined in StripesConstants.REQ_ATTR_ACTION_BEAN. The action bean is also set on the execution context.

HandlerResolution

The action bean's targeted event handler is resolved from the URL.

First, the getEventName() method is called on the ActionResolver implementation (the default is defined in AnnotatedClassActionResolver).[2] This method looks for the event name in the URL using the rules we saw on page 286. Internally, Stripes also looks for the event name in the "__stripes_event_name" request attribute (defined in StripesConstants.REQ_ATTR_EVENT_NAME).

---

2. To be clear, the default ActionResolver is NameBasedAnnotationResolver, but it extends AnnotatedClassActionResolver, and that's where getEventName() is implemented.

Second, Stripes calls ActionResolver.getHandler() to obtain the actual event handler Method object. If no event name was found in the previous step, this looks for a method annotated with @DefaultHandler or for the presence of exactly one event handler method.

The event name is set on the action bean context, and the event handler Method object is set on the execution context.

BindingAndValidation

At this stage, Stripes binds the request parameters to the corresponding properties of the action bean, performing validation and type conversion in the process. The work is done by the bind() method of the Action-BeanPropertyBinder implementation (the default is DefaultActionBeanProp-ertyBinder). ValidationErrors that occur are set on the action bean context.

CustomValidation

Custom validation methods (annotated with @ValidationMethod) are executed. If no resolution is returned and the action bean implements ValidationErrorHandler, handleValidationErrors() is called.

EventHandling

The action bean's event handler method is executed.

ResolutionExecution

The execute() method is called on the returned Resolution. Changing the resolution in an interceptor that runs at this stage can be done by calling setResolution() on the execution context before calling proceed(), *not* by returning a different resolution from the intercept() method. It's not possible to change the resolution *after* this stage, because by then it's too late—the resolution has already been executed!

There should be a resolution when this stage executes, because if the resolution is **null**, nothing happens. No response is given to the request, and the user's browser is left blank. Dead air. . . .

Unlike all previous life-cycle stages, the ResolutionExecution stage is executed regardless of a previous life-cycle stage returning a resolution. This makes sense—the resolution does have to be executed, after all.

RequestComplete

This life-cycle stage is executed at the end of the request, no matter what. All previous stages could be interrupted by an unhandled exception, but RequestComplete is executed in a **finally** block to ensure that it is called. An interceptor that executes at this stage is the perfect place for such things as releasing database connections, cleaning up resources, and so on.

What's Next?

You learned a ton about how the internals of Stripes work, including handling exceptions, customizing URL bindings, and writing code that intercepts the handling of a request at any life-cycle stage. This is very powerful stuff. Mastering Stripes and being able to tinker with the insides is good news for you, the developer. On the other hand, users messing with the insides of your application is bad news, and that's why we'll address security issues next.

Chapter 14

It's a Dangerous World: Adding Security

They say that the only way to be completely, absolutely, positively, 100 percent sure that a web application is secure is by not putting it on the Web. But that's no fun. So, let's give it our best shot to secure the webmail application.

Stripes has a few mechanisms for controlling what data goes in and out of an application. Validation and type conversion already provide some control to protect our model and database. But that's not enough. We need to account for security issues by thinking about what a malicious user might do to wreck our application and by putting up appropriate lines of defense.

14.1 Controlling Parameter Binding

One area concerning security is parameter binding. Even if we decide which parameters are sent in the forms and links of an application, it doesn't prevent users from tacking on additional parameters in URLs or in faked-out forms. We can use a few techniques to prevent parameters from being bound to properties.

Using @Validate(ignore=true)

By default, when a request is made to an action bean with a parameter someName=someValue, Stripes attempts to set the someName property, either directly or via a setter method.

However, in some situations we have setter methods in an action bean for purposes other than receiving request parameters. Users can invoke those methods by forging request parameters into URLs, unless we prevent that from happening. First, we can change the setter method's access modifier to anything except **public**: that is, **protected, private,** or no access modifier at all. If we need the method to remain **public**, we have another option: tell Stripes not to bind request parameters to the property by annotating it with @Validate(ignore=true). Stripes skips ignored properties in the request parameter binding process.

For example, say we have these methods in an action bean:

```
public void setOne(String one) {
    System.out.println("one=" + one);
}

@Validate(ignore=true)
public void setTwo(String two) {
    System.out.println("two=" + two);
}

protected void setThree(String three) {
    System.out.println("three=" + three);
}

void setFour(String four) {
    System.out.println("four=" + four);
}

private void setFive(String five) {
    System.out.println("five=" + five);
}
```

A user submits a request to the action bean with the parameters:

```
one=1&two=2&three=3&four=4&five=5
```

That results in the following output:

```
one=1
```

All other setter methods cannot be invoked by adding a parameter to the request, since they are either marked with @Validate(ignore=true) or marked with non-**public**.

Using @StrictBinding

Imagine that our registration process required users to activate their account by calling in and validating their identity. After doing that, our cheerful support staff would activate their account. Here's a simplified User class for this example:

```
security/src/stripesbook/model/User.java
```
```java
package stripesbook.model;
public class User {
    private String firstName;
    private String lastName;
    private boolean activated;

    /* getters and setters... */
}
```

The activated flag is **false** by default, and the support staff sets it to **true** when the user calls in and provides the appropriate information. Of course, we wouldn't include a user.activated field in the registration form, but a mischievous user could forge a form and then submit user.activated=true along with the rest of the registration information, effectively bypassing our activation process.

Annotating the user.activated property with @Validate(ignore=true) solves the problem. However, adding that to every single property that we want to block can become cumbersome. Another annotation that comes in handy when we want to allow certain properties and block "everything else" is @StrictBinding. When we annotate an action bean with @StrictBinding and use validations on the properties that are meant to be entered by the user, all other properties are automatically blocked:

```
security/src/stripesbook/action/UserFormActionBean.java
```
```java
package stripesbook.action;
@StrictBinding
public class UserFormActionBean extends BaseActionBean {
    @ValidateNestedProperties({
        @Validate(field="lastName", required=true, minlength=2),
        @Validate(field="firstName", minlength=2)
    })
    private User user;

    /* ... */
}
```

Now, user.activated is blocked from binding. Using @StrictBinding, this way is convenient when we are validating all user-entered fields. All nonvalidated fields are assumed to be for internal use only and so are not bound by request parameters.

That's great when we're validating *all* user-entered fields, but sometimes we want to prevent binding for some properties while still allowing other properties to be bound even though they are not validated. We have two options to achieve this.

The first option is to use an empty @Validate annotation on the property. This effectively allows the property to be bound without performing any actual validation.

The second option is to use the allow=, deny=, and defaultPolicy= attributes of @StrictBinding so that we can control exactly which properties are allowed and denied. In the previous example, say we weren't using any validation at all. We could specify which properties are allowed in the allow= attribute:

```
security/src/stripesbook/action/UserForm2ActionBean.java
package stripesbook.action;
@StrictBinding(allow={"user.firstName", "user.lastName"})
public class UserForm2ActionBean extends BaseActionBean {
    // No validation
    private User user;

    /* ... */
}
```

If there are many more allowed properties than denied properties, it becomes more convenient to allow all properties except for those indicated in the deny= attribute:

```
@StrictBinding(allow="user.*", deny="user.activated")
```

Notice the special * that matches all properties, *but not nested properties*. That's convenient to allow binding at one level but prevent users from injecting values into more deeply nested objects. If, on the other hand, we want to allow all levels of nested properties, we use **, as in allow="user.**".

So, what happens when a property matches *both* the allow= and deny= patterns or neither? That's when the value in the defaultPolicy= attribute is used for the final decision. The value can be Policy.ALLOW or Policy.DENY (DENY is the default).

In the previous example with no validated fields, the following won't work to block just the activated flag:

```
@StrictBinding(deny="user.activated")
```

When the user.firstName parameter comes in, Stripes sees that the property does not match the allow list or the deny list and is not validated. Since defaultPolicy=Policy.DENY, user.firstName is denied. Instead, we must either specify the allow= list as we did before or change the default policy:

```
@StrictBinding(defaultPolicy=Policy.ALLOW, deny="user.activated")
```

Remember that validated values are allowed by default, so think of them as being implicitly added to the allow= list of properties.

Another tidbit: when indicating more than one property in either of allow= or deny=, we can use a list of strings as in the previous examples, or we can use one string that contains the comma-separated list of properties. So, these two are equivalent:

```
@StrictBinding(allow={"user.firstName", "user.lastName"})
or
@StrictBinding(allow="user.firstName, user.lastName")
```

Finally, be aware that to prevent security issues, using * and ** cannot be used with partial strings. For example, we might be tempted to use allow="user.*Name" to match user.firstName and user.lastName or to use allow="user.info**" to match all properties and nested properties that start with info. Those types of patterns won't work and will just be ignored.

Using @DontBind

We already know that @DontValidate shuts off all validations, which is useful for such event handlers as those associated with ⎡Cancel⎤ buttons. Although no validations error occurs, parameter binding is nevertheless attempted when we use @DontValidate. For extra security, we can block all binding for an event handler by annotating it with @DontBind. This skips the BindingAndValidation life-cycle stage altogether, and when the event handler is called, all request parameters are ignored.

Note that @DontBind implies @DontValidate, so there's no need to use both annotations on the same event handler.

14.2 Preventing Cross-site Scripting Attacks

Let's move on to another security issue. Cross-site scripting (XSS) attacks consist of ill-intentioned users submitting scripts in input fields so that when the values are displayed, the scripts are executed.

Right now, the webmail application is vulnerable to such attacks. For example, if we go to the contact form and use the "Last name" field to enter this:

```
<script>alert('Oh no!')</script>
```

we'll see an "Oh no!" message pop up every time the contact is displayed in the contact list or contact view pages. Not good. Allowing such markup not only makes an application vulnerable to serious attacks but can also wreck a page's presentation when a user, even well-intentioned, makes a mistake in using formatting tags. For example, imagine what happens if a page that displays user-submitted comments is sent this input:

```
I <b>really like your website!
```

The user forgot to close the bold tag, causing *everything* after that comment to be displayed in bold!

Fortunately, XSS attacks and other markup-related headaches are fairly easy to prevent. The idea is to always filter user-entered values before displaying them. The filter escapes any HTML markup so that the following, for example,

```
<script>alert('Oh no!')</script>
```

becomes this:

```
&lt;script&gt;alert('Oh no!')&lt;/script&gt;
```

and so is displayed correctly and harmlessly.

First, there is the escapeXml() method in the *functions* part of the standard JSP tag library:

```
<%@taglib prefix="fn" uri="http://java.sun.com/jsp/jstl/functions"%>
${fn:escapeXml(value)}
```

This filters the contents of value before displaying it. To prevent XSS attacks in our JSPs, we just need to wrap user-entered values within fn:escapeXml(). For example, in the contact view page:

email_34/web/WEB-INF/jsp/contact_view.jsp

```
<tr>
  <td class="label"><s:label for="contact.firstName"/>:</td>
  <td class="value">
    ${fn:escapeXml(actionBean.contact.firstName)}
  </td>
</tr>
```

```
<tr>
  <td class="label"><s:label for="contact.lastName"/>:</td>
  <td class="value">
    ${fn:escapeXml(actionBean.contact.lastName)}
  </td>
</tr>
```

and so on for all other fields.

Second, we have to filter messages that are created by action beans and contain values entered by the user, such as confirmation messages. If, for example, we display "Message sent to *Somebody*" after the user has sent an email, with the *Somebody* part being what the user entered in the To field, it is vulnerable to XSS attacks. Stripes provides a helper method, HtmlUtil.encode(), to filter values before they are displayed:

email_34/src/stripesbook/action/MessageComposeActionBean.java

```
getContext().getMessages().add(
    getLocalizableMessage("messageSentTo",
        HtmlUtil.encode(message.getTo())));
```

Filtering values with ${fn:escapeXml(value)} and HtmlUtil.encode() protects your application from XSS attacks.

14.3 Using Encryption

Let's take stock. We've controlled which properties are allowed to be bound from request parameters and have filtered the values that are entered by the user before displaying them to prevent harmful scripting. Next on our security to-do list: using encryption for sensitive data.

Hashing Passwords

Did you notice something when you looked at Figure 12.1, on page 241? The password is stored in the database in clear text. Not a good idea! What we should do is hash the password before storing it in the database. That way, it won't be usable if it falls into the wrong hands.

What we'll do is create a PasswordTypeConverter, which converts a clear-text password into a hashed password. The type converter will *not* be in an extension package, and we'll use it only on password fields via @Validate(converter=PasswordTypeConverter.class). To hash the password, we'll use Java's MessageDigest class and Stripes' Base64 class.

email_34/src/stripesbook/nonext/PasswordTypeConverter.java

```java
package stripesbook.nonext;
public class PasswordTypeConverter implements TypeConverter<String> {
    public String convert(String input, Class<? extends String> cls,
        Collection<ValidationError> errors)
    {
        return hash(input);
    }
    public String hash(String password) {
        try {
            MessageDigest md = MessageDigest.getInstance("SHA-1");
            byte[] bytes = md.digest(password.getBytes());
            return Base64.encodeBytes(bytes);
        }
        catch (NoSuchAlgorithmException exc) {
            throw new IllegalArgumentException(exc);
        }
    }
    public void setLocale(Locale locale) { }
}
```

We're using the SHA-1 algorithm to hash the password.[1] Next, let's tell Stripes to use PasswordTypeConverter for the password fields:

email_34/src/stripesbook/action/RegisterActionBean.java

```java
@ValidateNestedProperties({
    @Validate(field="firstName", required=true),
    @Validate(field="lastName",  required=true),
    @Validate(field="username",  required=true),
    @Validate(field="password",  required=true,
        converter=PasswordTypeConverter.class)
})
private User user;

@Validate(required=true, converter=PasswordTypeConverter.class)
private String confirmPassword;
```

Now, instead of "nadia", this is the value that will be stored in the database:

Y9nEX5AlXnnpgnRsC8tAOD8gH8c=

There's not much anyone can do with that sequence of characters!

---

1. See http://en.wikipedia.org/wiki/SHA for more information on SHA and other hashing algorithms.

> ### A Note About Encryption Keys
>
> By default, Stripes generates a random encryption key to encrypt values. These values are not decryptable when you restart the web application or if your application is deployed in a cluster of nodes.
>
> To make encrypted values reusable across restarts and cluster nodes, you must set a specific encryption key, as explained Section A.3, *Stripes.EncryptionKey*, on page 373.

Encrypting Parameters

Loading model objects from ID parameters, whether it's with a custom type converter or with the magic of Stripersist, is pretty cool. Unfortunately, it's also a security issue. When you see a URL such as this:

```
/ContactList.action?view=&contact=2
```

you don't have to be a world-class hacker to figure out that this shows the information of contact ID 2. It's tempting to resubmit the request with different values for the contact ID.

Such parameters can be encrypted to prevent users from submitting random values. The encrypted=true attribute of @Validate does the work:

```
@Validate(encrypted=true)
private Contact contact;
```

Now, the contact parameter will be encrypted, as follows:

```
/ContactList.action?view=&contact=HaAi8A_XHzs%3D
```

If the user tries to submit a random value, Stripes detects that it is not a correctly encrypted value and does not bind the parameter.

A little later, in Section 14.5, *Showing Users Their Data, Not Other People's*, on page 313, we'll see how we continue letting users manually enter values for parameters while still preventing them from seeing data that is not their own.

14.4 Ensuring the User Is Logged In

Although the webmail application starts at the Login page and requires the user to log in before entering, we still need to prevent users who are not logged in from accessing pages within the application. Otherwise, they could still enter simply by typing the appropriate URL.

We saw a sneak preview of how to do this when we discussed interceptors. After the action bean has been resolved, we check whether it's one of the allowed action beans (Login and Register) and for the presence of the User object in the action bean context. Here is the login interceptor again, this time with an additional feature (can you spot it?):

`email_34/src/stripesbook/ext/LoginInterceptor.java`

```
package stripesbook.ext;
@Intercepts(LifecycleStage.ActionBeanResolution)
public class LoginInterceptor implements Interceptor {
    @SuppressWarnings("unchecked")
    private static final List<Class<? extends BaseActionBean>> ALLOW =
        Arrays.asList(
            LoginActionBean.class,
            RegisterActionBean.class
        );
    public Resolution intercept(ExecutionContext execContext)
        throws Exception
    {
        Resolution resolution = execContext.proceed();

        MyActionBeanContext ctx =
            (MyActionBeanContext) execContext.getActionBeanContext();

        BaseActionBean actionBean = (BaseActionBean)
            execContext.getActionBean();

        Class<? extends ActionBean> cls = actionBean.getClass();

        if (ctx.getUser() == null && !ALLOW.contains(cls)) {
            resolution = new RedirectResolution(LoginActionBean.class);
            if (ctx.getRequest().getMethod().equalsIgnoreCase("GET")) {
                ((RedirectResolution) resolution)
                    .addParameter("loginUrl", actionBean.getLastUrl());
            }
        }
        return resolution;
    }
}
```

When users who are not logged in are bounced to the Login page, the loginUrl parameter is set to the URL that the user was trying to use.[2]

---

2. Notice the check for a GET request. Sending the user to the URL for a POST request won't work, because the parameters won't be in the URL. Besides, it's better not to reissue a POST request after login and instead just let the user start over.

That way, we can send them to that page after a successful login. To do that, we just need to add a hidden parameter for loginUrl in the login form:

`email_34/web/WEB-INF/jsp/login.jsp`

```
<s:form beanclass="stripesbook.action.LoginActionBean">
  <%-- ... --%>
  <s:hidden name="loginUrl"/>
</s:form>
```

Finally, we add a loginUrl property in LoginActionBean and use it after a successful login. If the user went straight to the Login page, there is no loginUrl, and we send the user to the Message List page in that case.

`email_34/src/stripesbook/action/LoginActionBean.java`

```
public Resolution login() {
    getContext().setUser(user);
    if (loginUrl != null) {
        return new RedirectResolution(loginUrl);
    }
    return new RedirectResolution(MessageListActionBean.class);
}
public String loginUrl;
```

Logged-in users have to be able to log out, too. It's simple to implement a LogoutActionBean that delegates the session-handling details to MyActionBeanContext:

`email_34/src/stripesbook/action/LogoutActionBean.java`

```
package stripesbook.action;
public class LogoutActionBean extends BaseActionBean {
    public Resolution logout() {
        getContext().logout();
        return new RedirectResolution(LoginActionBean.class);
    }
}
```

`email_34/src/stripesbook/ext/MyActionBeanContext.java`

```
public void logout() {
    setUser(null);

    HttpSession session = getRequest().getSession();
    if (session != null) {
        session.invalidate();
    }
}
```

The user is removed from the action bean context, and the session is invalidated.

Finally, we add a Logout link to the menu:

email_34/src/stripesbook/action/MenuViewHelper.java

```java
public enum Section {
    MessageList(MessageListActionBean.class),
    ContactList(ContactListActionBean.class),
    Compose(MessageComposeActionBean.class),
▶   Logout(LogoutActionBean.class);
}
```

Just like that, the Logout link appears in the menu, as shown here:

Message List   Messages   Contact List   Compose   Logout

Preventing Browser Page Caching

When the user logs out from, say, the Message List page, hitting the browser's Back button goes back to showing the list of messages—even though the user is no longer logged in. Can we do something about that?

The problem is that the pages within the application are being cached by the browser. When the user clicks Back, the browser displays the page from its cache without issuing a request to our server, and the login interceptor doesn't get a chance to do its work.

Fortunately, we can tell the browser not to cache certain pages by adding HTTP headers to the response. The @HttpCache annotation does that for us. By annotating an action bean with @HttpCache(allow=false), the page will not be cached by the browser:

email_34/src/stripesbook/action/MessageListActionBean.java

```java
@HttpCache(allow=false)
public class MessageListActionBean extends BaseActionBean {
```

Now, when the user logs out from the Message List page and hits the Back button, the browser does not show a cached Message List page. Instead, it reissues a request, and the login interceptor sends the user to the Login page.

Besides disallowing page caching, you can also allow caching but *limit* the period of time. After the limit, the page expires, and the browser reissues a request. To do that, indicate the number of seconds in the expires= attribute, as in @HttpCache(expires=120) to expire the page after two minutes.

> ⚡ **Joe Asks...**
>
> ### What Happens If I Use @HttpCache(allow=false, expires=120)?
>
> The default value for allow= is **true**, which is why @Http-Cache(expires=120) works to allow caching for two minutes. If you set allow= to **false**, you are disallowing caching completely, and whatever value that you set for the expires= attribute will be ignored.

Action beans inherit the @HttpCache annotation from parent classes. So, for example, we can annotate ContactBaseActionBean with @Http-Cache(allow=false), and its subclasses, ContactListActionBean and ContactFormActionBean, will not be cached.

You can also use @HttpCache on event handler methods of action beans to have different settings for different events. When you use @HttpCache on both an action bean class and some of its event handlers, the annotation on an event handler has priority over the annotation on the class. That way, you can put the default setting on the class and override it as necessary on specific event handlers.

14.5 Showing Users *Their* Data, Not Other People's

Being logged in is all well and good, but once users are inside, we don't want to let them see the folders, messages, and contacts of other users. Earlier, in Section 14.3, *Encrypting Parameters*, on page 309, we saw how we can use @Validate(encrypted=true) to prevent users from entering random parameters. But say we wanted to keep plain parameters and let users change them, while still making sure that they view only their own data. Then what?

We just have to implement the logic that checks whether the data being loaded is owned by the current user. Only if that verification passes do we display the data to the user. In the webmail application, this applies to folders, messages, and contacts. Each model class for those objects provides methods to retrieve the user who owns the data; for example, Folder has a getUser() method. If the returned User object does not match the User that is logged in, the data is not set in the action bean and therefore not shown to the user.

The verifications are done in each setter method, because that is what gets called after the data has been loaded from the database. Here's how we prevent users from seeing other people's folders:

email_34/src/stripesbook/action/BaseActionBean.java

```
public void setFolder(Folder folder) {
    if (getUser().equals(folder.getUser())) {
        getContext().setCurrentFolder(folder);
    }
}
```

If the folder is owned by another user, it is not set as the current folder and not shown in the JSP. Similarly, from a Message, we can get the corresponding Folder and, from there, the owning User, and we can use the same logic in the setter method for a Message:

email_34/src/stripesbook/action/MessageDetailsActionBean.java

```
public void setMessage(Message message) {
    if (getUser().equals(message.getFolder().getUser())) {
        this.message = message;
    }
}
```

Finally, preventing users from seeing other people's contacts works almost in the same way, except that we also have to check that the User is not **null**. Indeed, when the user is creating a new contact, set-Contact() is called before the contact is saved so the user has not been associated to the contact yet.

email_34/src/stripesbook/action/ContactBaseActionBean.java

```
public void setContact(Contact contact) {
    User user = contact.getUser();
    if (user == null || getUser().equals(user)) {
        this.contact = contact;
    }
}
```

With these checks for ownership, users cannot meddle in other people's business. We now have some pretty good security measures in the webmail application.

14.6 Using Roles

The security boundaries are very clearly defined when you're restricting users to viewing their own data. Each user sees their own stuff, and that's it. Sometimes, though, you need a more flexible way of expressing *who* has access to *what*. One way of addressing this security issue is to use *roles*, such as Administrator, Developer, User, Guest, and so on. By assigning roles to users of your application and permitting access to different parts according to these roles, you can easily control who gets to see what.

Adding Roles in the Webmail Application

Let's define two roles for the webmail application: Administrator and User. Administrators have access to everything, and users have access only to their own data.

To use roles, we'll add a simple Role class in the model with a name property:

email_35/src/stripesbook/model/Role.java

```
package stripesbook.model;
@Entity
public class Role extends ModelBase {
    private String name;

    public Role() {
    }
    public Role(String name) {
        this.name = name;
    }
    /* getters and setters, equals, hashCode */

    @Override
    public String toString() {
        return name;
    }
}
```

We'll initialize the list of roles when the application starts up. Stripersist provides the StripersistInit interface for such tasks; just implement the interface, place the code in the init() method, and you're good to go:

email_35/src/stripesbook/ext/init/DataInit.java

```
package stripesbook.ext.init;
public class DataInit implements StripersistInit {
    private RoleDao roleDao = new RoleDaoImpl();
```

```
public void init() {
    if (roleDao.read().isEmpty()) {
        roleDao.save(new Role("User"));
        roleDao.save(new Role("Administrator"));
        roleDao.commit();
    }
}
}
```

Stripersist finds StripersistInit implementations through the extension packages mechanism or with the StripersistInit.Classes initialization parameter to StripesFilter in web.xml.

Next, we'll add a roles property to the User class. Users can have more than one role, and more than one user can have the same role, so it's a many-to-many relationship:

email_35/src/stripesbook/model/User.java

```
package stripesbook.model;
@Entity
public class User extends ModelBase {
    private String firstName;
    private String lastName;
    private String username;
    private String password;
    @ManyToMany
    private List<Role> roles;

    /* getters and setters... */

    @Override
    public String toString() {
        return String.format("%s %s", firstName, lastName);
    }
}
```

The roles are ready to go.

A Page with Restricted Access

To manage assigning roles to users and demonstrate the use of roles at the same time, let's add a User List page, as shown in Figure 14.1, on the facing page. The page shows the users with their roles and allows us to change which users have which roles. Only administrators are allowed to use this page. The application loads an administrator as a starting point; when users register, they are initially given the User role.

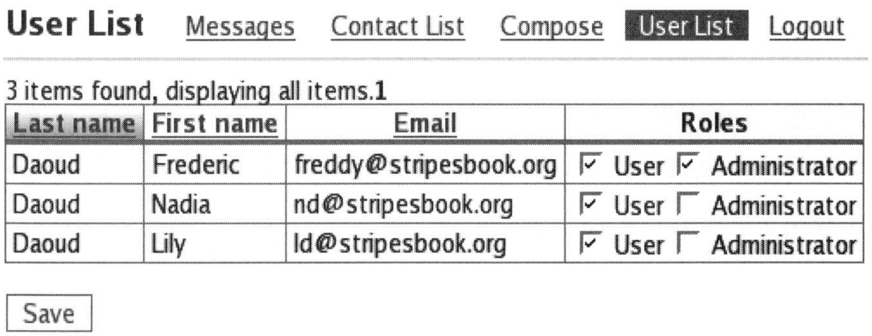

User List   Messages   Contact List   Compose   User List   Logout

3 items found, displaying all items.**1**

Last name	First name	Email	Roles
Daoud	Frederic	freddy@stripesbook.org	☑ User ☑ Administrator
Daoud	Nadia	nd@stripesbook.org	☑ User ☐ Administrator
Daoud	Lily	ld@stripesbook.org	☑ User ☐ Administrator

Save

Figure 14.1: USER LIST PAGE FOR ADMINISTRATORS ONLY

Here are the action bean and JSP for the User List page:

email_35/src/stripesbook/action/UserListActionBean.java

```java
package stripesbook.action;
@HttpCache(allow=false)
public class UserListActionBean extends BaseActionBean {
    private static final String VIEW = "/WEB-INF/jsp/user_list.jsp";

    @DefaultHandler
    public Resolution view() {
        return new ForwardResolution(VIEW);
    }
    public Resolution save() {
        for (User user : users) {
            userDao.save(user);
        }
        userDao.commit();
        getContext().getMessages().add(
            new LocalizableMessage("userList.saved"));
        return new RedirectResolution(getClass());
    }
    private List<User> users = userDao.read();
    public List<User> getUsers() {
        return users;
    }
    public void setUsers(List<User> users) {
        this.users = users;
    }
    public List<Role> getRoles() {
        return roleDao.read();
    }
}
```

email_35/web/WEB-INF/jsp/user_list.jsp

```
<c:set var="index" value="0"/>
<s:form beanclass="stripesbook.action.UserListActionBean">
  <d:table name="${actionBean.users}" id="user" requestURI=""
    defaultsort="1" pagesize="10">
    <d:column titleKey="user.lastName" sortable="true">
      ${fn:escapeXml(user.lastName)}
    </d:column>
    <d:column titleKey="user.firstName" sortable="true">
      ${fn:escapeXml(user.firstName)}
    </d:column>
    <d:column titleKey="user.email" sortable="true">
      ${fn:escapeXml(user.username)}@stripesbook.org
    </d:column>
    <d:column titleKey="user.roles">
      <c:forEach var="role" items="${actionBean.roles}">
        <s:checkbox name="users[${index}].roles"
          value="${role}" checked="${user.roles}"/>
        ${role}
      </c:forEach>
      <c:set var="index" value="${index + 1}"/>
    </d:column>
  </d:table>
  <br>
  <s:submit name="save"/>
</s:form>
```

Including UserListActionBean in MenuViewHelper adds it to the menu:

email_35/src/stripesbook/action/MenuViewHelper.java

```
public enum Section {
    MessageList(MessageListActionBean.class),
    ContactList(ContactListActionBean.class),
    Compose(MessageComposeActionBean.class),
▶   UserList(UserListActionBean.class),
    Logout(LogoutActionBean.class);
}
```

Now that the User List page is ready, let's see how we restrict access to it by requiring the Administrator role.

Restricting Access with the Stripes-Security plug-In

Oscar Westra van Holthe-Kind developed a neat plug-in called *Stripes-Security*, available at http://www.stripes-stuff.org. It includes an interceptor, a simple API, and a tag library to easily control *authorization* in a Stripes application. It leaves the *authentication* up to you—we have already covered that with our Login page.

Stripes Never Ceases to Amaze Me

So, I was building the User List page for this example and wanted to generate checkboxes next to each user to show which roles each user has. As I was iterating over the list of roles provided by the action bean, I was trying to figure out how to make the checkbox checked if the user's list of roles contains the current role in the iteration.

I was hoping for a contains operator or something similar in the JSP EL so that I could write ${user.roles contains role}, but no such luck. Then, I wrote a small JSP custom tag library with a function so that I could use ${myfn:userHasRole(user,role)}. That involved writing a class with a static method, declaring the tag library in a TLD file, and importing the tag library with a **taglib** directive in taglibs.jsp. As I was doing this, I was dreading having to explain it all. . .

. . . until I had a closer look at the documentation for the Stripes *<s:checkbox>* tag. It turns out that Stripes is smart enough to recognize this often-needed functionality of having a check-box be checked if the current value is contained in a collection. All I had to do was put the user's roles in the checked= attribute and the current role in the value= attribute, like this:

```
<s:checkbox name="..." value="${role}" checked="${user.roles}"/>
```

The checkbox is checked if ${user.roles} contains ${role}. Awe-some! No wonder I like Stripes so much. Happy with that simple and elegant solution, I went off to get rid of all that unneeded tag library code with a big smile on my face.

Besides that it is simple and flexible, what makes the Stripes-Security plug-in attractive is that it supports using roles with standard Java annotations. We'll get to that in a minute—let's start by setting up the plug-in. First, add org.stripesstuff.plugin.security to the extension packages:

email_35/web/WEB-INF/web.xml

```
<init-param>
  <param-name>Extension.Packages</param-name>
  <param-value>
    stripesbook.ext,
    org.stripesstuff.stripersist,
    org.stripesstuff.plugin.security
  </param-value>
</init-param>
```

This loads the Stripes-Security plug-in's main workhorse, implemented as an interceptor. Next, we need an implementation of the SecurityManager interface, which defines one method to determine whether a user is allowed access to the specified action bean and event handler:

```
public interface SecurityManager {
    Boolean getAccessAllowed(ActionBean bean, Method handler);
}
```

By implementing this interface, you can pretty much use any logic you want to control access to action beans and event handlers. Then, specify the fully qualified class name of the SecurityManager implementation as an initialization parameter to the Stripes filter in web.xml:

```
<init-param>
  <param-name>SecurityManager.Class</param-name>
  <param-value>your.pkg.YourSecurityManager</param-value>
</init-param>
```

That completes the setup of the Stripes-Security plug-in. Oscar doesn't leave you high and dry, though. The plug-in comes with two implementations of SecurityManager: J2EESecurityManager and InstanceBasedSecurityManager.

Using J2EESecurityManager

The first implementation, J2EESecurityManager, takes advantage of the annotations defined in Java's JSR-250:[3]

```
@DenyAll
@PermitAll
@RolesAllowed("Administrator")
@RolesAllowed({"Administrator", "User"})
```

These annotations can be used on classes and event handler methods. The first two deny and permit access for all roles, while @RolesAllowed specifies a list of roles that are allowed access.

J2EESecurityManager reads these annotations on event handler methods first, then on action bean classes, and finally on parent classes. Access is granted or denied according to the following criteria, in order of priority:

- If the @DenyAll annotation is found, access is denied.
- If the @PermitAll annotation is found, access is granted *provided that the user is authenticated.*

---

3. JSR-250 is available as a separate API (included in the book's source bundle) and is standard in Java EE 5.

- If the @RolesAllowed annotation is found, access is granted *if the user has at least one of the roles listed in the annotation.*
- If no annotation is found, access is granted.

To determine whether the user is authenticated and whether the user has a given role, J2EESecurityManager defines protected methods with default implementations:

```java
public class J2EESecurityManager implements SecurityManager {
  /* ... */

  protected Boolean isUserAuthenticated(ActionBean bean, Method handler) {
    return bean.getContext().getRequest().getUserPrincipal() != null;
  }
  protected Boolean hasRole(ActionBean bean, Method handler,
    String role)
  {
    return bean.getContext().getRequest().isUserInRole(role);
  }
}
```

HttpRequest.getUserPrincipal() and HttpRequest.isUserInRole(role) use the servlet container's configuration. In our case, however, authentication is performed in the Login page. Roles are stored in the database and are associated to the User object. We can subclass J2EESecurityManager and provide our own implementation for isUserAuthenticated() and hasRole():

email_35/src/stripesbook/nonext/MySecurityManager.java

```java
package stripesbook.nonext;
public class MySecurityManager extends J2EESecurityManager {
    @Override
    protected Boolean isUserAuthenticated(ActionBean bean, Method handler) {
        return getUser(bean) != null;
    }
    @Override
    protected boolean hasRole(ActionBean actionBean, Method handler,
        String role)
    {
        User user = getUser(bean);
        if (user != null) {
            Collection<Role> roles = user.getRoles();
            return roles != null && roles.contains(new Role(role));
        }
        return false;
    }
    private User getUser(ActionBean bean) {
        return ((BaseActionBean) bean).getContext().getUser();
    }
}
```

Joe Asks...

Why Isn't the SecurityManager Implementation Loaded via the Extension Packages mechanism?

All classes of the Stripes-Security plug-in are in the same package. This includes, among other things, the interceptor and two SecurityManager implementations. By adding that package to the extensions, the interceptor is automatically loaded. But we wouldn't want the two SecurityManager implementations to be loaded as well. One, there must be exactly *one* implementation, and two, we have to be able to provide our own.

Putting the two SecurityManager implementations in separate packages just to solve the extension packages issue would be, well, rather lame. Besides, you'd still have to indicate one of those packages in web.xml, so you wouldn't be saving any configuration. Since you have to add a parameter either way, it may as well just be the class that implements SecurityManager; it's clear and explicit.

We'll tell Stripes-Security to use our security manager by configuring it in web.xml:

email_35/web/WEB-INF/web.xml

```
<init-param>
    <param-name>SecurityManager.Class</param-name>
    <param-value>
        stripesbook.nonext.MySecurityManager
    </param-value>
</init-param>
```

Now that MySecurityManager is ready to go, we can use @DenyAll, @PermitAll, and @RolesAllowed on action beans and event handlers to control access rights. Here's how we grant access to UserListActionBean only if the user has the Administrator role:

email_35/src/stripesbook/action/UserListActionBean.java

```
@RolesAllowed("Administrator")
public class UserListActionBean extends BaseActionBean {
```

Just like that, people without the Administrator role are denied access to UserListActionBean. It's simple and straightforward, and we're reusing standard Java annotations instead of introducing new ones.

HTTP ERROR: 401

UNAUTHORIZED

RequestURI=/email_35/UserList.action

Figure 14.2: THE 401 (UNAUTHORIZED) HTTP ERROR CODE

We can even decide to remove the LoginInterceptor and instead use @PermitAll on the action beans for which the user must be logged in:

```
@PermitAll
public class MessageListActionBean ...

@PermitAll
public class MessageDetailsActionBean ...

@PermitAll
public class MessageComposeActionBean ...

@PermitAll
public class ContactBaseActionBean ...
```

Note that annotating ContactBaseActionBean takes care of both ContactListActionBean and ContactFormActionBean because they inherit the annotation from the parent class.

So, what happens if unauthenticated users try to access a protected page or if nonadministrator users link to the User List page? They are greeted with the 401 (Unauthorized) HTTP error code, as shown in Figure 14.2.

That's not very nice, but that's what they get for trying to access a forbidden page, right? Well, that's up to you to decide. You can leave it as is and be blunt with unauthorized users, or you can show them a custom page. If you choose the latter, create a JSP, and configure it as being the page for the 401 error code in web.xml:

email_35/web/WEB-INF/jsp/unauthorized.jsp
```
<%@include file="/WEB-INF/jsp/common/taglibs.jsp"%>
<fmt:message var="title" key="unauthorized.title"/>
<s:layout-render name="/WEB-INF/jsp/common/layout_main.jsp"
  title="${title}">
  <s:layout-component name="body">
    <p style="color: red">
      <fmt:message key="unauthorized.message"/>
    </p>
```

```
    <s:link href="/">
      <fmt:message key="exception.startOver"/>
    </s:link>
  </s:layout-component>
</s:layout-render>
```

email_35/web/WEB-INF/web.xml

```
<error-page>
  <error-code>401</error-code>
  <location>/WEB-INF/jsp/unauthorized.jsp</location>
</error-page>
```

Unauthorized users now see the page in Figure 14.3, on the facing page. Of course, you can display whatever message you want in this page. For extra security, you might prefer to be less specific and just use a "page not found" message, thus giving potential hackers the least possible amount of information.

If you've been paying attention (and I'm sure you have), you probably noticed that by getting rid of our login interceptor, we lost the feature of sending unauthenticated users back to the Login page with the URL that they were trying to access. Don't worry, we can easily put that back. When we implement SecurityManager, we can optionally implement SecurityHandler as well and determine what to do when access has been denied:

email_35/src/stripesbook/nonext/MySecurityManager.java

```
public class MySecurityManager
    extends J2EESecurityManager
    implements SecurityHandler
{
    public Resolution handleAccessDenied(ActionBean bean,
        Method handler)
    {
        if (!isUserAuthenticated(bean, handler)) {
            RedirectResolution resolution =
                new RedirectResolution(LoginActionBean.class);
            if (bean.getContext().getRequest().getMethod()
                .equalsIgnoreCase("GET"))
            {
                String loginUrl = ((BaseActionBean) bean).getLastUrl();
                resolution.addParameter("loginUrl", loginUrl);
            }
            return resolution;
        }
        return new ErrorResolution(HttpServletResponse.SC_UNAUTHORIZED);
    }
    /* ... */
}
```

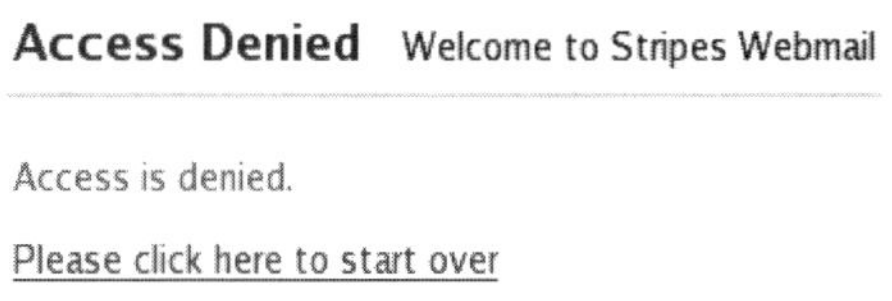

Access Denied Welcome to Stripes Webmail

Access is denied.

Please click here to start over

Figure 14.3: A NICER (BUT STILL BLUNT) PAGE FOR UNAUTHORIZED ACCESS

If the user is not authenticated, we redirect to the Login page with the URL to use after the user logs in. So, that will work as before. On the other hand, when access is denied to an authenticated user, there's no point in making them log in—we just return the 401 error code and show the "Access Denied" page.

Using InstanceBasedSecurityManager

The second SecurityManager implementation included in Stripes-Security is InstanceBasedSecurityManager, which extends J2EESecurityManager and adds support for restricting areas of the application not only by role name but also by an EL expression, like this:

```
@RolesAllowed("RoleName if ${expression}")
```

This grants access only if the user has the role RoleName and expression evaluates to **true**.

Because InstanceBasedSecurityManager extends J2EESecurityManager and overrides hasRole() to add support for EL expressions, it adds another method, hasRoleName(), which can be overridden to provide the logic that determines whether a user has a role. So, to extend InstanceBasedSecurityManager and not clobber its hasRole() implementation, we have to move our role-finding code from hasRole() to hasRoleName(). Here is the final MySecurityManager class:

email_35/src/stripesbook/nonext/MySecurityManager.java

```java
package stripesbook.nonext;
public class MySecurityManager
    extends InstanceBasedSecurityManager
    implements SecurityHandler
{
    @Override
    protected Boolean isUserAuthenticated(ActionBean bean, Method handler) {
        return getUser(bean) != null;
    }
}
```

```
        @Override
▶       protected Boolean hasRoleName(ActionBean bean, Method handler,
            String role)
        {
            User user = getUser(bean);
            if (user != null) {
                Collection<Role> roles = user.getRoles();
                return roles != null && roles.contains(new Role(role));
            }
            return false;
        }
        public Resolution handleAccessDenied(ActionBean bean,
            Method handler)
        {
            if (!isUserAuthenticated(bean, handler)) {
                RedirectResolution resolution =
                    new RedirectResolution(LoginActionBean.class);
                if (bean.getContext().getRequest().getMethod()
                    .equalsIgnoreCase("GET"))
                {
                    String loginUrl = ((BaseActionBean) bean).getLastUrl();
                    resolution.addParameter("loginUrl", loginUrl);
                }
                return resolution;
            }
            return new ErrorResolution(HttpServletResponse.SC_UNAUTHORIZED);
        }
        private User getUser(ActionBean bean) {
            return ((BaseActionBean) bean).getContext().getUser();
        }
    }
```

This allows us to do some pretty cool things with EL expressions. For example, recall how we previously restricted users to seeing their own data, including their own messages in MessageDetailsActionBean:

email_34/src/stripesbook/action/MessageDetailsActionBean.java

```
public void setMessage(Message message) {
    if (getUser().equals(message.getFolder().getUser())) {
        this.message = message;
    }
}
```

Say we wanted to keep restricting users to their own messages but let administrators see other users' messages. We could accomplish that by putting the setter method back to just a plain setter and annotating MessageDetailsActionBean.

email_35/src/stripesbook/action/MessageDetailsActionBean.java

```java
@RolesAllowed({
  "Administrator",
  "User if ${user eq message.folder.user}"
})
public class MessageDetailsActionBean extends BaseActionBean {
    public void setMessage(Message message) {
        this.message = message;
    }
}
```

Administrators are granted access no matter what, and users can get access only if the message belongs to them. How cool is that?

Hiding Restricted Content in JSPs

We're now controlling access to action beans according to roles. For the User List page, it seems unfair to show the link in the menu to nonadministrator users, only to show them an "Access is denied" message if they click the link.

Stripes-Security also includes a tag library so that you can show or hide content in JSPs according to the user's authorization. We'll declare the tag library in taglibs.jsp:

email_35/web/WEB-INF/jsp/common/taglibs.jsp

```
<%@taglib prefix="security"
  uri="http://www.stripes-stuff.org/security.tld"%>
```

The library includes two tags. The <security:allowed> tag renders its body if the user is allowed to use the default event of the current action bean. We can also use a different action bean by indicating its ID in the bean= attribute and can use a different event with its name in the event= attribute:

```
<security:allowed>
  <!--this appears only if the user is authorized access to the
  default event handler of the current action bean-->
</security:allowed>

<s:useActionBean id="beanId" beanclass="..."/>
<security:allowed bean="beanId">
  <!--same as above, but use the action bean who's ID is "beanId"-->
</security:allowed>

<security:allowed event="someEvent">
  <!--use "someEvent" event handler of the current action bean-->
</security:allowed>
```

```
<security:allowed bean="beanId" event="someEvent">
  <!--use "someEvent" event handler of "beanId" action bean-->
</security:allowed>
```

We want to omit the User List link from the menu when the user isn't allowed to see the page. Within the loop that displays the sections, we'll assign the target action bean to the "bean" ID and enclose the code that renders the section within the <*security:allowed*> tag:

email_35/web/WEB-INF/jsp/common/menu.jsp

```
<c:forEach var="section" items="${actionBean.sections}">
►   <s:useActionBean id="bean" beanclass="${section.beanclass}"/>
►   <security:allowed bean="bean">
      <fmt:message var="text" key="${section.textKey}"/>
      <c:choose>
        <c:when test="${section eq actionBean.currentSection}">
          <span class="currentSection">${text}</span>
        </c:when>
        <c:otherwise>
          <s:link beanclass="${section.beanclass}" class="sectionLink">
            ${text}
          </s:link>
        </c:otherwise>
      </c:choose>
►   </security:allowed>
  </c:forEach>
```

Now, the User List link appears in the menu only if the user is authorized access to the page. In fact, the same goes for each section of the menu. We can add more sections with security restrictions, and the menu will automatically display the appropriate links.

The other tag in the Stripes-Security library is <*security:notAllowed*>, which works just like <*security:allowed*> except that it renders its body if the user is *not* authorized access. That way, instead of completely hiding links from unauthorized users, we can display grayed-out plain text:

```
<c:forEach var="section" items="${actionBean.sections}">
  <s:useActionBean id="bean" beanclass="${section.beanclass}"/>
  <fmt:message var="text" key="${section.textKey}"/>
  <security:allowed bean="bean">
    <%-- same as before... --%>
  </security:allowed>
  <security:notAllowed bean="bean">
    <span class="grayedOut">${text}</span>
  </security:notAllowed>
</c:forEach>
```

> ## Joe Asks...
> ### What About Other Security Mechanisms for Java Applications?
>
> The specifications for Java web applications define standard ways of implementing security mechanisms. I prefer simpler and more lightweight solutions such as the ones I presented in this chapter. Nevertheless, it's worth knowing your options. *The Java EE 5 Tutorial* (JBC+06) is a good reference for all things Java EE, including security mechanisms. I didn't cover them because I wanted to present solutions that are more tightly integrated with Stripes.
>
> *Spring Security* (http://www.springframework.org/spring-security) and *JSecurity* (http://www.jsecurity.org) are other interesting solutions for adding security to Java applications. Using them with Stripes is not difficult, but again, I did not cover them to avoid spending too much time on frameworks that are completely orthogonal to Stripes.

A Sense of Security

We've put up several lines of defense to prevent malicious users from harming the webmail application. We won't be staying up at night worrying about security issues.

*Every day you may make progress. Every step may be
fruitful. Yet there will stretch out before you an
ever-lengthening, ever-ascending, ever-improving path. You
know you will never get to the end of the journey. But this,
so far from discouraging, only adds to the joy and glory of
the climb.*
> ▶ Sir Winston Churchill

Chapter 15

Using JavaScript and Ajax

Ajax (Asynchronous JavaScript and XML) is one of those buzzwords
that you simply can't ignore these days. A little bit of Ajax can really
spice up an application by making it more responsive and fun to use.

In a nutshell, Ajax lets you issue a request that it is *asynchronous*
and refreshes only a *portion* of the current page. This contrasts with
a traditional request for which the user has to wait for the response
before doing anything else and which reloads the whole page.

Consider this simple example. You have two select boxes in a form, and
the list of choices from the second box depends on what is selected in
the first box. You want to populate the second box as soon as the selection in the first box changes. Without Ajax, the whole page is refreshed,
causing flickering and even scrolling if the boxes are near the bottom of
a long page. With Ajax, only the portion that contains the second box
is refreshed. What's more, the user interface is not blocked during the
request-response exchange.

We'll look at how to use Ajax with Stripes for this and many other
examples. Using Ajax without a good JavaScript library is much like
developing a web application without a good framework—possible but
much more work than necessary—so I'll be using Prototype (http://www.
prototypejs.org) and jQuery (http://jquery.com) in the examples. If neither
of those is your favorite, have no fear—Stripes has absolutely no dependency on any specific Ajax framework.

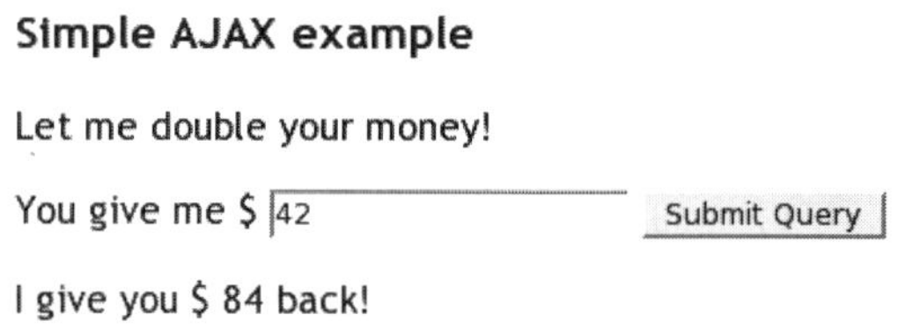

Simple AJAX example

Let me double your money!

You give me $ |42 | Submit Query |

I give you $ 84 back!

Figure 15.1: A SIMPLE AJAX EXAMPLE

15.1 Using JavaScriptResolution

We'll start with a simple reusable layout that loads the Prototype library and has components to put content in the *<head>* and *<body>* sections of the page:

```
ajax/web/WEB-INF/jsp/common/layout_main.jsp

<s:layout-definition>
  <!DOCTYPE HTML PUBLIC "-//W3C//DTD HTML 4.01//EN"
    "http://www.w3.org/TR/html4/strict.dtd">
  <html>
    <head>
      <title>${title}</title>
      <script src="${contextPath}/js/prototype.js"
        type="text/javascript"></script>
      <s:layout-component name="head"/>
    </head>
    <body>
      <h3>${title}</h3>
      <s:layout-component name="body"/>
    </body>
  </html>
</s:layout-definition>
```

We'll put JavaScript code in the head component and the page content in the body component.

We're ready to try a simple Ajax example. A page with a text field is shown in Figure 15.1. As the user types an amount, the text below refreshes to display double the amount. This happens after each keystroke, without having to click the [Submit Query] button.

Look at the source for the JSP, and then we'll discuss how it all works:

`ajax/web/WEB-INF/jsp/hello.jsp`

```
<s:layout-render name="/WEB-INF/jsp/common/layout_main.jsp"
  title="Simple AJAX example">
  <s:layout-component name="head">
    <script type="text/javascript">
❶     function sendMoney(control) { //
        var form = control.form;
        new Ajax.Request(form.action,
          { method: 'post',
            parameters: form.serialize(),
            onSuccess: receiveResponse
          }
        );
      }
      // xhr is the XMLHttpRequest, which is a core AJAX object
❷     function receiveResponse(xhr) { //
        var result = eval(xhr.responseText);
        $('iGiveYou').update(result);
      }
    </script>
  </s:layout-component>
  <s:layout-component name="body">
    <p>Let me double your money!</p>
    <p>
      <s:form beanclass="stripesbook.action.HelloAjaxActionBean">
        You give me $
❸       <s:text name="youGiveMe" onkeyup="sendMoney(this);"/>
        <s:submit name="doubleMoney"/>
      </s:form>
    </p>
    <p>
❹     I give you $ <span id="iGiveYou"></span> back!
    </p>
  </s:layout-component>
</s:layout-render>
```

We start with a regular Stripes form and text field. At ❸, the field's onkeyup= event calls the sendMoney() JavaScript function defined at ❶. Since the text field is passed as a parameter, it's easy to retrieve the corresponding form. Then, with Prototype's Ajax.Request, we issue an Ajax request to the form's action, passing the form's inputs as parameters and the name of the JavaScript function that will be called when the server responds to the request. That function is receiveResponse (❷), which is passed the data that the server sent as a response. That data is wrapped with a call to eval() to obtain the result as a JavaScript object. Finally, the <span> with id="iGiveYou" (❹) is updated with the value of the result.

So, what exactly is the data that the server sends as a response? Here is the code for the action bean to which the form is sent:

`ajax/src/stripesbook/action/HelloAjaxActionBean.java`

```java
package stripesbook.action;
public class HelloAjaxActionBean extends BaseActionBean {
    public int youGiveMe;

    public Resolution doubleMoney() {
        return new JavaScriptResolution(new Integer(youGiveMe * 2));
    }
}
```

Very simple: youGiveMe is received as a parameter, and doubleMoney() sends a response with 2× the value. That's the interesting part: JavaScriptResolution, helped behind the scenes by its buddy JavaScriptBuilder, converts a Java object into JavaScript code and returns it as a resolution so that the data can be turned back into a JavaScript object with the eval() function.

Remember that the Ajax request is sent as the user types characters into the text field, without clicking the submit button. However, serializing the form with form.serialize() includes the name= of the submit button, doubleMoney, in the request parameters. That causes the request to target the doubleMoney() event handler. It's not necessary to include a button just to indicate which event handler we want to call; we'll talk about that a little later. Right now I also want to point out that if you *do* click the submit button, you get to see exactly what data is sent by the JavaScriptResolution. For example, if you enter 42, the response data is 84;. That's not very exciting, but that's really all that's needed to get the value 84 in JavaScript.

Now that we've gotten our feet wet, let's try using a model object with JavaScriptResolution, such as an instance of this Money class:

`ajax/src/stripesbook/model/Money.java`

```java
package stripesbook.model;
public class Money {
    private int youGaveMe;
    private int andIGiveYou;

    public Money(int youGaveMe, int andIGiveYou) {
        this.youGaveMe = youGaveMe;
        this.andIGiveYou = andIGiveYou;
    }
    /* getters and setters... */
}
```

Instead of just returning a plain integer value, we'll return a Money object that contains both the amount that the user entered (youGaveMe) and the value given back (andIGiveYou):

`ajax/src/stripesbook/action/JavaScriptResolutionActionBean.java`

```java
public Resolution doubleMoney() {
    Money money = new Money(youGiveMe, youGiveMe * 2);
    return new JavaScriptResolution(money);
}
```

We can display the two values in separate places by using a different placeholder for each value:

`ajax/web/WEB-INF/jsp/javascript_resolution.jsp`

```
You gave me $ <span id="youGaveMe"></span>,
and I give you $ <span id="andIGiveYou"></span> back!
```

When the response is received, the JavaScript object returned by eval() contains the same properties as the Money object. We can then refer to these properties with the dot notation:

`ajax/web/WEB-INF/jsp/javascript_resolution.jsp`

```javascript
function receiveResponse(data) {
  var result = eval(data.responseText);
  $('youGaveMe').update(result.youGaveMe);
  $('andIGiveYou').update(result.andIGiveYou);
}
```

That's very convenient. You can return rich Java model objects with JavaScriptResolution and get them back in JavaScript. All the object's properties, including nested properties and circular references, are correctly converted.

If you peek under the covers to see the actual response data by using the submit button, you'll see something a little more involved:

```javascript
var _sj_root_2050643542;
var _sj_22791880 = {andIGiveYou:84, youGaveMe:42};
_sj_root_2050643542 = _sj_22791880;
_sj_root_2050643542;
```

That's somewhat scary, but remember that this is generated code that is meant to be evaluated as a JavaScript object. If you look at the second line, that's where the Money object's properties are being translated to a JavaScript hash, which in turn lets you get the properties with the dot notation.

15.2 Working with Ajax Requests and Responses

Using JavaScriptResolution is convenient for using JavaScript on the client side to do something with the response to an Ajax request. You can also transfer data in other formats, such as JSON or XML.[1]

However, if all you're doing in response to an Ajax request is updating a portion of the page, it can become cumbersome to construct HTML in JavaScript code using the values obtained in the response. I'll go even further and say that doing this makes me feel like I'm back in 1998, with only servlets at my disposal and having to construct HTML in Java code!

Fortunately, there's a much easier way. You can send HTML *fragments* in response to Ajax requests and use them directly to update a portion of the page. What makes this very convenient is that you can construct the HTML in a regular JSP, using all the goodness of Stripes, action beans, and everything else you've learned. The only difference is that the JSP renders a fragment instead of a complete page.

Automatic Page Portion Update

The idea of updating a page portion with the HTML fragment returned by the server is illustrated in Figure 15.2, on page 338. Prototype's Ajax.Updater sends an Ajax request and automatically updates the identified element ('result', in this example) with the response data.

Continuing the "double your money" example, say we just had an empty element to contain the result:

```
ajax/web/WEB-INF/jsp/updater.jsp

    <p>Let me double your money!</p>
    <p>
      <s:form beanclass="stripesbook.action.UpdaterActionBean">
        You give me $
        <s:text name="youGiveMe" onkeyup="sendMoney(this);"/>
        <s:submit name="doubleMoney"/>
      </s:form>
    </p>
▶   <p id="result"></p>
  </s:layout-component>
</s:layout-render>
```

---

1. In fact, that's why it's "Asynchronous JavaScript and XML"; initially XML was the main format used when transferring data in Ajax responses. Other formats have emerged since then; besides JavaScript code such as returned by JavaScriptResolution, JavaScript Object Notation (JSON, http://www.json.org) is also popular.

Tim Says...

Why Use JavaScript Instead of JSON or XML?

JavaScriptResolution generates and returns JavaScript code—not JSON and definitely not XML. Often this leads to the question, why not just use JSON? Or even better: JSON is a standard, so why don't you use it? Certainly there are advantages to using JSON—it's a nice compact format, and it's pretty human-readable. For cases where you want to send strictly hierarchical data to the browser, JSON is great.

The main reason to use JavaScript instead is that it can handle circular references properly. No declarative format can do this, and that includes both JSON and XML. For example, if you have a FamilyMember object that has properties that refer to its parents and its children, you quickly end up with circular references (for example, Freddy's child is Lily, who's father is Freddy). Modern persistence technologies like JPA and Hibernate tend to encourage these well-connected models. Using JavaScript allows us to do the following sequentially:

1. Convert "Freddy" to a JavaScript object.

2. Convert "Lily" to a JavaScript object.

3. Link Lily in as Freddy's child.

4. Link Freddy in as Lily's parent.

The result is that you get a JavaScript object graph that is linked up exactly like the object graph was on the Java side.

If you're still worried that JSON is a standard and JavaScript isn't, I'll gently remind you that JavaScript is actually specified by a standard called ECMAScript!

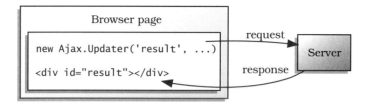

Figure 15.2: UPDATING A PAGE PORTION WITH THE SERVER'S RESPONSE

The 'result' ID is passed to the Ajax.Updater call:

`ajax/web/WEB-INF/jsp/updater.jsp`

```
new Ajax.Updater('result', form.action,
  { method: 'post',
    parameters: form.serialize()
  }
);
```

To respond to the request in the action bean, we can use a regular ForwardResolution to a JSP:

`ajax/src/stripesbook/action/UpdaterActionBean.java`

```
package stripesbook.action;
public class UpdaterActionBean extends BaseActionBean {
    private static final String RESULT = "/WEB-INF/jsp/result.jsp";
    public int youGiveMe;
    private Money money;

    public Money getMoney() {
        return money;
    }
    public Resolution doubleMoney() {
        money = new Money(youGiveMe, youGiveMe * 2);
        return new ForwardResolution(RESULT);
    }
}
```

In result.jsp, we'll render the fragment that is put back in the 'result' element. All the regular goodies are available, such as ${actionBean} to access the action bean's properties:

`ajax/web/WEB-INF/jsp/result.jsp`

```
You gave me $ ${actionBean.money.youGaveMe},
and I give you $ ${actionBean.money.andIGiveYou} back!
```

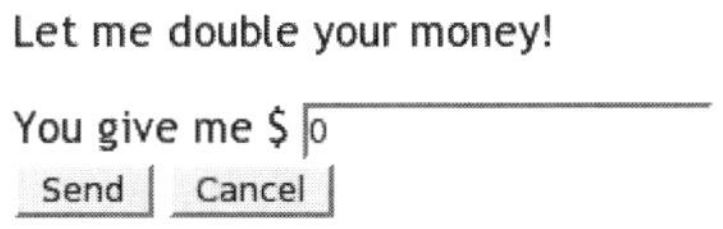

Let me double your money!

You give me $ |0

Send | Cancel |

Figure 15.3: AN AJAX FORM WITH MORE THAN ONE SUBMIT BUTTON

This is a simple example, but as these page fragments become more complex, you can imagine how much easier it is to use a ForwardResolution and a JSP rather than to return raw data and construct the page fragment in JavaScript.

Handling Multiple Submit Buttons

We've been issuing Ajax requests as the user is typing characters into a text field. Sometimes it's preferable to let the user finish entering values and submit the form only when the user clicks a submit button, while still using Ajax to send the request and handle the response.

Doing this with a form that has multiple submit buttons can be problematic if we're not careful. Consider the money example with a Send and a Cancel button, as shown in Figure 15.3.

When the form is serialized and posted, the default behavior is to include all inputs with their values, including all submit buttons no matter which one was clicked. Because Stripes relies on the parameter name matching an event name to determine which event handler to call, having all buttons present will wipe out the trail.

We can avoid this problem in a few ways. Prototype includes only one submit button in the form submission if we specify it as a parameter to form.serialize():

ajax/web/WEB-INF/jsp/multiple_submits.jsp

```
function sendMoney(control) {
  var form = control.form;
  new Ajax.Updater('result', form.action,
    { method: 'post',
      parameters: form.serialize({submit: control.name})
    }
  );
  return false;
}
```

Obviously, this solution is Prototype-specific. Although your favorite Ajax framework may also have an equivalent feature, it's good to know of a more general technique. One way is to include an _eventName request parameter with the name of the event handler, as in _eventName=save. Stripes uses that as the event name instead of looking at the names of the other request parameters. We saw other ways of specifying the event name in the request on page 286.

Besides taking multiple submit buttons into consideration, another important issue with Ajax form submission is to make sure that the JavaScript code returns **false** to prevent the browser from also submitting the form in the traditional (non-Ajax) way. In our example, sendMoney() returns false, which becomes the return value in the onclick= event of the submit button:

ajax/web/WEB-INF/jsp/multiple_submits.jsp

```
function sendMoney(control) {
  /* ... */
  return false;
}
  <s:submit name="doubleMoney" value="Send"
    onclick="return sendMoney(this);"/>
```

With these issues out of the way, we're ready to respond differently according to which button was clicked, Send or Cancel:

ajax/src/stripesbook/action/MultipleSubmitActionBean.java

```
private static final String RESULT = "/WEB-INF/jsp/result.jsp";
private static final String CANCEL = "/WEB-INF/jsp/cancel.jsp";
public Resolution doubleMoney() {
    money = new Money(youGiveMe, youGiveMe * 2);
    return new ForwardResolution(RESULT);
}
public Resolution cancel() {
    return new ForwardResolution(CANCEL);
}
```

The result.jsp file is the same as before, but cancel.jsp gives a different response to the user:

ajax/web/WEB-INF/jsp/cancel.jsp

```
Fine then, keep your money!
```

This message is displayed below the form if the user clicks the Cancel button, as illustrated in Figure 15.4, on the next page.

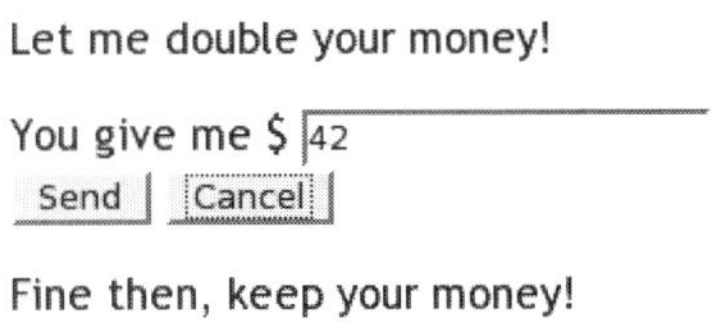

Let me double your money!

You give me $ 42

Send | Cancel

Fine then, keep your money!

Figure 15.4: RESPONSE AFTER CLICKING THE CANCEL BUTTON

Ajax and Validation Errors

When the user enters a money amount in the text field, it must be a valid integer value. What happens if the user enters something invalid? The whole form gets redisplayed in the 'result' element, producing the "double vision" effect illustrated in Figure 15.5, on the following page.

Why did this happen? Remember that when a validation error occurs, Stripes returns to the form instead of executing the event handler. That response is put back in the 'result' element by our Ajax response handler, so the form reappears. The validation error is not shown because we don't have the <s:errors/> tag in the form.

What we want to do is avoid returning the whole page and instead return just the fragment that displays the validation errors:

`ajax/web/WEB-INF/jsp/errors.jsp`

```
<s:errors/>
```

All that's left to do is implement ValidationErrorHandler in the action bean to override the default behavior of returning the source page resolution when validation errors occur. Instead, we'll return a resolution to errors.jsp:

`ajax/src/stripesbook/action/ErrorHandlingActionBean.java`

```
public class ErrorHandlingActionBean extends BaseActionBean
    implements ValidationErrorHandler
{
    private static final String ERRORS = "/WEB-INF/jsp/errors.jsp";
    public Resolution handleValidationErrors(ValidationErrors errors) {
        return new ForwardResolution(ERRORS);
    }
}
```

After submitting an invalid value, the error message is now shown within the page, as illustrated in Figure 15.6, on the next page. That's much better.

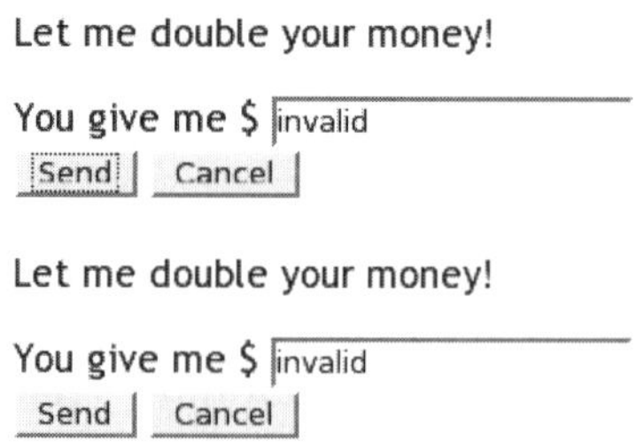

Let me double your money!

You give me $ |invalid_____
[Send] | Cancel |

Let me double your money!

You give me $ |invalid_____
Send | Cancel |

Figure 15.5: FORM GETTING REDISPLAYED ON INVALID INPUT

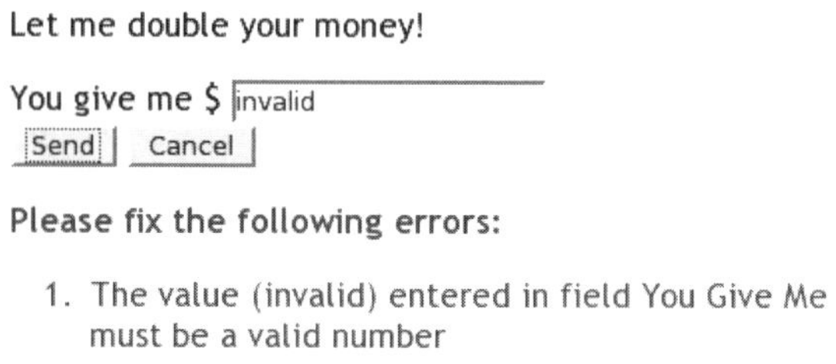

Let me double your money!

You give me $ |invalid_____
[Send] | Cancel |

Please fix the following errors:

1. The value (invalid) entered in field You Give Me
   must be a valid number

Figure 15.6: SHOWING VALIDATION ERRORS IN THE AJAX RESPONSE

Was That an Ajax Request?

By implementing the ValidationErrorHandler interface, you can return a resolution to a page fragment instead of the default getContext().getSourcePageResolution(). In this and other situations, you may want to do something different according to the request being Ajax or non-Ajax.

One way of finding out whether you're dealing with an Ajax request is by looking at the X-Requested-With request header. This header has a value of XMLHttpRequest for Ajax requests:

```
String header =
    getContext().getRequest().getHeader("X-Requested-With");

if (header != null && header.equalsIgnoreCase("XMLHttpRequest")) {
    // it's an AJAX request!
}
```

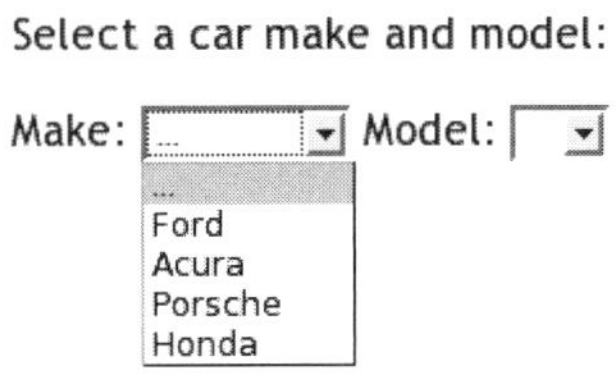

Select a car make and model:

Make: [... ▾] Model: [▾]

```
...
Ford
Acura
Porsche
Honda
```

Figure 15.7: INITIAL FORM BEFORE SELECTING A CAR MAKE

Using Partial Forms

By now you've realized that using Ajax and updating page fragments is easy and fun but also introduces new challenges. Another one of these is the use of page fragments with form input controls that are to be inserted back into an existing form, after an Ajax request.

Consider the form in Figure 15.7, which has select boxes to choose a car make and model. After a make is selected in the first box, an Ajax request is sent to update the models in the second box. The result after selecting a car make is shown in Figure 15.8, on the next page.

In Figure 15.9, on page 345, we can see how the onchange= event on the car make select box triggers an Ajax request with the make sent as a parameter. The server responds with the car model select box, populated with the models that correspond to the selected car make.

The model and action bean for this example are straightforward:

ajax/src/stripesbook/model/Cars.java

```java
package stripesbook.model;
public class Cars extends HashMap<String,List<String>> {
    public Cars() {
        put("Acura", Arrays.asList("CSX", "MDX", "TL", "TSX"));
        put("Ford", Arrays.asList("Escape", "Explorer", "Focus", "Mustang"));
        put("Honda", Arrays.asList("Accord", "Civic", "CR-V", "S2000"));
        put("Porsche", Arrays.asList("911 Carrera", "Boxster"));
    }
}
```

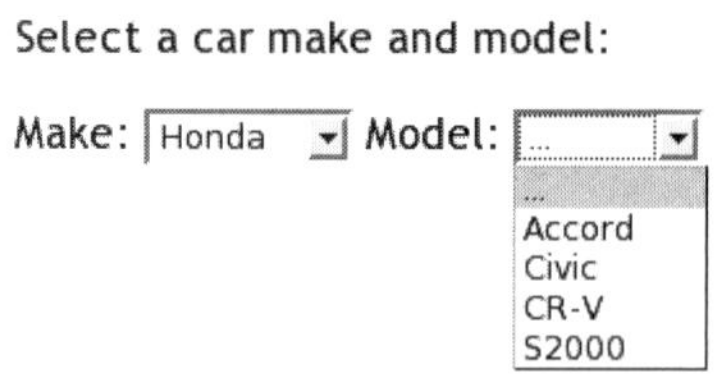

Select a car make and model:

Make: Honda ▾ Model: ... ▾
...
Accord
Civic
CR-V
S2000

Figure 15.8: Car models are populated after selecting a make.

ajax/src/stripesbook/action/PartialFormActionBean.java

```java
package stripesbook.action;
public class PartialFormActionBean extends BaseActionBean {
    private static final String VIEW = "/WEB-INF/jsp/cars.jsp";
    private static final String RESULT = "/WEB-INF/jsp/partial_form.jsp";
    private Cars cars = new Cars();
    public String make;
    private List<String> models;

    @DefaultHandler
    public Resolution view() {
        return new ForwardResolution(VIEW);
    }
    public Cars getCars() {
        return cars;
    }
    public List<String> getModels() {
        return models;
    }
    public Resolution updateModels() {
        models = cars.get(make);
        return new ForwardResolution(RESULT);
    }
}
```

The form contains the select box with the car makes and a 'model-Choices' placeholder for the car models:

ajax/web/WEB-INF/jsp/cars.jsp

```html
<s:form beanclass="stripesbook.action.PartialFormActionBean">
  Make:
  <s:select name="make" onchange="updateModels(this);">
    <s:option value="" label="..."/>
    <s:options-map map="${actionBean.cars}" label="key"/>
  </s:select>
  Model:
  <span id="modelChoices"><s:select name="models"/></span>
</s:form>
```

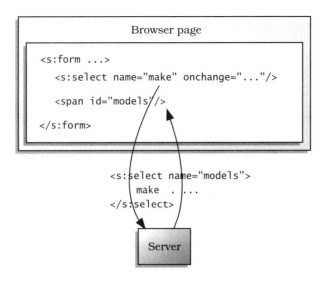

Figure 15.9: USING AJAX TO INSERTING FORM INPUT CONTROLS INTO AN
EXISTING FORM

When the user selects a car make, the onchange= event triggers a call to
updateModels(), which sends an Ajax request with the selected model.
The response is put back into the 'modelChoices' element:

ajax/web/WEB-INF/jsp/cars.jsp
```
function updateModels(control) {
  var form = control.form;
  var params =
    $H(form.serialize(true)).update({'_eventName':'updateModels'});

  new Ajax.Updater('modelChoices', form.action,
    { method: 'post',
      parameters: params
    }
  );
}
```

Notice how this time we're using the _eventName request attribute to
indicate the name of the event handler. The call to Prototype's $H() turns
the parameters into a hash, making it easy to add a key-value pair
before submitting the request.

The partial_form.jsp file contains the select box for the car models. Owing to the fact that it is being put back into an already-existing form, it's tempting to just return the select box:

ajax/web/WEB-INF/jsp/partial_form.jsp

```
<s:select name="models">
  <s:option value="" label="..."/>
  <s:options-collection collection="${actionBean.models}"/>
</s:select>
```

The problem is that Stripes doesn't know (or care) that we're working with Ajax here. When rendering partial_form.jsp, Stripes will complain that the <s:select> tag does not have a parent <s:form> tag. We can't very well say, "Yes, it does; it's sitting over there on the client side!" On the other hand, if we wrap the select box in an <s:form> tag, we're going to end up with *two* form tags, one nested inside the other.

To create form input controls that are going back into an existing form while still satisfying the requirement for a parent <s:form> tag, we just have to use the partial="true" attribute:

ajax/web/WEB-INF/jsp/partial_form.jsp

```
<s:form partial="true"
  beanclass="stripesbook.action.PartialFormActionBean">
  <s:select name="models">
    <s:option value="" label="..."/>
    <s:options-collection collection="${actionBean.models}"/>
  </s:select>
</s:form>
```

This tells Stripes not to render the HTML <form> tag or the special hidden inputs that Stripes normally renders in a form so that we don't end up with duplicate form tags. The example now works as expected.

15.3 Ajaxifying the Webmail Application

For the rest of this chapter, we'll use some Ajax in the webmail application to spice up the Contact List page. Instead of having separate Contact List, Contact Details, and Contact Form pages, we'll have everything in a single page and use Ajax to show, hide, and refresh different portions of the page.

Create a New Contact | Filter: [   ]

Last name	First name	Email	Action
Ballou	Jen	jb@stripesbook.org	❶ ❘ ✎ ❘ ⊗
Blair	Sammy	sb@stripesbook.org	❶ ❘ ✎ ❘ ⊗
Greene	Daniel	dg@stripesbook.org	❶ ❘ ✎ ❘ ⊗
Hawk	Lexi	lh@stripesbook.org	❶ ❘ ✎ ❘ ⊗
Hunter	Sophie	sh@stripesbook.org	❶ ❘ ✎ ❘ ⊗
McCallum	Donna	dm@stripesbook.org	❶ ❘ ✎ ❘ ⊗
Stocker	Betty	bs@stripesbook.org	❶ ❘ ✎ ❘ ⊗
Thompson	Lou	lt@stripesbook.org	❶ ❘ ✎ ❘ ⊗
Wells	George	gw@stripesbook.org	❶ ❘ ✎ ❘ ⊗
Wilson	Jason	jw@stripesbook.org	❶ ❘ ✎ ❘ ⊗

Figure 15.10: THE INITIAL AJAX CONTACT LIST PAGE

We'll be using jQuery for these examples, so the first thing to do is to import the library:

email_36/web/WEB-INF/jsp/common/layout_main.jsp

```
<script type="text/javascript"
  src="${contextPath}/js/jquery.js"></script>
```

The JSP for the contact list includes placeholders for the contact table, contact details, and contact form, which are all page *fragments* that are inserted into their respective containers:

email_36/web/WEB-INF/jsp/contact_list.jsp

```
<s:layout-render name="/WEB-INF/jsp/common/layout_menu.jsp"
  title="${title}" currentSection="ContactList">
  <s:layout-component name="body">
    <!-- ... -->
    <div id="contact_table" style="float: left">
      <%@include file="/WEB-INF/jsp/parts/contact_table.jsp"%>
    </div>
    <div id="contact_details" style="float: left"></div>
    <div style="clear: both"></div>
    <div id="contact_form"></div>
  </s:layout-component>
</s:layout-render>
```

The initial page is shown in Figure 15.10. Notice the Filter text field at the top and the icons for the View, Update, and Delete links. All controls will issue Ajax requests and modify portions of the page. Let's look at each feature, starting with the Filter field.

Create a New Contact | Filter: B

Last name	First name	Email	Action
Ballou	Jen	jb@stripesbook.org	❶ | ✎ | ⊗
Blair	Sammy	sb@stripesbook.org	❶ | ✎ | ⊗
Stocker	Betty	bs@stripesbook.org	❶ | ✎ | ⊗

Figure 15.11: FILTERING THE CONTACT LIST

Filtering the Contact List

As the user types characters in the Filter field, the contact list is filtered to show only the contacts for whom either the first name or the last name starts with the letters in the filter. An example is shown in Figure 15.11.

We can use a plain HTML text field with an onkeyup= event:

```
email_36/web/WEB-INF/jsp/contact_list.jsp
```
```
<s:url var="url"
  beanclass="stripesbook.action.ContactListActionBean"/>
<fmt:message key="contactList.filter"/>:
<input type="text" onkeyup="filterContacts(this, '${url}');"/>
```

The filterContacts() JavaScript method receives the text field and the URL to ContactListActionBean. A simple Ajax request to the findByName() event handler is made, passing the characters from the text field via the filter parameter. The response is the page fragment with the filtered contact table. It's easy to place the fragment back with a jQuery selector: '#contact_table' refers to the element with id="contact_table".

```
email_36/web/js/contact_list.js
```
```
function filterContacts(field, url) {
  $.get(url,
    { 'filter': $(field).val(),
      '_eventName': 'findByName'
    },
    function(data) {
      $('#contact_table').html(data);
    }
  );
}
```

In ContactListActionBean, we just have to receive the filter parameter and use it to retrieve the matching contacts in the findByName() event handler:

`email_36/src/stripesbook/action/ContactListActionBean.java`

```
public String filter;

public Resolution findByName() {
    if (filter != null && filter.length() > 0) {
        contacts = contactDao.findByName(filter, getUser());
    }
    return new ForwardResolution(TABLE);
}
```

Notice that we filter only if there is at least one character in the text field. That way, if the user deletes everything from the text field, the contact list goes back to being fully populated.

Finally, a simple query in the Contact DAO retrieves the list of contacts that match the filter:

`email_36/src/stripesbook/dao/impl/stripersist/ContactDaoImpl.java`

```
@SuppressWarnings("unchecked")
public List<Contact> findByName(String startsWith, User user) {
    return Stripersist.getEntityManager()
        .createQuery("select distinct c from "
          + getEntityClass().getName() + " c "
          + "where (c.firstName like '" + startsWith + "%' or "
          + "c.lastName like '" + startsWith + "%') "
          + "and c.user = :user"
        ).setParameter("user", user).getResultList();
}
```

The contact list now changes as the user types characters in the Filter field. Pretty spiffy!

Viewing Contact Details

To view the contact details, the user clicks the "i" icon in the column. The contact's information appears next to the table, as you can see in Figure 15.12, on the next page. A small "x" lets the user remove the details area from the page.

We used a plain HTML control for the Filter text field because there wasn't much to gain from using the Stripes equivalent. For the contact details link, however, we can take advantage of the <s:link> tag's features and attach an event to the onclick= attribute.

st name	Email	Action					First name: Jen
en	jb@stripesbook.org	❶	❘	✎	❘	⊗	Last name: Ballou
;ammy	sb@stripesbook.org	❶	❘	✎	❘	⊗	Email: jb@stripesbook.org
)aniel	dg@stripesbook.org	❶	❘	✎	❘	⊗	Phone number: 555-555-6495
.exi	lh@stripesbook.org	❶	❘	✎	❘	⊗	Birth date: 1982-08-30
:ophie	sh@stripesbook.org	❶	❘	✎	❘	⊗	Gender: Female

Figure 15.12: VIEWING A CONTACT'S DETAILS

email_36/web/WEB-INF/jsp/parts/contact_table.jsp

```
<s:link beanclass="stripesbook.action.ContactListActionBean"
  event="details"
  onclick="return ajaxLink(this, '#contact_details');">
  <s:param name="contact" value="${contact}"/>
  <img src="${contextPath}/images/info.gif" border="0"/>
</s:link> |
```

We're calling the JavaScript ajaxLink() function with the request URL and the ID of the page portion to be updated with the response. Can you guess what the ajaxLink() function looks like?

email_36/web/js/contact_list.js

```
function ajaxLink(link, update) {
  $.get(link, function(data) {
    $(update).html(data);
    $(update).show();
  });
  return false;
}
```

This function is easily reusable; it generically submits an Ajax request to the given link and updates the identified page portion with the fragment received in the response. For the contact details link, we're passing the contact ID with the contact parameter and calling the details() event handler on ContactListActionBean, which forwards to contact_details.jsp:

email_36/src/stripesbook/action/ContactBaseActionBean.java

```
public abstract class ContactBaseActionBean extends BaseActionBean {
    private Contact contact;

    public Contact getContact() {
        return contact;
    }
```

```
    public void setContact(Contact contact) {
        User user = contact.getUser();
        if (user == null || getUser().equals(user)) {
            this.contact = contact;
        }
    }
}
```

email_36/src/stripesbook/action/ContactListActionBean.java

```
public class ContactListActionBean extends ContactBaseActionBean {
    private static final String DETAILS =
        "/WEB-INF/jsp/parts/contact_details.jsp";

    public Resolution details() {
        return new ForwardResolution(DETAILS);
    }
}
```

The contact_details.jsp file renders the contact information exactly like before, but without the surrounding page layout. The JSP also includes the "x" icon at the bottom:

email_36/web/WEB-INF/jsp/parts/contact_details.jsp

```
<table class="view">
  <tr>
    <td class="label"><s:label for="contact.firstName"/>:</td>
    <td class="value">
      ${fn:escapeXml(actionBean.contact.firstName)}
    </td>
  </tr>
  <!-- same for other fields... -->
</table>
<a href="#" style="padding-left: 24px;"
  onclick="$('#contact_details').hide();">
  <img src="${contextPath}/images/close.png" border="0"/>
</a>
```

The fragment is put back into the #contact_details placeholder, next to the contact table, and we get the result from Figure 15.12, on the facing page. The user can click the "x" to remove the contact details portion from the page.

Instant Delete

Since we're making the contact list more clickety-click-click, let's shun that "Are you sure?" pop-up box and delete the contact when the user clicks the "x" icon, instantly refreshing the contact table.

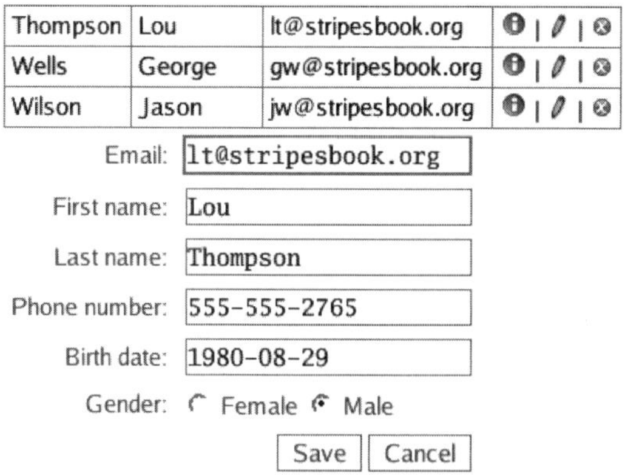

Thompson	Lou	lt@stripesbook.org	❶ | ✏ | ⊗
Wells	George	gw@stripesbook.org	❶ | ✏ | ⊗
Wilson	Jason	jw@stripesbook.org	❶ | ✏ | ⊗

Email: `lt@stripesbook.org`

First name: `Lou`

Last name: `Thompson`

Phone number: `555-555-2765`

Birth date: `1980-08-29`

Gender: ○ Female ⦿ Male

[Save] [Cancel]

Figure 15.13: THE CONTACT FORM APPEARS BELOW THE CONTACT TABLE.

```
email_36/web/WEB-INF/jsp/parts/contact_table.jsp
```
```
<s:link beanclass="stripesbook.action.ContactListActionBean"
  event="delete"
  onclick="return ajaxLink(this, '#contact_table');">
  <s:param name="contact" value="${contact}"/>
  <img src="${contextPath}/images/delete.gif" border="0"/>
</s:link>
```

Notice how we're reusing the ajaxLink() function. In fact, the delete link is quite similar to the contact details link. We're just using a different event on the action bean, updating a different portion of the page ('#contact_table' instead of '#contact_details'), and showing a different icon. In the action bean, the delete() event handler deletes the contact and returns a page fragment with the refreshed contact list table.

Ajaxifying the Contact Form

To complete the Ajaxification of the contact list, let's make the contact form appear below the table, as in Figure 15.13. The form is pre-populated when the user updates an existing contact and is blank for creating a new contact—same as before.

Making the contact form appear in the '#contact_form' placeholder works the same way as the other Ajax links we've created so far:

```
email_36/web/WEB-INF/jsp/parts/contact_table.jsp
```
```
<s:link beanclass="stripesbook.action.ContactFormActionBean"
  onclick="return ajaxLink(this, '#contact_form');">
```

```
<s:param name="contact" value="${contact}"/>
<img src="${contextPath}/images/update.png" border="0"/>
</s:link> |
```

For creating a new contact, the link is the same but without the contact parameter.

Now that the form is in place, rub your hands together because we're going to use a few neat tricks to submit the form via Ajax and handle the response.

First, we'll use the onclick= event on the Save button to call submitForm(), passing the button as a parameter:

email_36/web/WEB-INF/jsp/parts/contact_form.jsp

```
<s:submit name="save" onclick="return submitForm(this);"/>
```

In the JavaScript code, submitForm() serializes the form and adds the '_eventName' parameter with the name of the button:

email_36/web/js/contact_form.js

```
function submitForm(button) {
  var form = button.form;
  var params = $(form).serializeArray();
  params.push({name: '_eventName', value: button.name});

  $.post(form.action, params, function(data) {
    $('#contact_form').hide();
    $('#contact_table').html(data);
  });
  return false;
}
```

After creating the parameters, the form is posted via Ajax, and the result, which is the updated contact table, is put back into the '#contact_table' section, while the contact form, having done its task, is hidden again.

There's just one problem. . . can you figure out what it is?

What if the user submits the form with invalid input? As you know, the default Stripes behavior in that case is to redisplay the form with error messages. Since we're blindly putting the response into the contact table portion of the page, the table gets clobbered by a form with validation errors.

The problem is not that we're getting back the form instead of the contact table; rather, it's that we need to put the form back into the '#contact_form' portion instead of into '#contact_table'. In other words, we need some way of knowing *where* to put the response fragment, according to whether validation errors occurred.

My initial solution to this problem was to look for something in the contact form fragment that isn't in the contact table—the *<form>* tag, the error CSS class, or even an HTML comment that says, "There are validation errors!" Although this works, it's an ugly and brittle solution. Discussion with the friendly and talented Stripes community yielded a more elegant solution: use a header in the HTTP response to indicate that the form was successful. Upon receiving that header, the contact table is refreshed as before; otherwise, the form with validation error messages goes back into '#contact_form'.

OK, let's set a response header after successfully saving the contact. We can do this in the save() event handler, before returning the ForwardResolution:

email_36/src/stripesbook/action/ContactFormActionBean.java

```java
public Resolution save() {
    // save the contact...

    getContext().getResponse().setHeader("X-Stripes-Success","true");
    return new ForwardResolution(ContactListActionBean.class,
        "table");
}
```

Adding the response header in contact_table.jsp also works:

```jsp
<%= response.setHeader("X-Stripes-Success","true"); %>
```

I prefer adding the response in the action bean. I find that the intention of signaling success is clearer in the save() event handler method than it is in the JSP.

On the client side, we need to look for the response header in the Ajax callback function. Response headers are available in the standard XHR (XMLHttpRequest) object, which is the core object used when sending and receiving data with Ajax. With jQuery, the XHR object is returned from the function that sends the Ajax request—$.post, in our case. We can look for the 'X-Stripes-Success' with a call to getResponseHeader() on the XHR object:

email_36/web/js/contact_form.js

```javascript
function submitForm(button) {
  var form = button.form;
  var params = $(form).serializeArray();
  params.push({name: '_eventName', value: button.name});
```

```
  var xhr = $.post(form.action, params, function(data) {
▶    if (xhr.getResponseHeader('X-Stripes-Success')) {
      $('#contact_form').hide();
      $('#contact_table').html(data);
    }
    else {
      $('#contact_form').html(data);
    }
  });
  return false;
}
```

As you can see, upon finding the success response header, the form is hidden, and the contact table is refreshed. If the success indicator is not present, validation errors have occurred, and the contact form is redisplayed with error messages. Beautiful! The contact form is fully Ajaxified!

Hey, wait a minute, what about that Cancel button? Well, that's almost too easy. It just hides the form:

email_36/web/WEB-INF/jsp/parts/contact_form.jsp

```
<s:button name="cancel" onclick="$('#contact_form').hide();"/>
```

Now the contact form is fully Ajaxified.

15.4 Adding Client-Side Validation

With JavaScript, you can perform client-side form validation so that the user gets feedback before posting the form to the server. Although this does *not* replace server-side validation, it can improve the user's experience by giving more immediate validation information. It also saves bandwidth by not sending anything to the server until the form passes the validation being performed on the client.

The Stripes-Stuff project (http://www.stripesstuff.org) includes a plug-in by Aaron Porter that works with Stripes and jQuery to easily add client-side validation to a Stripes form. The plug-in discovers and applies the form's validation criteria as the user is filling out the form. This saves you a ton of work because you don't have to take all the validation rules that you've defined in the action bean and duplicate them in JavaScript code. The plug-in uses the validation metadata to dynamically do the work for you.

Back on page 201, we saw how ValidationMetadata provides runtime validation information. The <s:field-metadata> tag complements this by translating the validation metadata into JavaScript key-value pairs, as follows:

```
{
  'contact.email':
    {required:true,trim:true,typeConverter:'EmailTypeConverter'},
  'contact.firstName':
    {trim:true,maxlength:25,typeConverter:'StringTypeConverter'},
  'contact.lastName':
    {trim:true,minlength:2,maxlength:40,typeConverter:'StringTypeConverter'},
  'contact.phoneNumber':
    {typeConverter:'PhoneNumberTypeConverterFormatter'},
  'contact.birthDate':
    {type:'Date',trim:true,typeConverter:'DateTypeConverter'}
  'contact.gender':
    {typeConverter:'EnumeratedTypeConverter'},
}
```

The plug-in uses this information to validate the fields on the fly. Let's use it with the contact form as an example.

To set up the plug-in, import the JavaScript libraries, in order:

ajax/web/WEB-INF/jsp/client_side_validation.jsp

```
<script src="${contextPath}/js/jquery.js"
  type="text/javascript"></script>

<script src="${contextPath}/js/jquery.validation.js"
  type="text/javascript"></script>

<script src="${contextPath}/js/stripes.jquery.validation.js"
  type="text/javascript"></script>
```

Next, *right before the closing form tag*, add the <s:field-metadata> tag followed by a call to applyStripesValidation(), like this:

ajax/web/WEB-INF/jsp/client_side_validation.jsp

```
<s:form beanclass="stripesbook.action.ClientFormActionBean">
  <!-- form input controls... -->

  <s:field-metadata var="fmd"/>
  <script type="text/javascript">
    applyStripesValidation('${fmd.formId}', ${fmd});
  </script>
</s:form>
```

The <s:field-metadata> tag places the validation metadata in the variable, fmd. You can then access the information with ${fmd}, as well as the generated form ID with ${fmd.formId}. These two pieces of information must be passed to applyStripesValidation().

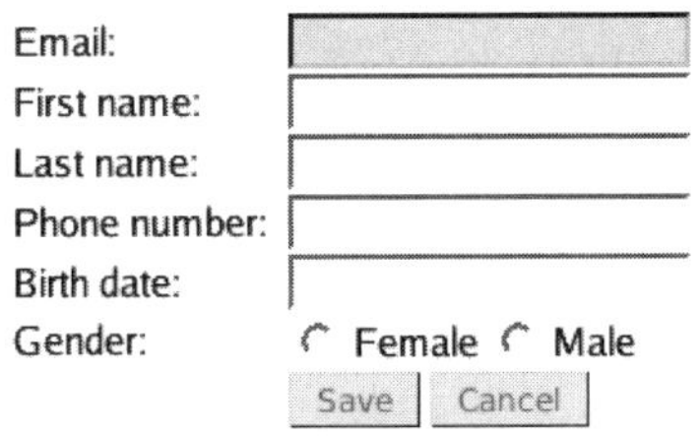

Figure 15.14: Initial contact form with client-side validation

Finally, the default behavior of the plug-in is to add the invalid CSS class to input controls that fail validation. So, we'll highlight them in the same way as we were doing with the Stripes error class:

ajax/web/css/style.css

```
input.error, input.invalid {
  border-color: red;
  background-color: #FFCCCC;
}
```

That's all there is to it. The initial form is shown in Figure 15.14. Notice that the Email field is highlighted because it fails validation—it is a required field. Also, the two submit buttons, Save and Cancel, are disabled because of the presence of validation errors.

As the user types values into the fields, these are highlighted (or not), and the submit buttons are enabled or disabled, according to the presence or absence of validation errors. When executing JavaScript code with each keystroke, it's best to turn off the browser's autocomplete feature with the autocomplete= attribute on the text fields. But wait—that attribute is not recognized by the *<s:text>* tag because it's not technically valid HTML. Are we out of luck? Of course not. Stripes includes another version of its tag library that accepts dynamic attributes:

ajax/web/WEB-INF/jsp/common/taglibs.jsp

```
<%@taglib prefix="s-dyn"
  uri="http://stripes.sourceforge.net/stripes-dynattr.tld"%>
```

We can keep using the original version and use this dynamic version whenever we need unrecognized attributes:

ajax/web/WEB-INF/jsp/client_side_validation.jsp

```
<s-dyn:text id="contact.email" name="contact.email"
  autocomplete="off"/>
```

Email:	fred@stripesbook.org
First name:	
Last name:	D
Phone number:	555-12
Birth date:	
Gender:	○ Female ○ Male
	Save Cancel

Figure 15.15: THE STATE OF THE CONTACT FORM AFTER ENTERING SOME VALUES

The form in Figure 15.15 shows the state after the user has typed something in. Notice that the "Last name" field is now in error; it is optional, but with a minimum length of 2. Therefore, entering a single character is not valid, and the field is in error.

The plug-in has a few limitations. Looking again at Figure 15.15, the phone number field is not in error despite the input being invalid. That's because we're using our own custom type converter, which the plug-in doesn't recognize. You'll also notice that the [Cancel] button is disabled even though it is associated with a @DontValidate event handler in the action bean.

These limitations very well may have been resolved by the time you read these lines, so check http://www.stripes-stuff.org for the latest version.

You can also pass options to the applyStripesValidation() function to customize the behavior of the plug-in. For example, we can tell the plug-in not to disable buttons. At the same time, we can specify the error CSS class so that it matches the one used by Stripes:

`ajax/web/WEB-INF/jsp/client_side_validation.jsp`

```
var options = {
  invalidClass: 'error',
  disableSubmit: false
};
applyStripesValidation('${fmd.formId}', ${fmd}, options);
```

The form is still validated on the client side when the user submits the form. The buttons are enabled, and a pop-up message appears if the form is submitted with validation errors, as illustrated in Figure 15.16, on the next page.

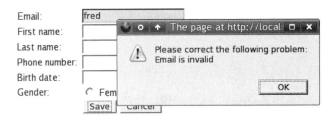

Figure 15.16: FORM BEING VALIDATED ON THE CLIENT SIDE WITH A POP-UP ERROR MESSAGE

Simulating Client-Side Validation with a Little Help from the Server

Client-side validation is nice, but you saw how it does have some limitations. Another strategy is to simulate client-side validation by issuing Ajax requests as the user is filling out the form, using the responses to show error messages instantly. The advantage of doing this is that we're reusing the server-side validation code; the drawback is that we're constantly sending and receiving data between the client and the server, so we're no longer saving bandwidth—quite the opposite. Nevertheless, let's have a look at this technique.

First we'll add a call to a JavaScript method in the onkeyup= event of the text fields:

ajax/web/WEB-INF/jsp/server_side_validation.jsp

```
<s-dyn:text id="contact.email" name="contact.email"
  autocomplete="off" onkeyup="validate(this.form);"/>
```

We'll also surround the <s:errors> tag with a container so that we have a place to put validation error messages:

ajax/web/WEB-INF/jsp/server_side_validation.jsp

```
<span id="contact_email" class="error">
  <s:errors field="contact.email"/>
</span>
```

Tim Says...

Stripes Has Two Tag Libraries. Wait, What?

The main Stripes tag library is imported, as Freddy showed in Chapter 2, *Stripes 101: Getting Started*, with the URI http://stripes.sourceforge.net/stripes.tld. There is a second, and largely identical, tag library that comes with Stripes that can be imported with the URI http://stripes.sourceforge.net/stripes-dynattr.tld. The main difference between these two tag libraries is that the input tags in the first tag library do not support JSP dynamic attributes, whereas the ones in the second do.

I advise everyone to use the first library almost all the time. In fact, for several versions, we had only the first tag library. It has the advantage of providing much better error checking. Because the set of attributes that a tag accepts is limited to a fixed and known set, the JSP compiler can provide compile-time checking of attribute names, and IDEs can usually spot errors immediately. This is especially helpful for attributes that are just passed through to the HTML, because Stripes won't complain if those attributes are misspelled. For instance, if you typed <s:text name="username" clas="important"/>, the mis-spelling of "class" would be flagged immediately, whereas with dynamic attributes the clas attribute would just get passed through to the HTML. You wouldn't be told about the typo in the IDE, and you'd notice the problem later only when the text field wouldn't be displayed with the "important" class.

Despite these advantages, there are times when you need HTML tags to have attributes that aren't technically valid HTML. This is quite common with Ajax or JavaScript libraries. For example, you might want to write <s:text name="friend" autocomplete="off"/>. Since "autocomplete" isn't valid HTML, the standard Stripes tag won't let you write it. For this you have to use the tag that supports dynamic attributes—this will pass any unknown attributes through to the HTML.

It's perfectly valid to import both tag libraries on the same page (with different prefixes) and intermingle them within the same form. That's why my advice is to use the standard library where possible—to get the best error checking possible—and then use the dynamic tag library just on the tags where it is needed.

The validate() JavaScript function submits the form to the validate()
event handler:

```
ajax/web/WEB-INF/jsp/server_side_validation.jsp
$(document).ready(function() {
  validate($('#${fmd.formId}'));
});
function validate(form) {
  var params = $(form).serializeArray();
  params.push({name: '_eventName', value: 'validate'});

  $.post(form.action, params, function(data) {
    /* ... */
  });
}
```

The action bean implements ValidationErrorHandler and checks for an
Ajax request. In that case, the validation error messages are put in
a map and returned in a JavaScriptResolution. With no validation errors,
validate() just returns an empty map:

```
ajax/src/stripesbook/action/ServerFormActionBean.java
public Resolution validate() {
    return new JavaScriptResolution(Collections.emptyMap());
}
public Resolution handleValidationErrors(ValidationErrors errors) {
    String header =
        getContext().getRequest().getHeader("X-Requested-With");

    if (header != null && header.equalsIgnoreCase("XMLHttpRequest")) {
        Map<String,List<String>> map = new HashMap<String,List<String>>();
        Locale locale = getContext().getLocale();
        for (String key : errors.keySet()) {
            List<ValidationError> errorList = errors.get(key);
            List<String> messages = new ArrayList<String>(errorList.size());
            for (ValidationError error : errorList) {
                messages.add(error.getMessage(locale));
            }
            map.put(key, messages);
        }
        return new JavaScriptResolution(map);
    }
    return null;
}
```

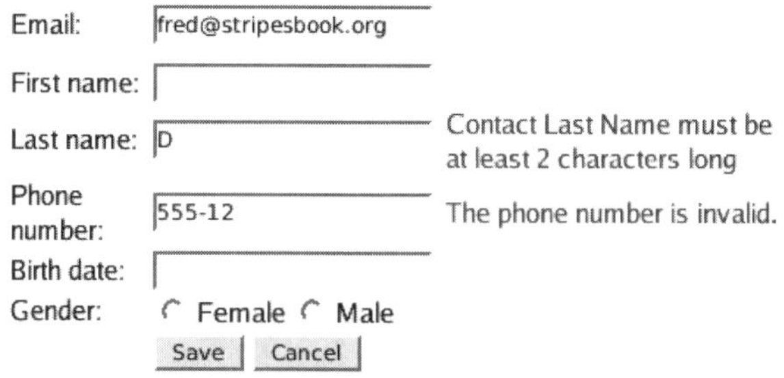

Email: fred@stripesbook.org

First name:

Last name: D   Contact Last Name must be
                   at least 2 characters long

Phone
number: 555-12   The phone number is invalid.

Birth date:

Gender: ○ Female ○ Male

Save   Cancel

Figure 15.17: FORM BEING VALIDATED BY THE SERVER SIDE AS THE
USER TYPES

Back on the client side, all that's left to do is to retrieve the response
and put the error messages in their placeholders:

ajax/web/WEB-INF/jsp/server_side_validation.jsp

```
$.post(form.action, params, function(data) {
  // Clear out any previous error messages
  var fieldMetadata = ${fmd};
  for (field in fieldMetadata) {
      $(getElement(field)).empty();
  }
  // Display current error messages
  var messages = eval(data);
  for (var field in messages) {
    var message = messages[field];
    var element = getElement(field);
    for (line in message) {
      $('<p></p>').text(message[line]).appendTo(element);
    }
  }
});
function getElement(field) {
  return '#' + field.replace(/\./g, "_");
}
```

Pretty simple. The only detail is that we have to change the dots to
underscores in the field name so that identifying the placeholder for
the error message works properly. Now, as you can see in Figure 15.17,
validation works even for our custom phone number type converter.

It works nicely, but it's not perfect. We're submitting the form at every
keystroke, so it's not really client-side validation. However, it's good to
know that you have different strategies to choose from when you want
to make forms more interactive.

A Little Ajax, or a Lot

You've seen how Ajax can make your web applications more responsive and more fun to use. What's nice about Ajax is that it's not an
all-or-nothing proposition; you can use just a little, or you can use a
lot. You don't need to do everything at once, either; you can start by
Ajaxifying just a small part of your application and convert other parts
progressively.

I Hope You've Enjoyed This Book!

It always somewhat bothers me when I read a computer book and the
last chapter ends just like all the other chapters. I feel like it's missing
some sort of closure.

So, allow me to say that I hope you've enjoyed reading this book and
that you'll love developing with Stripes as much as I do. If you have
any questions, drop us a line on the Stripes mailing list. You'll find a
friendly, helpful, and knowledgeable community. In the mood for something a little more "real time"? Drop by the #stripes IRC channel on the
freenode.net network. Hope to see you there.

Have fun with Stripes!

Configuration Reference

Stripes is very light on configuration: there's actually only one required configuration parameter. All others are optional. What's more, by using the Extension.Packages parameter and adding Stripes extensions to those packages, you've opened the door to customizing just about everything in Stripes without any additional configuration!

Nevertheless, you still have the option of using configuration parameters in web.xml to add extensions, as listed in Section A.2, *Extensions*, on the next page. Some default implementations also accept additional parameters; you will find those in Section A.3, *Settings*, on page 372. Finally, you'll be interested in Section A.4, *Interceptors*, on page 374 if you want to change the default interceptors or if you need your interceptors to run in a specific order.

A.1   Required Configuration

Only one configuration parameter is required by Stripes.

ActionResolver.Packages

This tells Stripes which packages to use when looking for action beans. Indicate each package *root*—subpackages are automatically included, so do *not* use .* at the end of the package name. For example:

```
<!-- Only one package root -->
<init-param>
  <param-name>ActionResolver.Packages</param-name>
  <param-value>stripesbook.action</param-value>
</init-param>
```

```
<!-- Multiple package roots are separated with commas -->
<init-param>
  <param-name>ActionResolver.Packages</param-name>
  <param-value>
    stripesbook.action,
    another.pkg
  </param-value>
</init-param>
```

A.2 Extensions

In this section, you will find the configuration parameters for Stripes *extensions*: classes that implement all subinterfaces of Configurable-Component, as well as Formatter and TypeConverter implementations. If you specify the Extension.Packages parameter shown next, *all* the following parameters are optional. Use them only if you prefer not to have your implementation automatically loaded by the extension packages mechanism.

Extension.Packages

This parameter is optional but *highly* recommended. By specifying the packages where your Stripes extensions live, you can add, change, and remove extensions in those packages without having to make any other configuration changes. Stripes automatically loads all extensions from those packages unless you've marked them with @DontAutoLoad.

For example:

```
<!-- Only one package root -->
<init-param>
  <param-name>Extension.Packages</param-name>
  <param-value>stripesbook.ext</param-value>
</init-param>
```

```
<!-- Multiple package roots are separated with commas -->
<init-param>
  <param-name>Extension.Packages</param-name>
  <param-value>
    stripesbook.ext,
    org.stripesstuff.stripersist
  </param-value>
</init-param>
```

ActionBeanContextFactory.Class

This is the implementation of the ActionBeanContextFactory interface, which is responsible for creating ActionBeanContext objects.

The default is DefaultActionBeanContextFactory. Here's an example:

```
<init-param>
  <param-name>ActionBeanContextFactory.Class</param-name>
  <param-value>
    stripesbook.nonext.MyActionBeanContextFactory
  </param-value>
</init-param>
```

ActionBeanContext.Class

This is the ActionBeanContext subclass to use instead of the default ActionBeanContext class. This is loaded by DefaultActionBeanContextFactory. Here's an example:

```
<init-param>
  <param-name>ActionBeanContext.Class</param-name>
  <param-value>stripesbook.nonext.MyActionBeanContext</param-value>
</init-param>
```

ActionBeanPropertyBinder.Class

This is the implementation of the ActionBeanPropertyBinder interface, responsible for validating, type converting, and binding request parameters. The default is DefaultActionBeanPropertyBinder. Here's an example:

```
<init-param>
  <param-name>ActionBeanPropertyBinder.Class</param-name>
  <param-value>
    stripesbook.nonext.MyActionBeanPropertyBinder
  </param-value>
</init-param>
```

ActionResolver.Class

This is the implementation of the ActionResolver interface, which determines the action bean and event handler method that handles a request. The default is NameBasedActionResolver. Here's an example:

```
<init-param>
  <param-name>ActionResolver.Class</param-name>
  <param-value>stripesbook.nonext.MyActionResolver</param-value>
</init-param>
```

Configuration.Class

This is the implementation of the Configuration interface. The default is RuntimeConfiguration. Note that this is the class that reads all other configuration parameters. You can provide your own implementation and use whatever strategy that you like to determine the implementations of all the modules used by Stripes. For example:

```
<init-param>
  <param-name>Configuration.Class</param-name>
  <param-value>stripesbook.nonext.MyConfiguration</param-value>
</init-param>
```

ExceptionHandler.Class

This is the ExceptionHandler implementation. The default is DefaultExceptionHandler. An alternate implementation is also available, DelegatingExceptionHandler, which you can use with the following:

```
<init-param>
  <param-name>ExceptionHandler.Class</param-name>
  <param-value>
    net.sourceforge.stripes.exception.DelegatingExceptionHandler
  </param-value>
</init-param>
```

DelegatingExceptionHandler works much like DefaultExceptionHandler except that you can use more than one exception-handling class. Each of those classes must implement AutoExceptionHandler (a marker interface) and implement methods with the same signature as exception-handling methods in DefaultExceptionHandler:

```
public Resolution methodName(Type exceptionType,
  HttpServletRequest request, HttpServletResponse response);
```

Returning a Resolution is optional; any other return type will be ignored.

DelegatingExceptionHandler discovers AutoExceptionHandler implementations via Extension.Packages, but you can also use DelegatingExceptionHandler.Packages to specify different packages:

```
<init-param>
  <param-name>DelegatingExceptionHandler.Packages</param-name>
  <param-value>stripesbook.exception</param-value>
</init-param>
```

FormatterFactory.Class

This is the FormatterFactory implementation. A custom formatter factory lets you control how Formatter instances are created and also allows you to register custom formatters outside the extension packages. For example:

```
<init-param>
  <param-name>FormatterFactory.Class</param-name>
  <param-value>stripesbook.nonext.MyFormatterFactory</param-value>
</init-param>
```

```
package stripesbook.nonext;
public class MyFormatterFactory extends DefaultFormatterFactory {
    @Override
    public void init(Configuration config) {
        super.init(config);
        add(MyType.class, MyTypeFormatter.class);
    }
}
```

LocalePicker.Class

This is the implementation of the LocalePicker interface, which decides which Locale to use for a request. The default is DefaultLocalePicker. Here's an example:

```
<init-param>
  <param-name>LocalePicker.Class</param-name>
  <param-value>stripesbook.nonext.MyLocalePicker</param-value>
</init-param>
```

LocalizationBundleFactory.Class

This is the implementation of the LocalizationBundleFactory interface, which returns the ResourceBundle for error messages and for form field labels. The default is DefaultLocalizationBundleFactory. Here's an example:

```
<init-param>
  <param-name>LocalizationBundleFactory.Class</param-name>
  <param-value>
    stripesbook.nonext.MyLocalizationBundleFactory
  </param-value>
</init-param>
```

MultipartWrapperFactory.Class

This is the implementation of the MultipartWrapperFactory interface, which is responsible for returning a MultiWrapper implementation for a request. The default is DefaultMultipartWrapperFactory. Here's an example:

```
<init-param>
  <param-name>MultipartWrapperFactory.Class</param-name>
  <param-value>
    stripesbook.nonext.MyMultipartWrapperFactory
  </param-value>
</init-param>
```

MultipartWrapper.Class

This is the implementation of the MultipartWrapper interface, which parses a multipart/form-data request. This parameter is used by Default-MultipartWrapperFactory. The default is CommonsMultipartWrapper if you have commons-fileupload.jar and commons-io.jar in the class path, or it's CosMultipartWrapper if you have cos.jar in the class path. If neither implementation can be loaded, a debugging message is logged. No exception is thrown because not all web applications need to support file uploads.

To use a different implementation, use the following:

```
<init-param>
  <param-name>MultipartWrapper.Class</param-name>
  <param-value>stripesbook.nonext.MyMultipartWrapper</param-value>
</init-param>
```

PopulationStrategy.Class

This is the implementation of the PopulationStrategy interface to populate the values of form input tags. The default is DefaultPopulationStrategy. As we saw on page 181, the BeanFirstPopulationStrategy is a useful alternative:

```
<init-param>
  <param-name>PopulationStrategy.Class</param-name>
  <param-value>
    net.sourceforge.stripes.tag.BeanFirstPopulationStrategy
  </param-value>
</init-param>
```

TagErrorRendererFactory.Class

This is the implementation of the TagErrorRendererFactory interface, which returns objects that implement TagErrorRenderer. The default is DefaultTagErrorRendererFactory. Here's an example:

```
<init-param>
  <param-name>TagErrorRendererFactory.Class</param-name>
  <param-value>
    stripesbook.nonext.MyTagErrorRendererFactory
  </param-value>
</init-param>
```

TagErrorRenderer.Class

This is the implementation of the TagErrorRenderer interface, which formats form input fields when they are in error. This parameter is loaded by DefaultTagErrorRendererFactory. The default is DefaultTagErrorRenderer. Here's an example:

```
<init-param>
  <param-name>TagErrorRenderer.Class</param-name>
  <param-value>stripesbook.nonext.MyTagErrorRenderer</param-value>
</init-param>
```

TypeConverterFactory.Class

This is the implementation of the TypeConverterFactory interface. The default is DefaultTypeConverterFactory. A custom type converter factory lets you control how TypeConverter instances are created and also allows you to register custom type converters outside of the extension packages. For example:

```
<init-param>
  <param-name>TypeConverterFactory.Class</param-name>
  <param-value>stripesbook.nonext.MyTypeConverterFactory</param-value>
</init-param>

package stripesbook.nonext;
public class MyTypeConverterFactory
    extends DefaultTypeConverterFactory
{
    @Override
    public void init(Configuration config) {
        super.init(config);
        add(MyType.class, MyTypeConverter.class);
    }
    @Override
    public TypeConverter getTypeConverter(Class forType, Locale locale)
        throws Exception
    {
        TypeConverter tc = super.getTypeConverter(forType, locale);

        ServletContext context =
            StripesFilter.getConfiguration().getServletContext();

        SpringHelper.injectBeans(tc, context);

        return tc;
    }
}
```

ValidationMetadataProvider.Class

This is the implementation of the ValidationMetadataProvider interface, which is responsible for returning ValidationMetadata for properties and nested properties of an action bean. The default is DefaultValidationMetadataProvider. Here's an example:

```
<init-param>
  <param-name>ValidationMetadataProvider.Class</param-name>
  <param-value>
    stripesbook.nonext.MyValidationMetadataProvider
  </param-value>
</init-param>
```

A.3 Settings

The parameters in this section change the default settings for some of the modules used by Stripes.

FileUpload.MaximumPostSize

This sets the maximum *total* size of the request data, including request headers, parameters, and uploaded files. A value without a suffix is in bytes; you can use the K, M, or G suffixes (case insensitive) to provide a value in kilobytes, megabytes, or gigabytes. Do *not* put any spaces between the value and the suffix. Any characters after the suffix are ignored.

```
<init-param>
  <param-name>FileUpload.MaximumPostSize</param-name>
  <!-- Sets the limit to 5 MB -->
  <!-- 5m, 5MB, 5megabytes, or 5242880 all have the same effect -->
  <param-value>5M</param-value>
</init-param>
```

LocalePicker.Locales

This is a comma-separated list of locales supported by the application. This parameter is loaded by DefaultLocalePicker. Locales can be in the ln, ln_CN, or ln_CN:ENC format, where ln is the language, CN is the country, and ENC is the encoding. For example:

```
<init-param>
  <param-name>LocalePicker.Locales</param-name>
  <param-value>en,fr_CA,es_MX:UTF-8</param-value>
</init-param>
```

LocalizationBundleFactory.ErrorMessageBundle

Loaded by DefaultLocalizationBundleFactory, this parameter indicates the name of the resource bundle for error messages. The default is Stripes-Resources.

Here's an example:

```
<init-param>
  <param-name>LocalizationBundleFactory.ErrorMessageBundle</param-name>
  <param-value>path/MyErrorMessageBundle</param-value>
</init-param>
```

LocalizationBundleFactory.FieldNameBundle

Loaded by DefaultLocalizationBundleFactory, this parameter indicates the name of the resource bundle for field names. The default is StripesResources. Here's an example:

```
<init-param>
  <param-name>LocalizationBundleFactory.FieldNameBundle</param-name>
  <param-value>path/MyFieldNameBundle</param-value>
</init-param>
```

Stripes.DebugMode

This sets a **true** or **false** flag (the default is false) to indicate that the application is running in debug mode. You can then retrieve this flag with StripesFilter.getConfiguration().isDebugMode(). For example:

```
<init-param>
  <param-name>Stripes.DebugMode</param-name>
  <param-value>true</param-value>
</init-param>
```

Stripes.EncryptionKey

This sets the key used to encrypt values in all sessions of the web application. You *must* set a key if you need encrypted values to be decryptable across cluster nodes or after the web application restarts. For example:

```
<init-param>
  <param-name>Stripes.EncryptionKey</param-name>
  <param-value>
    some very long string used as an encryption key
  </param-value>
</init-param>
```

You can also set the encryption key in Java code by creating an object that implements javax.crypto.SecretKey and calling CryptoUtil.setSecretKey(SecretKey) before any requests are made, as in a ServletContextListener.

Validation.InvokeValidateWhenErrorsExist

This flag indicates whether to continue executing validation methods when previous validations have produced errors. The default is **false**. Here's an example:

```
<init-param>
  <param-name>Validation.InvokeValidateWhenErrorsExist</param-name>
  <param-value>true</param-value>
</init-param>
```

A.4 Interceptors

Stripes automatically loads core interceptors. Moreover, all autodiscovered interceptors are also loaded, but in an unpredictable order. You can change these defaults with the parameters in this section.

CoreInterceptor.Classes

These are the Interceptor implementations to be automatically loaded before any other interceptors. The defaults are BeforeAfterMethodInterceptor (required to support @Before and @After), and HttpCacheInterceptor (required to support @HttpCache). For example, if you wanted to replace HttpCacheInterceptor with your own implementation, you could use this:

```
<init-param>
  <param-name>CoreInterceptor.Classes</param-name>
  <param-value>
    net.sourceforge.stripes.controller.BeforeAfterMethodInterceptor,
    stripesbook.nonext.MyHttpCacheInterceptor
  </param-value>
</init-param>
```

Interceptor.Classes

This is a comma-separated list of Interceptor implementations. Interceptors will be executed in the order that you list them, unlike extension-packaged interceptors for which the order is not guaranteed. For example, if it's important to execute Interceptor1 before Interceptor2, you would use this:

```
<init-param>
  <param-name>Interceptor.Classes</param-name>
  <param-value>
    stripesbook.nonext.Interceptor1,
    stripesbook.nonext.Interceptor2
  </param-value>
</init-param>
```

Appendix B

Resources

B.1 Stripes Online Resources

The Stripes Framework . . . . http://www.stripesframework.org
This is the official Stripes Framework home page.

The Stripes Book . . . . http://www.stripesbook.com
I use this website to talk about the book and offer more tips and tricks about
Stripes.

The Stripes Users Mailing List . . .
. . . http://news.gmane.org/gmane.comp.java.stripes.user
This is the place to go when you need help.

The Stripes Developers Mailing List . . .
. . . http://news.gmane.org/gmane.comp.java.stripes.devel
Follow this mailing list if you're interested in what's being developed in the
Stripes core.

Stripes Stuff . . . . http://www.stripes-stuff.org
This is a collection of Stripes plug-ins, including Stripersist, Stripes-Security,
a JavaScript client-side validation library, and more.

Stripes-Spring . . . . http://www.silvermindsoftware.com/stripes
This is the Stripes-Spring plug-in by Brandon Goodin.

B.2 Stripes Dependencies

Commons Logging . . . . http://commons.apache.org/logging
This is the only strictly required Stripes dependency. Other dependencies are
needed only if you use the corresponding features, as detailed in this appendix.
Also note that *all* dependencies are included in the Stripes distribution, but it's
still nice to know where they come from.

Commons FileUpload . . . . http://commons.apache.org/fileupload
This is required if you want to use CommonsMultipartWrapper for file uploads.
You'll also need Commons IO (http://commons.apache.org/io).

COS (com.oreilly.servlets) . . . . http://www.servlets.com/cos
This is Jason Hunter's file upload support. This is required if you want to use
CosMultipartWrapper for file uploads.

JavaMail . . . . http://java.sun.com/products/javamail
This is required if you use EmailTypeConverter to validate email addresses. If
you're not using Java 6 or newer, you'll also need the Java Activation Framework (http://java.sun.com/javase/technologies/desktop/javabeans/jaf).

B.3 Third-Party Frameworks, Libraries, and Tools

Display Tag . . . . http://displaytag.sourceforge.net
This is a library for easy creation of feature-rich HTML tables.

Log4J http://logging.apache.org/log4j
This is a popular and powerful logging framework. Used in the book's sample
code bundle.

HSQLDB . . . . http://www.hsqldb.org
This is an easy-to-use Java database engine.

Java Persistence API (JPA) . . .
. . . http://java.sun.com/javaee/technologies/persistence.jsp
This is the standard persistence-layer specification for Java EE 5.

Hibernate . . . . http://www.hibernate.org
This is a JPA-compliant ORM (Object-Relational Mapping) tool.

Spring . . . . http://www.springframework.org
The Spring framework includes, among other modules, a dependency injection
container.

Google Guice . . . . http://code.google.com/p/google-guice
This is a dependency injection library.

JUnit . . . . http://www.junit.org
This is a framework for automated unit tests.

Mockito . . . . http://www.mockito.org
This is a library for testing with mock objects.

jQuery . . . . http://www.jquery.com
This is a popular JavaScript and Ajax library.

Prototype . . . . http://www.prototypejs.org
This is another popular JavaScript and Ajax library.

B.4 Development Tools

Sun Java . . . . http://java.sun.com
This is the source for core Java development tools, including the Java Development Kit (JDK), and Java Enterprise Edition (EE).

VIM (Vi Improved) . . . . http://www.vim.org
This is an awesome editor. I used VIM to write this whole book, including all the text and most of the sample code.

Ant (Another Neat Tool) . . . . http://ant.apache.org
This is a Java build tool, used in the book's source code bundle.

Eclipse . . . . http://www.eclipse.org
This is the Eclipse IDE.

NetBeans . . . . http://www.netbeans.org
This is the NetBeans IDE.

Stripes NetBeans Plug-In . . .
. . . http://plugins.netbeans.org/PluginPortal/faces/PluginDetailPage.jsp?pluginid=5115
This is a Stripes plug-in for NetBeans.

IntelliJ IDEA . . . . http://www.jetbrains.com/idea
This is another popular IDE, IntelliJ IDEA.

IntelliStripes . . . . http://code.google.com/p/intellistripes
This is a Stripes plug-in for IntelliJ IDEA.

B.5 Bibliography

[Bec02]   Kent Beck. *Test Driven Development: By Example*. Addison-Wesley, Reading, MA, 2002.

[HT00]   Andrew Hunt and David Thomas. *The Pragmatic Programmer: From Journeyman to Master*. Addison-Wesley, Reading, MA, 2000.

[HT03]   Andrew Hunt and David Thomas. *Pragmatic Unit Testing In Java with JUnit*. The Pragmatic Programmers, LLC, Raleigh, NC, and Dallas, TX, 2003.

[JBC+06]   Eric Jendrock, Jennifer Ball, Debbie Carson, Ian Evans, Scott Fordin, and Kim Haase. *Java EE 5 Tutorial*. Prentice Hall PTR, Englewood Cliffs, NJ, third edition, 2006.

Index

Get Groovy

Expand your horizons with Groovy, and tame the wild Java VM.

Programming Groovy

Programming Groovy will help you learn the necessary fundamentals of programming in Groovy. You'll see how to use Groovy to do advanced programming techniques, including meta programming, builders, unit testing with mock objects, processing XML, working with databases and creating your own domain-specific languages (DSLs).

Programming Groovy Dynamic Productivity for the Java Developer
Venkat Subramaniam
(320 pages) ISBN: 978-1-9343560-9-8. $34.95
http://pragprog.com/titles/vslg

Groovy Recipes

See how to speed up nearly every aspect of the development process using *Groovy Recipes*. Groovy makes mundane file management tasks like copying and renaming files trivial. Reading and writing XML has never been easier with XmlParsers and XmlBuilders. Breathe new life into arrays, maps, and lists with a number of convenience methods. Learn all about Grails, and go beyond HTML into the world of Web Services: REST, JSON, Atom, Podcasting, and much much more.

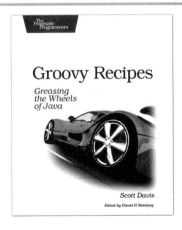

Groovy Recipes: Greasing the Wheels of Java
Scott Davis
(264 pages) ISBN: 978-0-9787392-9-4. $34.95
http://pragprog.com/titles/sdgrvr

The Pragmatic Bookshelf

The Pragmatic Bookshelf features books written by developers for developers. The titles continue the well-known Pragmatic Programmer style and continue to garner awards and rave reviews. As development gets more and more difficult, the Pragmatic Programmers will be there with more titles and products to help you stay on top of your game.

Visit Us Online

Stripes...and Java Web Development Is Fun Again's Home Page
http://pragprog.com/titles/fdstr
Source code from this book, errata, and other resources. Come give us feedback, too!

Register for Updates
http://pragprog.com/updates
Be notified when updates and new books become available.

Join the Community
http://pragprog.com/community
Read our weblogs, join our online discussions, participate in our mailing list, interact with our wiki, and benefit from the experience of other Pragmatic Programmers.

New and Noteworthy
http://pragprog.com/news
Check out the latest pragmatic developments in the news.

Save on the PDF

Save on the PDF version of this book. Owning the paper version of this book entitles you to purchase the PDF version at a terrific discount. The PDF is great for carrying around on your laptop. It's hyperlinked, has color, and is fully searchable.

Buy it now at pragprog.com/coupon.

Contact Us

Phone Orders:	1-800-699-PROG (+1 919 847 3884)
Online Orders:	www.pragprog.com/catalog
Customer Service:	orders@pragprog.com
Non-English Versions:	translations@pragprog.com
Pragmatic Teaching:	academic@pragprog.com
Author Proposals:	proposals@pragprog.com